HISTORY OF MODERN POLITICAL MOVEMENTS

HISTORY OF MODERN POLITICAL MOVEMENTS

Prasanta Kumar Nayak

AKANSHA PUBLISHING HOUSE
NEW DELHI-110 059 (INDIA)

AKANSHA PUBLISHING HOUSE
R 37-B, Vani Vihar, Uttam Nagar
New Delhi-110059
Email: ektabooks@yahoo.com
Ph. : 25640621

History of Modern Political Movements

First Edition 2003
ISBN 81-87606-40-1

PRINTED IN INDIA

Published by M.P. Misra for Akansha Publishing House, New Delhi and Printed at Tarun Offset Press, Delhi.

CONTENTS

PREFACE

This work throws light on the dynamics of a resurgent Orissa (1866-1947) on the basis of some of its political movements. Nationalism and the emergence of the democratic independent India was a part of the larger global nationalistic resurgence. Like the national scene, Orissa, a part of a great saga had a complex kind of story. The Na-anka' famine of 1866 in Orissa on one hand exposed the devastating economic impact of the British rule and the unsympathetic attitude of the Bengal government and on the other, acted as a catalyst for fermenting political consciousness and a birth-pangs of a more resurgent Orissa fired with the vigour of greater self-identity. Orissa presented the complexities of various political movements as the regional level under the aegis of India's freedom struggle. The nature of the nationalist struggle in Orissa was complex with three movements interlacing each other, namely the linguistic movement for formation of the separate province for Orissa, the movement for Indian Independence and the Prajamandal movements in the princely states against the continuance of medieval administration.

The complexities that these movements involved have been well addressed here. Even though good monographs on each of these movements have come up, very little is done to analyse their inter-relations. The issue like the nomenclature to be adopted for the various movements and specifically to analyse their nationalistic, democratic and popular contents, their inter-related contradictory and complementary elements and their nature and leadership pattern have not been dealt so far. A maiden attempt in this monograph has been made to theoretically conceptualise the dynamics of all these movements in a way estimating them in the framework of above characteristics vis-a-vis their absence in related published literature in a review work.

To construct the present study a thorough search has been undertaken. Sources in the form of original records, printed books, journals and periodicals have been consulted at the National Archives of India, New Delhi, Nehru Memorial Museum and Library, New Delhi, Indian Council of Historical Research Library, New Delhi, National Library, Calcutta; Central Library, University of Hyderabad; Hyderabad, Orissa State Archieves, Bhubaneswar, Orissa State Library, Bhubaneswar, Nabakrushna Choudhury Centre for Development Studies Library, Bhubaneswar, Parija Library, Utkal University, Bhubaneswar and Seminar Library, Department of History, Utkal University, Bhubaneswar. I express my profound thanks to the authorities of these institutions for their selfless help.

This book has grown out of my under the joint guidance of my reserved teachers–Prof. K.S. Behera, Vice-Chancellor, Fakir Mohan University, Balasore, Orissa and Prof. S.P. Pani, Director, College Development Council, Utkal University, Bhubaneswar, Orissa. I express my deep indebtedness to both of them for their meticulous care and scholastic supervision of the study. I also gratefully record my gratitude to my esteemed teacher Prof. M.N. Das, Ex-Vice Chancellor, Utkal University, Bhubaneswar for his kind suggestions at the stage of recasting the work into the present monograph. I am equally obliged to my respected teachers and members of the P.G. Department of History of the same University. I too acknowledge the inspiration from the Pincipal and other colleagues of Government College, Bomdila, Arunachal Pradesh.

I owe my profound indebtedness to Prof. Damodar Lenka, Dean Extension (Retd.), Orissa University of Agriculture and Technology, Bhubaneswar, my father-in-law and other relatives and friends for encouraging me to work on this study. But for the cooperation and inspiration of my wife Chinmoyee (Rinee), daughter Prachi Mrudula (Himani) and son Partha Prateem (Jubun), this work would not have been possible.

Department of History
Government College, Bomdila
Arunachal Pradesh

Prasanta Kumar Nayak

ABBREVIATIONS

AA	-	Asha
AAR	-	Annual Administrative Report
AICC	-	All India Congress Committee
AISPC	-	All India States' Peoples' Conference
BAR	-	Bengal Administrative Report
BOLC	-	Bihar and Orissa Legislative Council
CP	-	Central Provinces
GNML	-	Gandhi National Museum and Library
GRPI	-	General Report on Public Instruction
ICR	-	Indian Constitutional Reform
ILA	-	Imperial Legislative Assembly
ILC	-	Imperial Legislative Council
INC	-	Indian National Congress
ISC	-	Indian Statutory Commission
JPC	-	Joint Parliamentary Committee
NAI	-	National Archives of India
NMML	-	Nehru Memorial Museum and Library
ODG	-	Orissa District Gazetteers
OLAP	-	Orissa Legislative Assembly Proceedings
OSPC	-	Orissa States' Peoples' Conference
PCC	-	Provincial Congress Committee
PUS	-	Proceedings of Utkal Sammilani
UUC	-	Utkal Union Conference (Utkal Sammilani)
WWCC	-	Who's Who Compilation Committee

GLOSSARY

Ashram	-	Training centre for Congress workers
Babaji	-	Saint, sage
Begari	-	Forced labour
Bethi	-	Forced labour
Charkha	-	Spinning wheel
Chowkidar	-	Village watchman
Circar	-	Modern district
Darbar	-	A Raja's court, a royal Assembly
Debottar	-	Lands assigned for the worship of an idol
Dhoba	-	Washerman
Diwan	-	Chief Executive Officer in the state
Ganja	-	Raw intoxicant
Garjat	-	Lands constituted of mountain fortresses
Hartal	-	Strike, ceasework
Hat	-	Market
Hizrat	-	To move from place to place due to excessive oppression
Jogi	-	Saint, hermit
Karan	-	Kayastha, revenue officials
Kendera	-	A local variety of single string instrument
Khadar/Khadi	-	Home-spun coarse cotton cloth
Khasmahal	-	Management of estates directly by the officers of the government
Lathi	-	Big bamboo stick used by the police
Magan	-	Fees exacted by the Rajas from the tenants mostly on ceremonial occasions
Mahal	-	An estate, a revenue paying unit
Maharaja	-	Emperor
Malguzari	-	Revenue
Meli	-	Violent agitation

Mogulbandi	-	The territory under Mughal administration, that is the coastal plains comprising the modern districts of Balasore, Cuttack and Puri
Paik	-	Foot soldier of the Orissan kings holding land or tenure of military service
Pan	-	Betel leaf chewed with dried arecanut and lime
Pana	-	A man of low caste
Panchayat	-	Arbitration court of a village
Pandit	-	A scholar
Raj	-	Crown
Raja	-	King
Rani	-	Queen
Rasad	-	Provision of ration for the officer
Sadhu	-	Saint, hermit
Saheb	-	Englishman
Satyagraha	-	Protest demonstration in a peaceful manner
Satyagrahi	-	One who participates in satyagraha
Swadeshi	-	Indigenous
Swarajya	-	Freedom, self-government
Taluk	-	An estate, area
Tamakhu	-	Tobacco
Thana	-	Police station
Vanar Sena	-	Monkey Brigade
Zamindar	-	Proprietor of an estate who pays revenue directly to the government
Zamindari	-	The estate of a zamindar
Zilla	-	A district

INTRODUCTION

For nearly hundred years from the middle of the nineteenth century India experienced an unprecedented awakening of a new consciousness with socio-political dimensions. Every aspect of Indian life was touched and underwent nearly metamorphic changes. Nationalism and the emergence of a democratic independent India was a part of the larger global nationalistic upsurge. Orissa presently a state of India was a part of the great saga. Like the national scene the Orissan story was complex. The present study is an attempt to focus at the regional level with an emphasis on political movements. Orissa had witnessed several resistance movements against the British conquest. The nature of the nationalist struggle in Orissa was complex with three movements overlapping each other, namely, the linguistic movement for formation of the separate province for Orissa, the movement for Indian Independence and the movements in the princely states against the continuance of medieval administration. The assertion of Oriya identity and the demand for a separate province for the Oriya-speaking people placed under various presidencies dominated the scenario in first two decades of the twentieth century. This movement raises questions like whether it was nationalist, whether it was contradictory, cooperative or complimentary with the indian nationalist movement. Similarly the nature of the movements in the princely states and its inter-relation with the other two movements raises issues like the commitment of the Congress to the democratic ideas. Further there were leaders particularly associated with the movement for a separate province who were close to the British administration. One may question their nationalism or even their patriotism. In contrast, it is difficult to dismiss them as non-nationalist in view of their contribution for strengthening the Oriya identity and their passion for alround development of the province.

The present work attempts to discuss the complexities of these three movements. Even though good monographs on each of these movements have appeared, very little has been done to analyse their inter-relation. It is held that a theoretical framework is considered to be necessary for the proposed analysis. This forms a part of the first chapter of the book. A detailed attempt in surveying the growth of education, press, communication and political associations etc. forms the other part of the introductory chapter. This is followed by three chapters devoted to the three movements. The chapter titled 'The Nature, the Inter-relation and the Contradictions' is an attempt to present a holistic picture. It contains an evaluation of popular elements, class structure, nature of leadership, inter-relations and contradictions. This chapter also includes a brief review of conclusions and opinions expressed by various scholars on the issues raised in the present work. No full scale review of literature is taken up at the outset, as references to the existing literature have been made in the chapters concerning the movements. Based on the introductory theoretical framework the movements have been analysed. Broad conclusions are drawn at the end.

The work being chiefly one of analysis and interpretation, broadly accepts the known facts and the events as brought out from archival sources by the historians. However, primary sources such as, archival records, newspapers, journals and periodicals as listed in the bibliography have been consulted. Notwithstanding this the focus is never on contradictory views and the accuracy of the events. The secondary sources though have been used for narration of broad events, have principally been used for their interpretative value. The monographs, books, essays and articles have been enlisted in the bibliography. For greater readability abbreviations for sources have been used with full form when they occur first in the reference.

1

THE GENESIS: BIRTH OF MODERN ORISSA

A few words on the history of Orissa may be placed as a background to a study of popular movements of Orissa in modern times. The history of Orissa finds fleeting mention in the standard books of Indian history. Save the Kalinga War, the saga of Kharavela and the temple heritage notably of the Konark, nothing much from Orissa history adorn the pages of the same. A plethora of historical research studies at regional level now provide substantial details of Orissan history, though comprehensive works still elude the readers.

Orissa was predominantly the land of aboriginals and it is only after the 6th century B.C. that the process of so-called Aryanisation began in Orissa. Orissa being juxtaposed between south and north had been the melting-pot for synthesis of the Aryans, the Dravidians and the aboriginals. Orissa finds mention in the later Vedic literature and the epics. Leaving aside the prehistorical remnants, history of Orissa can be built up in fragments from the 6th century B.C. onwards. The first major political event in its history was the Ashokan conquest in 3rd century B.C. Kharavela the most illustrious ruler of Orissa ruled from Bhubaneswar in the 1st century A.D. The Guptas had defeated various Orissan rulers. Orissa formed a part of Harshavardhan's kingdom. She continued to be ruled by numerous independent and semi-independent dynasties right up to the Mughals. Notable among these dynasties were- the Sailodbhavas (7th century A.D.), the Bhaumakaras (8th to 10th century), the Somavamsis (10th to 11th century), the Gangas (11th to 15th century) and the Suryavamsis (15th and 16th century A.D.). It came under the Mughal empire from Akbar's time. On the decline of the Mughals, it passed into the hands of the Marathas.

With the discovery of sea-route to India, Orissa like the rest of the country came in contact with the West. Europeans established warehouses in Hariharpur (modern Jagatsinghpur), Pipli, Balasore etc. The presence of European merchant was negligible up to 18th century Orissa. Her political conquest by the British began in the first decade of nineteenth century. By 20's of the nineteenth century the whole of Orissa had come under direct or indirect British political control. The tragedy was the dismemberment of Orissa under various units of British authority; while the coastal Orissa remained under the Bengal Presidency, the Ganjam and Koraput tract remained under Madras Presidency and Sambalpur and the western region under Central Province and Berar. Of course, no motive can be ascribed to the British of anyone else for this political division. It was but natural that winds of change blew over Orissa with its opening to western contact and British Raj. The genesis of popular movements is to be searched in this quarter. However, before delving into various aspects of Orissan history to seek the genesis of the popular nationalist movements, one must provide a theoretical framework of nationalism. Thus the analysis of various aspects of Orissan history in nineteenth as well as twentieth century is preceded by the following discussion on nationalism.

Nationalism: An Analysis in Concept and Process

The present analysis of nationalism is broadly divided into three parts; concept of nationalism as enunciated by political thinkers, growth of nationalism in global perspective, the modern Indian concept of nationalism and growth of Indian nationalism.

The concept of nationalism is a dynamic one. Nationalism is also a complete historical process. As such it is not desirable to adopt a cut and dry definition. It is proposed to highlight the points of views of numerous political thinkers and then to adopt a synthetic view in the light of the historical process.

Nationalism is derived from the word 'nation' which in turn is taken from the Greek word 'Natio' that emphasizes 'birth' and 'race'. Nation is defined as 'a society' united under one government in a political state; alternately as a considerable group of people having common descent, history or language[1]. A nation is something more than a mere state. State is essentially a political and legal entity. State is defined as "a concept of political science and public law, is a community of persons more or less numerous, permanently occupying a definite portion of territory, independent or nearly so, of external control and possessing an organized government to which the great body of inhabitants render habitual obedience."[2] In other words, a state is distinct by its four features namely, population, territory, government and sovereignty. Every State may not be a nation and a state may contain more than one nationality. A nation is marked by a feeling of nationalism permeating amongst the people. Nationalism is essentially a water of feeling of distinctness arising out of a common descent or history or language or religion or culture or a combination of these. The feeling of oneness may persist in spite of contradictions like multiplicity of language, culture, religion etc. The cohesion makes a people a nation irrespective of the unity or diversity of variables noted above. Number of political scientists have emphasized this aspect. Lipson holds "when people do feel this way, that is, when they unite around a national symbol, they think and live and act and if necessary, die in warfare- not as Athenians or Romans or Christians, but as Americans or Frenchmen or Russians, they constitute a nation".[3] The common political aspiration, tradition, and memories strengthen nationalism. It involves emotional, psychological aspects coupled with political aspiration. This feeling, this emotional and psychological integration may be in the making in a nation. The feeling of nationalism is at times described as consciousness. Toynbee regards 'the will to be a nation' as the most important element of modern nationalism. Further this will has necessarily to be from within. Ernest holds "to have suffered, rejoiced and hoped together makes a people a nation".[4] J.S. Mill opines "The strongest of all (factors) is the identity of political antecedents; the possession of a national history and consequent community of recollections; collective pride and humiliation, pleasure and regret, connected with the same incidents in the past".[5] In fact, nationalism is still a historical process by which nationalities are being transformed into states asserting the legitimate right of a people of a nationality to form a distinct and vigorous nation-state. Lord Bryce observes "the sentiment of nationality is that feeling or group of feelings which makes an aggregate of men conscious of ties, not being wholly either political or religion which unite them in a community which is, either actually or potentially, a nation".[6] On the same lines, C.J.H. Hayes writes "a national state is always based on nationality, but nationality may exist without a national state. A state is essentially political, nationality is primarily cultural and only incidentally political".[7] Nationalism is increasingly being associated with national independence since the last century. Hence, it is defined as patriotic feeling, principle or efforts and as a policy of national independence.[8] It is increasingly also associated with the democratic principle. It holds that the collective personality of the nation is more important than the individual person of the monarch. It involves the ideal of the sovereignty of the people.[9] According to Ramsay Muir "as the rights of man primarily include the right to choose their own governors, it was a natural corollary that men had a right to be governed by their mutual sympathies and affinities in the organization of the state, and once this position is granted, the nationalist doctrine is established".[10]

In addition to the democratic concept national independence is emerging as the other important feature of nationalism. Nationalities not only assert their right of self-determination but also strongly desire to govern themselves to the exclusion of extra-territorial authority. In other words, nationalism denounces imperialism, it at the minimum can not accept territorial and political imperialism. Hence nationalism has been identified with freedom movements in the last century. Currently other aspects like economic rights of nations are being emphasized increasingly.

Various factors of nationalism have been identified. It may be reasserted that nationalism transcends these factors. The factors are not to be confused as absolutely essential for the making of a nation. However, in the absence of all the factors or most of the factors a nation can not exist. Geographical unity or a naturally defined territory like the Indian sub-continent or Italy etc. is asserted as a prime condition. However, Pakistan lasted for quarter of a century being separated by the vast country like India. In contrasts, Alaska and Hawaii are away from the mainland of America but are well integrated emotionally with the mainland. Common nativity is a great fostering factor. However, sometime, an over riding religious unity may bring together a people as in Israel. In the course of history man's allegiance has moved from his village, tribe or smaller geographical units to the nation as a whole. The allegiance to the national geographical units may co-exist in a colupative-co-operative allegiance to the village, city or a province.[11] In this sense, there is a strain and strain of allegiance and over-lapping of affinity. In extreme cases, the allegiance transcends even national boundaries when one identifies himself with a religious institution outside the national boundaries. A geographical unity and entity necessarily does not graduate itself to a nation. A geographical expression becomes a nation when a feeling of nationality spreads amongst the people of that geographical entity. Germany was only a geographical expression till mid-nineteenth century. The geographical unity is not conceived as an inert piece of land but as a living fatherland or a motherland. The love for the land makes it the motherland.

Racial purity or unity was held to be very important for a nationality. But it is rightly asserted that racial purity is non-existent. Every nation today is heterogenous in is own way. Mussolini, one of the strongest adherents of racial purity conceded that 'race is a feeling not a reality. Nothing will ever make me believe that biologically pure races can be shown to exist today'. Nationality actually cuts through and across race. The principle of primordial right of a race is narrow and no race is pure. Eventhough racial homogeneity is no longer accepted as a necessary precondition for formulation of a nation state, yet one has to concede that racial feelings may positively be used for strengthening nationalism.

Besides these two important factors unity of ideas, common culture, literature, art, education, history, and tradition and religion of late economic interests etc. are cited as factors of nationalism. Like racial purity, unity of language, culture, history etc. are not a precondition for birth, growth or sustenance of nationalism. Unity of any one factor definitely contributes to the growth of nationalism. Renan rejects the view of the essence of nationalities in the unity of race, language, religion, community of interests or geographical unity. It is basically a spiritual principle based primarily on a rich heritage of memories and keen desire to live together. People are a nation because they want to be a nation. Common subjugation has also bounded people together to a nationality. Subjugation may lead to identification and ultimately may lead to an assimilation with the ruling country.[12] Numerous examples may be cited of nationalism, transcending the variety of language, culture, faith, religion etc., but none better than India. The feeling of oneness must transcend all other feeling to make a people a nation. This does not necessarily mean patriotism or nationalistic feeling wipes out all other feelings and allegiances. It only asserts that it is the highest feeling - atleast politically. We may say a legitimate pride in the past, a wholesome confidence in the present, a buoyant hope for the future, all strengthen and sustain the national spirit transcending heterogenous forces that may work within a nation.

Reserving the proposition of a basket of ideas as a definition of nationalism to the end of this chapter, we may trace historically the growth of nationalism. This has to be necessarily very skeletal and the author may be required to indulge in sweeping generalisation.

As noted earlier nationalism is a complex historical process. Recognising the same Ebenstein notes "Since the French Revolution atleast, nationalism has been one of the driving forces of domestic, imperial and international politics. Complex in its origin, it has developed along many, and often contradictory lines. In its name some of the greatest acts of heroism and liberty have been committed, but also crimes of cruelty and fanaticism. In the first half of its existence from the late eighteenth to the middle of the nineteenth century, nationalism was essentially inspired by humanitarian, democratic ideas; this was the story of early French, American, Czech, Italian, Irish and polish nationalism. In the last eighty years, on the other hand, nationalism has tended to ally itself with parochialism, intolerance, bigotry, persecution of minorities, racialism and finally imperialism and aggression - the recoil of pan-Germanism, Hungarian imperialism, Japanese militarism and finally fascism".[13] Various principles of nationalism have developed over the centuries. In the process, certain negative aspects have emerged.

Conventionally the growth of nationalism is traced from the American War of Independence and French Revolution, one may push its antiquity back to another two more centuries. Henry VIII (1509-1547) invoked the principle of England being supreme in dealing with her own affairs, including that of ecclesiastic. He made Parliament a partner in this assertion. The process of democratisation and assertion of English nationalities was carried forward through the Tudor and Stuart period. Under Queen Elizabeth a feeling of nationality gripped the English in their fight against the Spaniards.

France was a great theatre of nationalism. Louis XIV enunciated the principle of geographical unity when he raised slogan 'France must expand to its natural boundaries'. French Revolution marked the clearest birth-pangs of nationalism. France rejected the divine sanction of government and it was now held that people have an inalienable right to govern themselves which they may transfer to a government of their choice. The principle of sovereignty of the people alongwith liberty, equality and fraternity emerged from the French Revolution. More important than these constitutional concepts was the over-riding upsurge of nationalistic feelings amongst the French. Napoleon emerged as the symbol of their aspiration. Whole of Europe was affected by this contagious nationalistic feeling. Hugh- Seton Watson writes the principle of nationalism emerged gradually in Western Europe and was theoretically formulated in revolutionary France.

Fourteen years before the French Revolution in far off America the colonists raised the slogan of 'no taxation without representation'. The American War of Independence and the formulation of the constitution marked the growth of democratic principle as a component of nationalism. A hundred years later the civil war carried forward the principle of equality as a part of American nationalism.

In the negotiations at Vienna in 1815 the doctrine that nationality should be the basis of independent statehood came strongly to the front in providing for the future of Poland, Italy and Germany. It was held that the Poles, the Italians and the Germans were each so homogenous racially as to furnish the natural material for a state. The eminent Niebuhr set the principle of race so high as gravely to argue that Saxony, in standing by Napoleon after all the other Germans had deserted him, had been guilty of treason to the German race and must pay the penalty in loss of autonomous life.[14] These far-reaching conceptions of national rights did not show any appreciable influence in the territorial arrangements actually effected at Vienna; but Poles and Italians and Germans voiced a loud chorus of protest against the violation of their ideals, and never ceased their denunciation till it had produced the most important results in both theory and fact.

By the middle of the century, when the revolutionary drama of 1848 was unfolded, nationalism was the central force in the whole great commotion, outside of France. Even Great Britain had to deal with the trouble-making principle, as it was invoked by the malcontents in Ireland. Middle Europe, from the Baltic to the Mediterranean, was a seething culdron of nationalistic aspiration.[15] In most cases the immediate end sought was the release of a self-conscious people from the control of a government that was felt to be alien. Along with this went a wild craving for the consolidation of hitherto separate communities of kindred speech into a single political system.

The principalities and provinces of the Italian peninsula flamed with hatred of their Habsburg and Bourbon rulers, drove them out, and groped excitedly about for union among themselves. But the time of Italian unity was not yet, and when the tumult and the shouting ceased Italy was still merely what Matternich had called it, a geographical expression. The Czechs at Prague demanded a revival of the ancient realm of Bohemia. The Magyars at Budapest deposed the Habsburger from the throne of Hungary. The Serbs of Croatia set up the standard of revolt against the Hungarians. Here again, however, the end of the troubles found the authority of the House of Habsburg practically intact, and its subjects as heterogenous as ever.[16]

At Frankfurt, in the Assembly that convened to frame a constitution for Germany, centred the most important of the nationalistic movements of this time. The popular demand that led to the meeting of the convention was irresistible both from its diffusion and its intensity. For a generation the growth of the idea of a unified and powerful Germany had been remarkable from both the sentimental and rational point of view. But the political unity of the German race on which this vision depended, required the dismemberment of the Austrian Empire and a notable expansion of the power of Prussia. Neither of these requirements could be secured in 1849, and the work of the Frankfurt Assembly went to shipwreck. Germany became again a disjointed congeries of political units, but the men and the ideas that were destined to realise the national desire had been revealed.

The ebullition of 1848 in both its nationalistic and constitutional phases, was largely controlled by sentiment and emotion. An influential and often dominant part was played by orators, poets, literary men and professors. Within twenty years after the failures of these men the principle of nationality achieved the wonderful triumphs manifested in a unified Italy, a unified Germany, and a unified United States; but the men most responsible for these results were of a different type from the leaders of 1848. Louis Napoleon, Otto von Bismarck, Camilio di Cavour and Abraham Lincoln were hard-headed politicians, whose methods subordinated the ideal and sentimental to the practical.[17] Hence the nationalism exhibited in the results of their work was hard to reconcile at some points with the doctrine of the earlier days. The German nation that Bismarck consolidated included many Germans who bitterly opposed his procedure, and left out the great masses of Germans who were subject to the Austrian Empire. The United States that Lincoln left included millions of Americans who had fought a bloody war to free themselves from his government. In the earlier conception of a nation it was the expression of the popular consciousness and will. In the conception that prevailed in the German and the American development nationality became an instrument of aggression and was used to justify the overriding of popular desires. Where race, geography and history were held to have decreed that there must be a single people under a single government, no adverse choice or preference of any fraction of the people was allowed to prevail.

Hence, nationalisms have become an effective force only in those countries where there has been national consciousness among atleast an important section of the people concerned. The partition of Poland, the American War of Independence, and the French Revolution were important factors for arising national consciousness. The spread of education, writings and utterances of great social and political philosophers gave a great impetus to nationalisms. Machiavelli may rightly be called the father of modern nationalism since he preached the creation of a united Italian state. Mazzini was the greatest of the philosophers of same nationalism. "Like Herder and Fichta", writes Hallowell, "Mazzini declared that every people has its nationality, like Hegel, Mazzini believed that the nation state was the medium and agency through which history manifests itself in its progressive development towards greater human freedom".[18]

Upto 1880, it is found nationalism identified with the crusade for free and democratic government- liberalism and nationalism marching together. Afterwards economic factors came into play and the capitalist class made one nation against another and one capitalist entity against another, in a struggle for materials and markets. It gave birth to a new form of nationalism which soon developed into economic imperialism. The new nationalism brought in its wake many wars. Nationalism reached its climax under fascism and nazism, resulting in second great world war.

The World War I provided a great impetus to the growth of nationalism in new theatres. The defeat of Turkey in the first world war became the source of inspiration for the advent of nationalism. It was indeed the first cry of nationalism in the middle east and in an Islamic country. The revolution in Russia was a nationalist movement of a different kind. Socialism like democracy followed road high with nationalism. Nationalist movement was carried to the Japanese and Chinese frontiers also. The political and national consciousness emerged in Africa and gained momentum in the post second World War era. The process of independent movements and their success is a continuous process since 1945. India gained her independence in 1947. Since then many countries like Burma, Sri Lanka, Indonesia, Bangladesh, Vietnam, Angola, Tanganyika, Kenya, Uganda, Mozambique etc. have followed suit; Namibia too. Nationalism is brooking new frontiers. The abolition of apartheid in South Africa and emergence of black majority rule under

Nelson Mandela is a new chapter. The state of Palestine is yet another star of hope on the horizon of nationalism.

Before rounding off the discussion on the growth of nationalism a word of caution needs to be added. Nationalisms at times have raised an ugly head of exclusiveness and aggressiveness. Mankind has to evolve a balance between the needs of the universal man and the national citizen. We must recognise that mankind organises itself in many groups other than national. Sub-national, socio-religious, cultural, economic, political and even international groupings have their rightful place. Mankind in order to survive and survive better must recognise that we are a part of each other.

Indian Philosophers

The modern struggle of India was not without its theoreticians. A number of thinkers from Raja Rammohan Roy to Mahatma Gandhi, not only provided the theoretical framework necessary for growth of nationalism but also enriched universal heritage of political thought and metaphysics. Raja Rammohun Roy (1772-1833) was one of the earliest thinkers of Indian nationalism. Though religious and social reformers dominated his life and work, he was indeed a champion of rights of men, liberty and equality. He rejoiced at the success of 1830 revolution. Though he did not advocate immediate independence and accepted the British connection and divine ordain, he rejected the idea of India's unending subjection to the British rule as a necessary condition for the amelioration of the Indian people. He pleaded for freedom of press as an essential ingredient for a good government, separation of judiciary from the executive, equality before law and he also was fascinated by the ideas of universal spiritualism. Being inspired by the Vedantas Rammohun proved that Indian nationalism was emerging from within eventhough the necessary stimuli may have come from the west. In the evolution of modern nationalist political philosophy, Rammohun Roy was the foremost torchbearer.

Dayanand Saraswati (1824-1883) was another socio-religious reformer who hailed from a traditional Brahmin family and was inspired by the vedic works and those of Panini, Patanjali, Shankara, Ramanuja and Sankaracharya. He propounded a political philosophy which was a mixture of the ideas of *Manusmriti* and Western democracy. Though this was crude, yet he exhibited a tremendous nationalistic feeling and wanted the Indians to help themselves. He created a consciousness amongst the

Indians by instilling a faith in their own cultural tradition. At times, he was aggressive.

Rabindra Nath Tagore (1861-1941), predominantly a poet was also a prophet of universal way and a philosopher of spontaneity and worshipper of nature. He asserted the rights of men and their freedom. In *Gitanjali,* highlighting the ideal he held for India, he writes,

"Where the mind is without fear and the head is held high;

Where knowledge is free;

Where the world has not been broken up into fragments by narrow domestic walls;

Where words come out from the depth of truth;

Where tireless striving stretches its arms towards perfection;

Where the clear stream of reason has not lost its way into the dreary desert sand of dead habit;

Where the mind is led forward by Thee into ever-widening thought and action-

Into that heaven of freedom, my Father, let my country awake."[19]

Even though Tagore did not actively participate in the freedom struggle he surrendered his Knighthood as a protest against the Jallianwalabagh massacre. He pleaded for self- government. Tagore was the first in India to recognise the conflict between nationalism and internationalism.

Dadabhai Naoroji (1825-1917) was the foremost patriarch of Indian nationalism. He was unique not merely for dominating the Indian political scene but also for building up the theory of the economic foundations of Indian nationalism. He pleaded for the natural rights of Indians to protect their own economy from drain. Though Dadabhai initially accepted the British connection as divine ordain he threw his weight in favour of the extremists like Aurobindo Ghosh and Tilak in getting their resolution in Swadeshi, Swaraj, national education and boycott approved in the Calcutta Session of Indian National Congress in 1906.

Vivekananda (1863 - 1902) like Dayanand was essentially a socio-religious reformer and a vedantist who believed in humanism as the essence of all religions. Though he was not directly involved in the nationalist movement he reaffirmed the faith of Indians in their own civilization and their common history and culture; this in turn facilitated the growth of nationalism. Further he criticised the early Congress policy of dependence on the British for the same. He placed greater faith in awakened mass of India.

Gopal Krishna Gokhle (1866-1915) symbolised the political philosophy of early Congress leadership termed as moderates. He accepted that India was a nation in making. He wanted to retain the British connection till such time Indians made themselves ready for introduction of a representative government. He too pleaded for liberty, equality, social justice and democracy.

Aurobindo (1872-1950) was the most complete thinker of the freedom struggle of India. He struck a new direction by emphasising the principle of self-determination and right to self- governance. Tilak and Aurobindo, the pioneers of new thinking in Indian nationalism pleaded for complete independence and based their argument on the right of a people to govern themselves. They did not accept the British connection, they were definitely anti-imperialists and considered the right to national independence as a fundamental birth right. In extreme ways they even claimed the right to bad self-governance. They did not accept any period of probation as necessary precondition for national independence. Aurobindo considered nationalism in India to be the spirit of time and India a living mother.

M.K. Gandhi (1869-1948) was the chief architect of India's freedom struggle. Gokhle's plank was Gandhi's foundation. Yet, he developed a unique political philosophy of his own. His plan for nationalism was founded on the principle of self-rule. He carried forward the principle of democracy to the village level and was champion of humanism. Jawaharlal Nehru (1889-1964) alongwith M.N.Roy and J.P. Narain introduced the socialistic philosophy into the stream of nationalism. He dreamt of an industrialised, secular and technological advanced independent India with its rightful place in international politics.

Genesis of Indian Nationalism

A brief on the genesis and evolution of Indian nationalism is a necessary component of the background of our present study. The basic inspiration came out of contact with the west was manifold. The British rule and her colonial policy transformed the Indian scenario. It was transferred into a major market for British manufacturers, a source of raw material and food-stuff; and a field for investment of British capital.

Her economy and social development were completely subordinated to that of Britain. India had become one of the most underdeveloped and leading backward colonial countries. In spite of increasing pressure on land negligible commercialization of agriculture, decline of handicrafts and near collapse of village economy, limited development took place in the field of growth of communication and transport as well as in the introduction of new agricultural products and emergence of an industrial capitalistic economy.

Indian nationalism was shaped by the changing social milieu from the mid-nineteenth century. The peasantry was the worst sufferer under the British imperialism. Thus, the pauperised Indian peasantry realised the impact of imperialism and ultimately provided to mass-base the Indian nationalism.

The English introduced western education partly to foster their self-interest. However, this led to the emergence of a very small section of educated Indians. The microscopic Indian intelligentsia exposed the socio-economic and political structure of British India and were inspired by ideas of democracy, freedom of press, speech and association and the right to criticise the rulers. This modern rationalism filtered into important aspects of Indian society like art, literature, press, education etc.

During the later part of British rule in India a small class of Indian capitalists emerged which desired to safeguard the Indian economy and realised that only a nationalist government would be able to provide the necessary protection and create an atmosphere for their growth. This class provided the sap to the Indian National Movement. Growth of industry created a new class of labourers, urban, easily organisable and more susceptible to the ideas of socialism and nationalism.

The earliest political associations were established in the first half of the nineteenth century by the landlords to protect their class interests. The number of associations like British Indian Association, East India Association, Poona Sarvajanik Sabha, Indian Association, Bombay Presidency Association had emerged before the birth of Indian National Congress in 1885. The Congress and other political associations created, sustained and led the freedom struggle of India.

The spread of education and re-examination of India's culture, heritage and religion led to an upsurge of socio-religious reform movements. Man like Rammohun Roy and Vivekananda reaffirmed the faith of Indians in their own culture and created a pride in the common historical and cultural past. Common memory which is the foremost ingredient of nationalism was provided by the new indologists, historians, comparative philologists and socio-religious reformers. Introduction of modern education, emergence of Indian intelligentsia, capitalist class, labour class, the pauperised peasantry, introduction of railways, posts and telegraphs, press, importation of ideas of democracy, liberty, equality and fraternity and rights of men, growth of political associations, etc. were like rivulets that drained into the stream of Indian nationalism which flooded the pages of Indian history in the first half of twentieth century like a brawling river of revolt.

Phases of Indian Nationalism

The 1857 movement was the last attempt of the Indian feudal element to wrest power from the Britishers. Eventhough, it aspired to reestablish the Mughal rule, it was still a nascent call for nationalism for it had atleast one essential element of it namely the desire to replace a foreign by a native government. The 1857 movement had been preceded by numerous civil rebellions, tribal uprisings and peasant movements. With the failure of the 1857 movement the baton for the race for freedom was transferred to the hands of Indian intelligentsia. The movement was carried forward through various political associations amongst which the Indian National Congress was the most notable and leading. The first phase was led by Moderates.[20] They had an inexplicable faith in the British desire for change in India. Their agenda included arousal and consolidation of national feeling organising the educated Indians for nationalist politics and political agitation and struggle for gradual implementation of the democratic principle and ultimate attainment of national independence. The hopes of the moderates were belied for Britain could not behave in a way other than that of an imperialist ruling nation. Serving through their failures the moderate phase gave way to a new thinking. Tilak, Aurobindo, Lajpat Rai and Bipin Chandra Pal symbolised the new thinking.[21] Going beyond the constitutional methods of agitation, the new group aspired to bring in the Indian mass to the freedom struggle. It had a better understanding of the nature of British imperialism and was naturally bolder than the earlier phase. A discussion of methods of various groups is excluded from the present work. Yet its importance is well-recognised. From 1915 the personality of Gandhi, his policies and methods dominated the Indian freedom struggle. Any detailed discussion on his contribution is naturally excluded from the present context. India's struggle for freedom was spread over a century covering many phases and was a complex process crowded by individuals, political associations, constitutional agitationists, revolutionaries, Extremists, Gandhians, Socialists, Communists and individual patriots.

For a better analysis the above background discussion needs to be summarised in two segments; a theoretical framework in concept in global and Indian perspective and the other of the Indian nationalist movement. Eventhough the scholar is cognizant of the dangers of sweeping generalisations, it is felt necessary that such a summary shall be helpful.

To form a theoretical framework and to adopt a synthetic view on nationalism, the features of nationalism may be derived from the preceding discussion.

(i) Nationalism involves the feeling of a people as having a common descent, language or history etc.

(ii) Nationalism is an emotional and psychological issue which involves a feeling of oneness and a will for self-rule. In contrast, state is more legal.

(iii) Common political aspiration, memoirs and traditions strengthen nationalism.

(iv) The inspiration for nationalism has to be essentially from within though inspiration from outside may facilitate the growth of the former.

(v) It is increasingly associated with national independence–the desire to be governed by the own people to its exclusion of foreigners.

(vi) Principles of democracy, equality are the new corollaries of nationalism.

(vii) A geographical unity, not necessarily absolute is helpful.

(viii) Nationalism does not negate allegiance to other groups including universal ones.

(ix) Racial, cultural, linguistic, art, literary and traditions foster nationalism. Yet, nationalism does not demand unity of any of the above.

(x) Economic interests, common subjugation have also strengthened nationalism.

(xi) Nationalism recognises subnationalism and internationalism.

(xii) The race of humanity need not be from nationality to bestiality, the world must develop an international mind, goodwill and friendship. The highest of nationalism will be an ideal international world where nations live at their best.

Similarly, the following generalisation on Indian nationalist movement can be drawn with reservations.

(i) The contact with west and western ideals of nationalism, liberalism and democracy fostered the growth of the same in India. This was accelerated with the spread of institutional educational system, growth of vernacular and English press and the consequent dawn of modern Indian literatures.

(ii) Equally important factor was the re-examination and rediscovery of India's history and heritage. The much needed sense of identification was provided by it. To this European and Indian scholars, the nineteenth and early twentieth century social reformers and socio-religious thinkers contributed in no small measure.

(iii) The nationalist movement in India progressed through various phases, the earliest phase was marked by various resistance movements both by the ex-ruling class and general mass culminating in the 1857 movement. This was followed by political associations ultimately resulting in the birth of Indian National Congress in 1885. The middle-class elite-led movement moved on constitutional methods accepting wholly the British West Minister model, yet agreeing on a period of probation under the English tutelage. By the first decade of the 20th century ultra and aggressive nationalists and extremists offered an alternate to the early Congress ideals. Basing the claims for independence on the rights of self-governance and self-determination not going to the extreme of ruling out violent methods. At a later stage, a small section of Indians was inspired by socialistic and Russian revolution. The socialistic ideals flowed into the concepts of democracy, capitalism and even welfare state. Ill-governance, protest, religious as well as regional identities, anti-foreign feelings, all got entangled with the broad nationalist movement.

Having generally surveyed the Indian scene and adopted a theoretically framework on nationalism, one may turn to the Orissan milieu.

The growth and development of an educated class, emergence of press, modern Oriya literature and political associations coupled with socio-economic developments in the nineteenth century contributed to the genesis of popular and nationalist movements in Orissa. The present discussion and analysis of the genesis shall include highlighting the 1866 famine as a catalyst for change, a matter of fact, presentation of the growth of press, literature and political association and spread of education, an analysis of British economic impact and economic development in Orissa and the growth of Oriya identity as a prelude to growth of national identity. At the end of the chapter an attempt shall be made to contrast the Orissan picture with that of other provinces. Before taking up the above mentioned issues a fundamental observation may be made. Orissa had a distinct identity of its own right from the earliest time.

Odradesa, Kalinga, Utkal and Orissa were the various nomenclatures by which it was known . Under the Mughals Orissa existed as a separate suba with Cuttack as its headquarters. Under the Marathas the situation did not change much save Ganjam and Koraput tract being transferred to the Nizam of Hyderabad, a feudatory of the Mughals. In 1765 when the East India Company obtained the Zamindari of Bengal, Bihar and Orissa, effectively only Midnapore of Orissa suba came under their control, the rest they had to conquer from the Marathas and obtain from the Nizam. Though in about a century Midnapore lost its identity from Orissa and culturally got entangled with Bengal, yet even to-day, it is not fully culturally integrated with Bengal and it retains its link with Orissa. As a whole, it would be wrong to suggest that the basic identity of Orissa was created by the British or was a 19th century phenomenon. However, it is equally true that in the first half of the 19th century when Orissa was placed under various British India units there was no opposition and the people as a whole, were not conscious of the same. This was not surprising for in past not only Orissa but various other provinces of India had been placed in such situations and such an identity just did not exist. Even under the British rule the linguistic identity was not uniformly respected in formation of political or administrative units. Thus, the genesis of the growth of linguistic identity of the Oriyas and their demand for a separate province is to be sought from the 19th century scenario only.

In the 19th century, the concept of nationalism slowly emerged on the horizon of Orissa too. Although there was no visible 'Oriya Nation' as such, for it was tagged on to the Bengal Presidency and other provinces, yet a conscious sense of oneness in culture and society started growing. Such nationalistic feelings in the regional context were not peculiar to Orissa alone. It was but a natural sentiment flowing freely in a number of regions of India and brought about administrative reorganisation in various parts at various times. As to the genesis of these feelings, it is generally accepted that the renaissance in the 19th century ushered in a general progress in the realm of education and in particular led to the development of vernacular literature which in turn contributed appreciably towards a revival of various cultural groups. Interestingly enough, the very nature of the political-administrative units into which the British government divided this country, also helped strengthen the regional nationalism. Divisions of British India into presidencies were mere agglomeration of more than one cultural groups in which one particular cultural or linguistic groups enjoyed many more privileges than the other constituent groups due to location of administrative headquarters which consistently made the other groups aware of the plight of their communication that logically progressed into currents underneath of individual nationalistic feeling.

Before going into further details one may raise the issue of regional-nationalism. One may question the very concept, so it is difficult to reconcile both. One important aspect of nationalism is the self-awareness of the community. India being a multi-linguistic and multi-cultural nation - its nationalism involves these identities. At times, it seems that people became aware of these identities or separation before developing a full-fledged nationalist identity. It involved both a contradiction and a complementation. It was a prelude to nationalism and for sometime it was hampering the growth of nationalism. In other words, it is suggested here that the Oriya identity movement or the movement for a separate province was a prelude to the nationalist movement in Orissa, it was also hampering the growth of nationalism in Orissa and at the end, the contradiction was synthesised with independence and by the acceptance of regional identity by the nationalist movement. The scholar shall examine the above hypotheses at the end.

Genesis of the New Awakening in Orissa

The 'Na Anka' Famine

The great famine of 1865-1866 considerably affected the course of history of Orissa. It is generally referred to 'Na Anka' as it occurred during the 9th regnal year of the king Divyasimha Deva of Puri. The catastrophic famine caught both the government and the people unaware and took a merciless toll of human lives. Some of the causes commonly attributed for this outbreak were the failure of crops due to the insufficient premature cessation of rainfall, shortage of foodgrains in the stores as a result of export in 1865, abnormal rise in the price of rice, lack of foresight on the part of the information machinery of the Government, geographical isolation of Orissa and the apathy of the landlords.[22] Mr. G.N. Barlow, the experienced Collector of Puri, left in October 1866. Mr. Manspratt took over as the Collector of Balasore in 1865 and Mr. Cornell was appointed Collector of Cuttack in February 1866. Mr. T.E. Ravenshaw succeeded Mr. Shore as Commissioner in July 1865.[23] This reshuffling in the Civil department added to the cacophony and dimension of the calamity since these men were yet to get acquainted with the problems of the region and they could not react quickly in the early stages of the famine. The separation of police from the general administration also made it difficult for them to acquire first-hand information about the situation. There was also no local newspaper either in Oriya or in English which could have given a word of caution to the administration, and no organisation of the people to transmit their grievance to the government. Thus, the information media was virtually absent.[24] Consequently, the situation became grievous. A Famine Commission was set up in 1867 which reported that the famine had affected about 12,000 sq. miles with a population of 40 millions taking a heavy toll of 10 million lives, worst affecting the three districts of Puri, Cuttack and Balasore.[25]

It would be pertinent to examine the role of this natural calamity in arousing a nationalistic sentiment and its importance in bringing in its train a number of far-reaching administrative and socio-political changes.

The famine of 1866 was not an unmixed evil. After the censure which the Bengal Government received from Stafford Northcote the Secretary of State for India, they evinced more zeal for the material progress of Orissa. In his letter to the Governor-General in India in Council dated 25 July 1867 he gave expression to some of his ideas.[26] He suggested that Assam and possibly Orissa should be separated from the Bengal Presidency to constitute into a Commissionership.[27]

John Lawrence, the then Governor-General of India consequently wrote to the Lt.-Governor of Bengal apprising him the feasibility of a separate Commissionership for Orissa provided the financial burden became viable. The Lt.-Governor on his part, virtually followed the line of the Governor-General and expressed his inability to agree to the proposal of Northcote. In response to such reactions, Northcote in his letter of 16 January 1868 to the Governor-General wrote that the question of the formation of separate Commissionerships including that of Orissa in the province of Bengal was a matter whose approval rested only with the Governor-General.[28] Finally, the Governor-General decided to constitute Assam and some other districts into a separate Commissionership but maintained the status quo for Orissa.

Northcote's suggestion for making Orissa a separate independent unit in 1867 came out releasing Bengal's territorial indigestion and administrative inefficiency. But the significance of his report was immense for the cause of the Oriya nationalism. It marked a unique watershed in the history of Orissa since the Government started taking initiative for the progress of this region and the people too relied most upon the same. This emotional confidence of the Oriyas ailed to some extent their suffering in the famine which ultimately paved the way for imparting Oriya nationalism.

This Na Anka famine proved to be a boon in disguise for the Oriyas. The agony of the famine was so much so that realisation set in motion in almost all the levels. The administration realised its several loopholes to tackle and handle the situation tactfully, the Government was convinced of its absence of strict adherence and noticing to the dilapidating recourse of the famine and the public was well aware of the step-motherly treatment meted out to them both by the above. The public as well as the administration desired to render Orissa a separate provincehood since they realised that had Orissa been a separate province, the misery of the famine on Orissa would not have been to that extent. The people commonly held that apathetic attitudes of the Bengal as well as the British had put them in troubles since it was held that due to their carelessness that the situation did aggravate more. The famine blessed Oriyas with the tendency, initiation and cooperation among themselves to form several political organisation, the first lesson of this sort to fulfil their demands, interest and benefits to be placed before their authorities in an organised, planned and disciplinary manner. This loosened the caste feeling particularly among the poorer sections who ate at the common public kitchen run by the government. This led to the rising of the self-consciousness which altogether found culmination in the growth of nationalism among themselves. The famine expressed the poverty of the Orissan peasantry, the low pace of agricultural development and the economic decline in general due to foreign rule and paved the way for the introduction of modern technology in agricultural production and for the growth of transport and communication because it was due to the bleak and intractable communication system, the distribution of the famine relief could not reach the victims living in the remotest rural areas. So the famine acted like a catalytic agent to foster political consciousness among the Oriyas which brought in the long run for them, a kind of bonafide result. At the official level also for the first time the need for a separate administrative unit for Orissa was realised.

Growth of Education

In the field of education, no interest was evinced by the Company though the missionaries had begun their educational activities in 1823 by establishing an English Charity School at Cuttack. The Government took over the management of the said school in February 1841. Nothing more was done for a number of years except starting a few vernacular schools. In some quarters of Orissa there was a demand for English education. For example, the people of Balasore petitioned several times for an English school in their town, but their prayer was turned down. In 1854 the number of schools directly managed by the Government in Orissa Division was only three English and eight vernacular schools. The Wood's Despatch of 1854 on Education which marked the beginning of a new phase in the education policy of the Government, brought no advantage to Orissa. In 1856, G.F. Cockpurn, the Commissioner of Cuttack, tried to improve the position and he pleaded for the creation of a separate post of Inspector of Schools for Orissa, and suggested the establishment of several Government schools and a Normal school to impart training to teachers. But the Lieutenant-Governor of Bengal turned a deaf ear to his suggestions. Thus the condition of education in Orissa at the end of the Company's rule was quite lamentable. The report of the Inspector of Schools, South-West Bengal for the year 1857-58 gave the following picture: There were three Zilla Schools in the headquarters of the three districts and the number of pupils on roll were: Balasore English School - 80, Cuttack - 113 and Puri - 89. There was one Anglo-Vernacular School at Bhadrak which received a grant-in aid of thirty rupees per month from the Government. Besides, there were only 16 vernacular schools in the whole province.[29] In 1852, an English School was set up in Sambalpur[30] and another in Ganjam about the same time.

Soon after the famine, T.E. Ravenshaw took keen interest for the spread of education in Orissa. He advocated for a separate Inspector of Schools for the Orissa Division. He pointed out that one such officer posted in Orissa "would be able to devote his whole attention towards the province introducing Oriya as the medium of instruction".[31] On his recommendations, a Joint School Inspector was appointed for Orissa in 1873 to assist the Inspector in controlling educational affairs of the Division. In 1867 the Government declared that the Cuttack Zilla School would be raised to the status of a 'High School' (Intermediate college affiliated to the Calcutta University), and on 20th January 1868, the 'High School' classes were started only with six students.[32] In that year Madhusudan Das, the foremost leader of modern Orissa, passed F.A. and in 1870, he passed B.A. from Calcutta University, the first graduate of Orissa. He was also the first Oriya to pass M.A. in 1873 and first Oriya to obtain the degree of B.L. in 1878 from the Calcutta University. The Cuttack High School was made a College in 1876. In both the years, 1878 and 1879, none could pass B.A. from the Cuttack College. In 1880, Durga Charan Sahu alone passed the B.A. examination from that college. In 1885 Gopal Ballabh Das, the brother of Madhusudan Das, passed Post Graduation in Botany from the Calcutta University, the second Oriya to be crowned with such degree.[33]

Mention may be made over here that with much financial constraints B.A. classes were opened in January 1879. The public donated Rs.30,000[34] and Maharaja Sriram Chandra Bhanjadeo donated Rs. 5,000 in 1877 for the improvement of the Cuttack College and Cuttack Medical School which was established by Ravenshaw in 1876 with the help of Dr. W.T. Stewart, Civil Surgeon of Cuttack.[35] Two years later, he donated Rs. 20,000 for the extension of the Cuttack College which was named as Ravenshaw College according to his suggestion.[36] It was a landmark in the growth of western education in Orissa.

Thus, many educational institutions grew up by the munificence of the rajas, maharajas and zamindars. It is said that the Ravenshaw College played the same role in Orissa as the Hindu College of Calcutta played in Bengal in creating a sense of self- consciousness and a strong sense of national spirit. It became a cradle for the germination of new ideas.

Women's education was very much neglected in Orissa for a long time. The Christian missionaries took initiative for the spread of female education in Orissa. They allowed the girls study in their school meant for the boys, of course in a separate room. The Balasore Mission School, where Fakir Mohan Senapati was the Headmaster for sometime, managed a girls' wing. He said "In all my humble efforts at the spread of female education in Balasore and improvement of the Oriya language, I had excellent support and patronage from the Collector, John Beams."[37]

In 1871, the Cuttack Hindu Valika Vidyalaya was established but attendance was very low. In November 1881, there were only 25 pupils in the school, out of which four were Oriya girls. The pupils of Jaleswar Girls' School in Balasore, started by Miss Crawford, an American lady, took M. E. examinations for the first time in 1882. The Ravenshaw Girls School was started at Cuttack in 1890. By the end of the 19th century many other girls schools sprang up at different places, but co-education continued in almost all schools. The orthodox section of the society opposed the education of girls. Thus the progress of education in Orissa was rather very slow, and the number of educated persons was rather insignificant. However, this enlightened and educated minority formed the 'hard core' of the socio-political movements in Orissa during the last decade of the 19th century.

Political consciousness was aroused in Orissa, partly due to the spread of English education and partly as a protest against the Bengali agitation against Oriya language and domination in higher appointments. Between 1868 and 1872, some Bengalis attempted to replace Oriya by Bengali as the medium of instruction in the schools in Orissa. They made an agitation that education would not spread in Orissa unless Bengali was introduced, as text books were not available in Oriya. This unjust agitation was relevantly opposed in Orissa.[38] Mr. Ravenshaw, the Commissioner encouraged setting up of more schools and writing up of text books in Oriya language. He also favoured the introduction of Oriya language alongside Bengali as a medium of instruction in the schools.

The impetus given to the vernacular teaching in Orissa now generated an apprehension among the Bengalis. They were afraid that once the local people started receiving higher education, the Oriyas would pose a threat to their economic and social status. They tried to prevail upon the Education Department that the medium of instruction in Oriya in Orissa would be a disastrous experiment considering the fact that there were quite a huge number of Bengalis in Orissa for whom it would be more convenient to have only the Bengali medium. The need for providing Bengali medium instruction was realised for the large section of students who naturally hailed from that community. It is noteworthy to point out here that the first elite class in Orissa was a mixture of Zamindars and Bengali Officials. Moreover, the problems of insufficient text books in the local vernacular language was not so acute as it was made out to be and that it was the Government who were responsible for the poor show with regard to the text-book. Indeed, had not the missionaries come to Orissa and set up the press, there would not have been even a single vernacular text-book. The comments of Utkal Dipika helped generate a concern among the Oriyas and a number of letters and complaints to the paper followed.[39] The lack of text books was partly due to lack of a demand in the absence of schools and non-promotion of Oriya as a medium of instruction, partly due to insufficient number of printing press and lack of Oriya letterhead and partly lack of authors for an educated Oriya elite class was only slowly emerging.

Mr. Ravenshaw supported the cause of the Oriya language wholeheartedly and urged in his speech in a prize distribution ceremony at Cuttack High School, that the Bengali outsiders should learn the local language, and if anybody was interested in a foreign language, he could come to the English school to learn. He also further commented that it was not necessary to continue with a second language apart from Oriya.[40] The opinion of the Commissioner was a great tory stockade in saving the Oriya language from extinction. However, a concerted attempt by many, including the historian Dr. Rajendra Lal Mitra, Umanath Haldar, the Deputy Inspector of Schools and Kantilal Bhattacharya, Deputy Inspector of Schools at Balasore to name a few, all Bengalis was being incessantly made to abolish Oriya from the schools in Orissa.

In the later part of the nineteenth century the Government of India started taking greater interest in the culture of india and decided to bring out a catalogue and compile a short history of the main Hindu Art and Sculpture. Dr. Rajendra Lal Mitra, a historian and antiquarian from Bengal requested the Government to appoint him to compile a book on the antiquities of Orissa.[41] The Government's permission to him to carry out the mission elated the Oriyas since they thought it to be an appreciation of their great cultural heritage. Educated people got prepared to extend all possible help required by Dr. Mitra. However, all the expectations and enthusiasm of the people evaporated when Dr. Mitra, in one of his speeches of Cuttack mentioned that as long as Oriya language was not abolished, there would not be any progress of the land. He even went on elaborating and emphasising his point.[42] In another occasion he also highlighted, "the Oriya language which is a mere dialect of Bengali and spoken by twenty lakhs of people of the coast, would not develop on account of the dearth of books. While in Bengal three hundred books were written and published in the preceding three years, only three to four books have been published in Orissa".[43] He further argued that if Bengali could successfully replace Oriya in the district of Midnapore then it should be equally potent in other districts as well.

The Oriyas were perplexed at Dr. Mitra's contention which accounted for only the Mughal-bandi areas, leaving aside a big section of Oriya-speaking population lived in Midnapore in the north, Ganjam in the south and Sambalpur in the west.[44] Dr. Mitra's arguments were thoroughly baseless, misleading and seemed to be ill-motivated.

The speech of Dr. Mitra made at Cuttack furthered the Oriya-Bengali dispute in Orissa. Dr. Mitra was a leading exponent in Indian history and his earnest request brought him the appointment to survey the rich socio-cultural ethos of Orissa. But instead of going deep into the cultural heritage of Orissa he prepared the layout for the elimination of such from Orissa in particular and India in general. His sincere and blatant exposition against the Oriya language itself showed his strong refusal to the British claims that India did not have any architectural and sculptural tradition of her own. This clearly proved his respect for and belief in the Oriya tradition and culture. His remark about the abolition of the Oriya language was apparently based on the wrong conclusion that was fed to him by the Bengalis in Orissa, as Dr. Mitra himself admitted before M.S. Das, an eminent Oriya leader later on.[45] In the course of the agitation attempts were not only made to prove that the Oriya language did not have a separate identity but books and articles were printed which distorted the history of the land.

Gourishankar Ray and Kalipada Banerjee, two leading Bengali figures through their Oriya journals *'Utkal Dipika'* and *'Utkal Hitaisini'* counteracted the campaign for subordination of Oriya language. It took a very bad turn when Uma Charan Haldar suggested that Oriya should be written in Bengali scripts.[46] But just at this time the government appointed the Cuttack School Book Society[47] for the preparation and publication of Oriya text books. On account of strong official support of Ravenshaw to the Oriya cause, the British Government unequivocally declared Oriya to be an independent language and not a mere dialect of Bengali as was being attempted to prove. It is significant that people like Gaurisankar Ray were guided not by their ancestral language but by the genuineness of the cause and became pioneering leaders of Oriya nationalism.

Nationalism possesses many elements, each of which could be justified if the people were willing. Language, religion, geography, race - all these may contribute to the claim of nationalism, though each one might prove disastrous if stretched too far without the popular desire. A German disciple of Rousseau, Herder (1744-1803) had thought that each man could be himself only by thinking and creating in his own mother-tongue and the rights of nationality were above all, the rights of language.[48] It was this trait of the linguistic nationalism that became most evident during the early phase of the struggle in Orissa.[49]

A parallel of such linguistic nationalism was to be witnessed in East Pakistan (later Bangladesh) where eventhough 54.6% people spoke Bengali and only 7.2% Urdu, the Federal Government of Pakistan decided to thrust Urdu as the national language soon after the partition. On March 19, 1948 when M.A. Jinnah visited Dacca, he too advocated the use of Urdu as their national language. The students rose in revolt but ignoring the popular sentiment of the East Pakistan the Federal Government proceeded resolutely with its language policy. The plan was not only to make Urdu the national language of Pakistan but to introduce Arabic script for the Bengali Language as well. The students and teachers of Dacca University came forward to oppose the move that was directed to strike at the very root of their culture - so atleast the people of East Pakistan understood. In February 1952, a mammoth general strike forced the Government to stall their plan and to accept Bengali as one of the national languages.[50] Ultimately Bangladesh emerged out of East Bengal.

Development of Press and Communication

With the blossoming of linguistic nationalism in Orissa, the educated people started exploring other possibilities to bolster up their stand. The necessary outcome of the spirit of liberation has been the active press and the formation of intellectual societies which has been the trend since the nineteenth century when nationalism started playing a unique role in many countries. The spirited Belgian youth for example, expressed his views through "Courrier des Pays-Bas" in Brussels and the "Mathieu Landsberg" in Liege, to name a few in order to spread their nationalistic sentiments.[51]

In Orissa, the missionaries were the pioneers in establishing the modern press. The Orissa Mission press was established at Cuttack in 1838 and the missionaries published a periodical named 'Jnanaruna' in 1849 for propagating their religious ideas. Other periodicals which existed earlier to the famine included 'Arunodaya' (1861) and 'Probodha Chandrika' (1856). But the most important journal of Orissa in the second half of the nineteenth century which moulded public opinion and ventilated their feelings was 'Utkal Dipika' edited by Gouri Sankar Ray, a champion of socio-political reforms. It came out on 4 August 1866 as a weekly paper from the Cuttack Printing Press, established by Bichitrananda Das. The third Press, the Utkal Press was set up in Balasore in 1868 by Fakir Mohan Senapati which published 'Bodha- Dayini' and 'Balasore Sambad Vahika'. The fourth press, known as the De's Press was also set up in Balasore by Raja Baikuntha Nath De in 1873.[52] Under his patronage, a literary journal, 'Utkal Darpana' was published. By the close of the nineteenth century, as many as 16 printing presses had appeared in Orissa of which prominence was gained by the Utkal Hitaisini Press (1873) of Kalipada Banerjee at Cuttack, the Victoria press (1885) at Cuttack managed by Jagannath Rao, the Sudhal Press of Bamra started by Raja Basudev Sudhal Dev, and the Mayurbhanj Press at Baripada.[53] But Balasore and Cuttack were the centres of intellectual awakening in Orissa in the second half of the 19th century. It was at the former place that the modern Oriya literature found its greatest culmination.

From 1870, the number of newspapers and journals began to increase rapidly. The Sudhal Press published the 'Sambalpur Hitaisini' at Bamra edited by Nilamani Vidyaratna on 30th May, 1889 which gave expression to public opinion and moulded their views in Western Orissa. Equally great was the influence of 'Utkal Sahitya' edited by Biswanath Kar. Besides these there were a number of other journals and periodicals which became defunct in no time. They were the media of the nascent socio- political consciousness of the people. The names and years of publication of some of these papers are given below.[54]

'Cuttack Argus' (January, 1869), 'Cuttack Star' (February, 1869), 'Utkal Hitaisini' (February, 1869) 'Cuttack Standard' (November, 1869), 'Cuttack Chronicle' (March, 1871), 'Utkal Darpan' (January, 1873), 'Utkal Putra' (April, 1873), 'Utkal Samskarak' (August, 1874), 'Utkal Madhupa' (April, 1878), 'Prajabandhu' (1882), 'Sebaka' (Sept, 1883), 'Pradipa' (Jan., 1885), 'Oriya and Navasambad' (Jan, 1888), 'Oriya Patriot' (April, 1888), 'Utkal Prava' (April, 1891), 'Ganjam News' (August, 1896), and 'Orissa Times' (June, 1898).[55]

Most of them were published from Cuttack the headquarters of the Orissa Division, where the educated Oriyas worked and made joint efforts to reach certain common ends. Gradually however some other places, particularly the Feudatory States and the outlying districts did not remain unresponsive. The 'Mayurbhanj Fortnightly' from Baripada appeared in April 1879, 'Purusottama Patrika' came out from Puri in April 1882 which however went out of publication after 1884. The 'Ganjam News' came out in August 1896 under the editorship of Syamsundar Rajguru and was patronised by the Parla chief, Padmanabha Narayan Dev. In June 1899, 'the Ganjam Odia Hitabadini' started from Berhampur edited by Sri R. Gunnia Shastri.[56] Some newspapers appeared too with a view to mobilizing public opinion in favour of Bengali language. The most important of them was the 'Utkal Hitaisini' or 'Orissa Patriot' which was founded in 1869. During the language agitation this paper took the lead against Utkal Dipika's vociferous support of Vernacular language. The same stand was also taken by another paper, called 'Utkal Star', an English weekly in February 1869. A couple of papers which came out during the language conflict, disappeared after the agitation had subsided. The publication of this spate of newspaper was made possible through numerous printing presses which were established in Orissa after the great famine of 1866. The newspapers aroused political awareness of the people and drew their attention to various problems of local and national interest. In addition, the progressive education in the western style also started widening the horizon of the common people. All these created congenial climate for like-minded people to come together for exchanging ideas on a number of issues.[57]

The Associations

The energy of the people found vent in several organisations devoted to the course of all-round improvement of the people. Those organisations tried to bring almost much-needed social reforms in several directions.

The first such organisation was the Mutual Improvement Society at Cuttack which was started in 1859.[58] Some Englishmen residing at Cuttack also attended the meeting of this society and discussed socio-cultural problems. After the famine of 1866, the number of organisations in different parts of Orissa increased rapidly. In November 1866 an association known as 'The Utkal Bhasa Unnati Bidhayini Sabha' was founded at Balasore and appears to be one of the earliest to come into being, Subsequently, 'Utkal Dipika' in its edition of 25 April 1868 informed that some learned and aristocratic people of Cuttack also had formed an association since two months and that it was sitting regularly at the Cuttack High School where discussions were held on various social and scientific topics. Facilities were also provided to its members for reading newspapers. In fact, the Commissioner Mr. Ravenshaw also attended a meeting of the association on April 15, 1868 and encouraged its member.[59] Abinas Chatterjee was the founder of this 'Cuttack Society' which attempted to widen its base and to this end, contacted various important personalities of the states including the landlords.

In the second half of the 19th century, various societies sprang up. They were known as Sabhas, Samajas and Samitis. Some of them were purely cultural and literary, while others were engaged in social reforms or activities relating to common welfare.[60] A list of such association is given below.[61]

Mutual Improvement Society, Cuttack (1859), Utkal Bhasa Unnati Vidhayini Sabha, Balasore (1866), Utkal Bhasoddipani Samaj, Cuttack (1867), Cuttack Debating Club (1869),[62] Cuttack Young Men's Association (1869),[63] Utkalollasini Sabha, Cuttack (1869), Utkal Brahmo Samaj, Cuttack (1869), Puri Society, (1870), Ganjam Utkal Hitabadini Sabha, Berhampur (1872), Utkal Bhasa Uddipani Sabha, Cuttack (1874),[64] Bhadrak Desh Hitaisini Sabha, Bhadrak (1874), Ganjam Nisha Nishedhini Sabha, (1875), Orissa Islam Association, Cuttack (1875), Utkal Sabha, Cuttack (1877), National Society, Balasore (1878), Unity Association, Balasore (1881), Utkal Hitaisini Sabha, Parlakhemindi (1881), Dhenkanal Hitaisini Sabha (1881), Orissa People's Association (1882), Puri Student's Association (1882), Anti-Corruption and Prohibition Sabha (1884), Utkal Sahitya Sammilani, Cuttack (1886), Orissa Graduate and Under-Graduate Association (1888), Baripada Reading Club (1889), Kayastha Sabha (1889-90), Cuttack Union Club (1891), Alochana Sabha, Cuttack (1893), B. Dey's Social Club, Balasore (1895), Bamalochani Sabha, Talcher (1895), Observer Club, Cuttack (1896), Orissa Christian Association (1896), Sikshabibardhini Sabha, Angul (1897) and Fraser Club, Sambalpur (1905).

Many of these organisations met extinct within their short span of life and could not materialise their aim to carry out splendid efforts for the dynamic sound-political change. But a little doubt remains that they succeeded in resuscitating the people as well as the society from the deep slumber and prinked the cocoon of their self-complacent existence. And the nationalism which had taken birth already, drew a lot of strength from these associations and newspapers.

Cuttack proved to be the cynosure of several organisations and associations which spearheaded variety of aspects leading to the resurgence of socio-political consciousness in Orissa. The elite of Orissa was influenced by outside political events. In 1870, Ravenshaw's attempts to unite all the associations with a view to forming the Orissa society failed.[65] In the same year when the National Society was established in Calcutta, attempts were made to set up a branch of it at Cuttack,[66] but there was no marked response. In 1876, the Indian Association was established in Calcutta by S.N. Banerjee.

Once again attempts were made at Cuttack[67] and Balasore[68] to form its branches. All associations of Cuttack, Balasore and Puri warm welcomed its foundation in Calcutta. Although no regular branch of the Indian Association was formed in Orissa, all these activities may be regarded as pioneering efforts towards political awakening. But the actual beginning of political activities in Orissa began with the establishment of the Utkal Sabha or Orissa Association in 1882.

The Orissa Association started functioning with no ambitious plan and programme. It was meant to be forum only for encouraging literary discussions in an informal manner. The sessions sat regularly and monthly meetings were held. One such monthly session of the Orissa Association was held in October 1879 at the building of the Cuttack Printing Company where, Ramsankar Ray read an article on 'Unity and Orissa' and Sudarsana Das was the President.[69] The Orissa Association gradually attracted the educated people of Cuttack into its fold and its activities went on with a good deal of zeal and zest.

Political consciousness of the people in Orissa was sufficiently roused by 1882 when Lord Ripon introduced the new scheme of Local Self-Government in India. A big public meeting was organised at Cuttack on 30 June 1882 to celebrate the occasion and to thank the Governor-General for his benevolent measure. The meeting was attempted by the zamindars, Government servants, pleaders and businessmen, etc. M.S. Das, Hariballabha Ghose, Priyanath Chatterjee, Madhusudan Rao, Bipin Behari Mitra etc. spoke on the occasion. The speakers strongly supported the measure of Local Self-Government initiated by Lord Ripon and pointed out that the people were prepared to shoulder the responsibilities entrusted to them. They desired that the people should elect their representatives to the local bodies in order to make them more effective.[70] A public meeting in this connection was also held in Puri in the first week of August 1882, and similar decisions were taken.[71]

The Orissa Association assumed greater prominence in 1882 when M.S. Das, a man of great moral courage, self-respect and determination, deeply influenced by the philosophy of Edmund Burke and John Stuart Mill,[72] Gourisankar Ray and Chaudhury Kasinath Das decided to incorporate more constructive ideas into its programme. The Bhingarpur Zamindar Chaudhury Kasinath Das became its President and Gourisankar Ray, a Calcutta-returned lawyer, its Vice-President. The Utkal Sabha became an exponent political organ of Orissa in the 19th century.

Gourisankar Ray mooted the ideas of organising a branch of the Indian Association at Cuttack,[73] but M.S. Das was of the opinion that Orissa's problems were quite different from that of Bengal although she was under the Bengal Presidency. Like the Madras Mahajan Sabha (May, 1884)[74] and Poona Sarvajanik Sabha (1887)[75], the Indian Association of Calcutta was local association although it was called Indian. Orissa should have an association of her own to spearhead the political activities of the people. Gourisankar seemed to have been convinced.

A special meeting of the Utkal Sabha was convened on 21 May 1883 to discuss the controversial Ilbert Bill of Lord Ripon. The members unanimously agreed to support it and passed a resolution demanding the appointment of the Indians as session judges with power to try the European offenders.[76] It further decided to send a petition to the Governor-General for the acceptance of the Bill. On other occasions, the Utkal Sabha of Cuttack and the Balasore National Society criticised the conspiracy of the Anglo-Indians against Ripon for having passed the Ilbert Bill.[77] While the Local Self-Government created a spirit of the civic sense, the Ilbert Bill controversy taught the people the lessons of organisations.[78] In another meeting on 19 December 1886, the Utkal Sabha decided to petition the Government to introduce liberal reforms for reconstituting the Legislative Councils in order to bring the real representatives of the Indian people into those bodies.[79] Thus the people in Orissa had begun to clamour for political rights as was the case elsewhere in India during the last quarter of the 19th century.

No prominent delegate from Orissa attended the first session of the Indian National Congress held in December, 1885 in Bombay. But to the second session of December, 1886 in Calcutta, presided over by Dadabhai Naoroji, the Utkal Sabha sent its four selected representatives. They were M.S. Das, Golak Chandra Bose, Hari Ballava Bose and Kalipada Banerjee. Besides, the National Society of Balasore also sent three delegates, Baikuntha Nath De, Bhagaban Chandra Das, and Ramesh Chandra Mandal for participation in the Congress session.[80] Rev. Shem Sahu, John Samson Rout, Mushi Mahammed Athar, Bhagaban Ch. Das, Ramesh Chandra Mandal, Gourisankar Ray and M.S. Das took keen interest in the activities of the Congress in its early years. Especially the leaders of the Utkal Sabha like M.S. Das and Gourisankar Ray were pioneers in bringing the message of the Congress and its liberal ideas to Orissa in the last two decades of the 19th century. They laid the foundation of constitutional struggle of the people against the British authorities.

The larger question involved here is - why the Orissa leaders did not join the Congress-led movement in late 19th century ? They were opposed to the Ilbert Bill as much as the rest of the country. They were committed to democracy and had welcomed the introduction of local self-government. It seems that the leaders felt that the Bengali elite which was dominating the Congress was unsympathetic to the aspiration of Oriyas for assertion of their regional and linguistic identity. The growing consciousness was initially directed against the Bengalees more than the British. Besides the issue of formation of a separate province was high on the agenda of the Oriya elites.

The problem which agitated the enlightened Oriyas for a longtime was the amalgamation of Oriya-speaking tracts into one administrative unit and then the formation of a separate province[81] which led to the emergence of an organised political movement- a sustained struggle for many years in a institutional way to achieve the said objective.

The suggestion for amalgamation of Oriya-speaking tracts under one administration came from official sources as early as 1841. Mr. Cooke, the Commissioner of Orissa in his Administrative Report of Orissa Division for 1894 mentioned that in the map of India of 1841 the Oriya-speaking areas of Madras and Central Province were shown included on Orissa.[82] But the people of Orissa at that time were not politically so conscious to catch the clue to make an organised attempt to form popular opinion and press their demand.

The first non-official proposal for the unification of the scattered Oriya-speaking tracts under one single administration came from Raja Baikuntha Nath De and Bichitrananda Patnaik in 1876 in which they presented a memorandum to the Government asking it to take necessary steps in this matter[83]. In November 1885 Sir Stewart Colvin Bayley the Lt.-Governor of Bengal visited Orissa. He was presented a memorial by the Utkal Sabha of Cuttack and among other things, he was requested to give attention to the problem of uniting the Oriya-speaking territories of Madras, Central Province, and Bengal in one administrative unit so that its all-round development would not be hampered. However, the Lt-Governor rejected the proposal in his reply to the memorial.[84]

The language issue came into surface at Balasore in 1870, when a Bengali teacher of Balasore Zilla School, named Kantichandra Bhattacharya wrote a booklet, 'Odia Swatantra Bhasa Nay' in order to prove that Oriya was a dialect of Bengali :[85]Some Bengalees at the same time clandestinely carried on the signature campaign urging the introduction of Bengali as the medium of instruction in schools.[86] Fakir Mohan Senapati who was then a mere primary school teacher spearheaded a counter-attack against this move. Interestingly, however, a section of the Bengali elite domiciled in Orissa, supported the view that Oriya was a rich language with a separate alphabet. They even counteracted the arguments of the anti-Oriya Officers. Bhudev Mukhopadhyaya, a Bengali educationist and a literati, also expressed the baselessness of Kantichandra's arguments,[87] and pointed out that Assamese, Bengali and Oriya did have some close affinities on account of their common origin. It was supported by John Beams, Collector of Balasore (1869-73) who established the historicity of the Oriya language by a scientific analysis of its grammar and phonetic by criticising Kantichandra's thesis as "profoundly destitute of philological arguments".[88] Fakir Mohan Senapati says in his autobiography, "At that time, to the good fortune of the Oriyas, all the British officials and the English Christian missionaries were in our favour. They all now supported our countermove".[89] Emphasising the independence and antiquity of the Oriya language, Beams published a brochure and advocated that adequate steps should be taken for its development. T.E. Ravenshaw, the Commissioner supported Beams. Oriya was allowed to remain in its former position. Fakir Mohan thus saved his mother-language, spoken by more than 20 lakhs of people, from the impending linguistic guillotine by the neighbours and proved himself as the real senapati[90] of his race. The language movement in Orissa led to the growth of the Oriya language and literature.

A different situation cropped up in 1895. The Chief Commissioner of the Central Provinces, John Woodburn decided to abolish the Oriya language from official use in the district of Sambalpur. Such a decision against the interest of the majority of Oriya population in the district raised a storm of protest not only in that district but also throughout

Orissa. On June 20, 1895, the Utkal Sabha sent a memorial to Lord Elgin, the Governor-General, protesting against this unjust and arbitrary measure. They asserted that the denial to the people "of the use of their mother tongue, is the worst form of gagging and is yet unknown even in the most despotic form of Government".[91] They hoped that such a decision would not be put into effect. However, all protests were in vain, and by the end of 1895 Oriya was discontinued as the language of courts in Sambalpur. This very much axed at the sentiments of the Oriya-speaking people and from that year they started continuous agitation in all fronts for the amalgamation of Oriya-speaking tracts. It is curious to note that in 1895 the Commissioner of Orissa Division in his Annual Administrative Report wrote : "As a question of administrative reform for which there is much to be said, I have to advocate the extension of the divisional boundaries so as to include the whole area populated by races speaking the Oriya language, or at any rate, some definite areas adjoining Orissa where the Oriya language prevails". As regards the areas to be united with the Orissa Division, he said : "The areas that I prefer to are the Sambalpur district of the Chhatisgarh Division of the Central Provinces with the tributary states of Patna, Sonepur, Rairokhol, Bamra, Kalahandi and the whole or part of the Ganjam District with the states of Kimidi and Ghumsur".[92]The suggestion of the Commissioner was completely ignored.

The agitation in Sambalpur for the restoration of Oriya as the court language continued unabated and in July 1901 the leading men of Sambalpur proceeded to Nagpur in a delegation to apprise the situation to the new Chief Commissioner, A. Fraser. They said that "if it was thought impossible to have Oriya as the language of one Central Provinces' district, they would prefer to be transferred to Orissa".[93] The Commissioner accepted the proposal and urged the Government of India to transfer Sambalpur to Orissa Division. M.S. Das as who was a member of the Bengal Legislative Council by this time, informed Lord Curzon, the Governor- General that the people of Orissa fully supported the memorial submitted to Sir Andrew Fraser, and it was their desire that the Oriya territories should be placed under a Chief Commissioner. A deputation from Sambalpur consisting of Madan Mohan Mishra, Balabhadra Suar, Braja Mohan Patnaik, Bihari Das Mahant and Sripati Misra also met the Governor-General at Shimla to acquaint him with their problems.[94] It is reported that in 1900, M.S. Das also called on the Viceroy there. He narrated the misfortune of the Oriya in such an appealing manner that Curzon was greatly moved. He promised to do whatever could be done and also agreed to visit Orissa on M.S. Das' request. The same year on his way back from Madras and enroute to Calcutta he visited Orissa, and was apparently charmed by her art and natural beauty.[95] On 2 September 1901, M.S. Das sent a telegram to the Private Secretary to the Viceroy, who was resting in Shimla describing in brief the case of Sambalpur.[96] He wrote that he had heard about the new Chief Commissioner's visit to Shimla to discuss the memorial presented to their office in 1895 by the people at Sambalpur protesting against the order of "abolishing Oriya as court and official language". He reminded that Oriya Association too had submitted a memorial of the same nature in June 1895. His telegram "...... the people of Orissa fully support the memorial now submitted by Sambalpur people" underlined clearly the fact that the interest in Sambalpur was not confined to the people of that district alone, it was a matter of concern to the people of Orissa as well. This was because Sambalpur had all along been considered by them as a part of Orissa. He hoped, "Curzon being the first Viceroy to visit Orissa, will vouchsafe personal attention to this grievances". The reply which he received from the Private Secretary to the Viceroy on 12 September 1901[97] indicated the Secretary's sympathy with the issue. He wrote that he had shown everything to the viceroy and due considerations would be given. However, the Govt. of India did not consider it feasible to transfer Sambalpur to the Orissa Division or to create a Chief Commissionership for Orissa at that time, though they restored Oriya to its rightful place in the Sambalpur district from 1 January 1903.[98]

During the later half of 1902, the Oriyas of Ganjam sent a mammoth memorial to Lord Curzon, in which they spoke of themselves as dissociated from their Oriya brethren, and of Orissa as "a limb separated from the body", and they prayed "not for a patch-work redistribution but that the Govt. of India will be graciously pleased to bring together the scattered divisions inhabited by Oriya-speaking people, i.e., Ganjam in Madras, Sambalpur in the C.P., and Orissa in Bengal, under the Government of Bengal or under any one Govt. and one University."[99]

Ganjam was once the centre of the Oriya literature and culture. Great Oriya poets like Upendra Bhanja, Kavisurya Baladev Rath and Gopalkrishna were born here. Their contributions to the Oriya literature are inestimable.[100] All the zamindars of the Ganjam and Koraput districts were of Oriya origin. They maintained matrimonial relationship with the feudatory Chiefs and zamindars of Orissa. The Raja of Parlakhemindi had blood relationship with the Raja of Puri. All the zamindars and their subjects, therefore, cherished a natural desire to be united with the Orissa Division. Their desire became quite intense in the last decades of the 19th century.

In 1870, Janardan Das of Ghumsar complained that the Oriyas were harshly treated by the Telugus in the offices.[101] He further called upon the Oriyas to agitate against this maltreatment. To ventilate the grievances of the Oriyas, William Mohanty started an Oriya Weekly, named Swadeshi in 1876. He complained that there were no adequate educational facilities for the Oriyas. Secondly, Oriya was not used in the offices.[102] On popular demands, the Madras University recognised the indepedent status of the Oriya language by making it a subject of study. In 1890, the Govt. of Madras recognised Oriya as the official language in Ganjam.[103] From this year, the people of Ganjam began to agitate for their union with Orissa. Harihar Mardaraj Deo, the Raja of Khallikote took leadership of the movement.

By the beginning of the 20th century, the attitude of the people all over Orissa had started changing. They had become increasingly conscious of their problems, the successful language agitation and the struggle in Sambalpur for reviving their mother- tongue instilled a hope in them- a hope for the metamorphosis of their present loathsome condition. Meanwhile, there was a deep rethinking on the part of the Government about the territorial redistribution and they were toying with the idea of amalgamating Sambalpur with Orissa and of putting them together under the Central Provinces.[104] At this juncture Berar was ceded by the Nizam of Hyderabad to the Government and the Government took a trial decision to make the territorial readjustment in India on a more rational basis.

Role of Intellectuals

The intellectuals, be they philosophers, novelists, poets, play wrights or historians have traditionally played significant role in all the nationalist revolutions of the world. Not only do they reach the minds of the people through their writings, they also subject every institution of the society to the test of reason and through that foster the idea of change and progress.

On the Indian scene, those who had comparatively earlier contacts with the Britishers and consequently had a longer exposure to the western style of education imbibed the idea of progressiveness and formed an enlightened class. Raja Rammohun Roy of Bengal was the leader of this group and he was venerated as "The father of modern India."

In Orissa, the wind of change was yet to be felt. It was only after the language agitation in the 19th century that the need for awakening was seriously felt. Just as the British impact unwillingly germinated the Indian nationalism, the Oriya nationalist feeling drew inspiration to some extent from the Bengali renaissance and their social reform ideas. The Oriya literary and social ideas in the late 19th century centred around three figures - Radhanath Ray, Fakir Mohan Senapati and Madhusudan Rao.

Radhanath Ray, a Bengali government official had begun writing in Bengali but subsequently switched over to Oriya. He pioneered the modern Oriya poetry. His love for nature, ecology of Orissa's land, flora and fauna and popular myths endeared him to a large readers. He freed himself from the traditional Oriya poetic metre and themes of epic and devotion. He was well-conversant with English literature and the new waves in Bengali. He was also a nationalist lyricist, his 'Sarvesam nno Bharata Janani' is still popular in orissa. His principal works include the 'Chilika', 'Mahajatra', 'Darabara', 'Bharata Gitika' etc. Through some of his writings, he always attempted to convey the Oriya readers the ideas of western philosophers.[105]

Madhusudan Rao, a great believer in Brahmo Samaj was influenced by the enlightened ideas of the west and contributed a great deal towards social reformation through his writings. He also displayed a natural penchant for independent thought and strove towards freedom from religious dogmas. Deep nationalistic feelings run through his poems, 'Pruthibi Prati' and 'Janmabhumi'. Another collection of poems by him, 'Utkala gatha' centred round the Oriya nationalistic ideas. Some of these were chosen by the Utkal Union Conference to be sung during its sessions.[106] The credit of compiling a 'first book' for beginners in Oriya language also goes to Madhusudan Rao. This book although narrow in scope, manifests his distinct style and he attempted to bring upon the young minds the essence of nationalism with the help of such simple word formations and imageries that it is considered by many to belong to the genre of Classics.

Fakir Mohan's imagination was greatly stirred by the language crisis and he vowed to take it upon himself to add a new dimension and respectability to Oriya literature.[107] He has indeed been regarded as the 'father of modern Oriya literature', 'father of modern Oriya prose, short story and novel'. His writings depict in an innovative, inimitable, colloquial style, the conditions that prevailed in the society, its superstitions and also the political chaos that confronted Orissa. His autobiography brought to light in a lucid manner all the darkness prevailing in the feudatory areas where he had worked for a long time. It also gave graphic descriptions of the exploitation by the rulers and the abject-backwardness of their subjects.[108] His poetic creations like 'Utkala Krusaka', 'Utkala Bhumi', 'Utkala Yubaka' were the products of his deep involvement in the Oriya nationalistic ideas and inspired thousands of his fellowmen with their message.[109] He was the one who freed himself from Sanskritised Oriya and wrote his literary pieces in simple and understandable language so much so that, they attracted larger readership in Orissa. His role in setting up the printing press with Oriya letterhead and in subsequent publication of text books was noteworthy.

The language of the common urban people under this influence was fast losing its distinctiveness. Fakir Mohan recognised this dangerous trend and was determined to stall this process of language. He very meticulously chose the words which were current amongst the unsophisticated villagers. This, among other things, encouraged the readers to shake off their diffidence in using their mother-tongue in its genuine form. Moreover, colloquial style instantly touched the heart of the masses as well as other fellow writings. His writings enjoy a classic status in the Oriya literature till date.

Close to the pedestal of the trio, appeared the famous lyricist of the late 19th and early 20th century, Gangadhar Meher of Sambalpur a prolific nature poet. Though he received no modern education, his writings expressed in spontaneity and natural freshness of a poetic genius that is still a proud possession of the Oriya literature. The Oriya agitation which was quite intense in Sambalpur in the late 19th century produced as has been noted, a tremendous impact on Oriya literature. During this agitation Gangadhar Meher wrote his appealing poems which were so poignant that they immediately caught on.[110] The traditional values and the sacred duty to uphold them was the theme of many of his poems and the poet tried to instigate amongst the common people a sense of attachment to their motherland.[111] His writings therefore did not betray a special fancy for western ideas instead, they were very much home-bound and appealed to the people tremendously.

The period following that of Gangadhar Meher was dominated by the duo, Nand Kishore Bal and Gopal Chandra Praharaj. These two tried to represent through their writings the Oriya culture in its true nature. Nand kishore Bal immortalised as the 'Village Bard' of Orissa, set his poems against the background of unsophisticated, serene beauty of the Oriya countryside and gave a special status to the day-to-day lives in villages through his writings.[112] Gopal Chandra Praharaj, the compiler of most authentic and voluminous dictionary in the Oriya language was a gifted essayist who treated extremely serious issues of the society with rare wit.[113] Praharaj was very closely associated with the activity of the problems facing the Oriyas.

M.S. Das' speech and writings also helped to intensify the spirit of nationalism in literature in the early 20th century. Laxmikanta Mohapatra, Padma Charan Patnaik, Dinabandhu Mohanty, Kuntala Kumari Sabat, Sribatsa Panda, Balukeswar Misra, Harihar Dash and Biswanath Kar were a few of the notable writers and poets who illuminated the Oriya literary scene in the early 20th century. And each of them dealt with some aspects of the nationalist problem of Orissa. In this context much attention must be paid to the 'Satyavadi tradition' initiated by Gopabandhu Das which had a tremendous impact on literature dealing with nationalism and the social reformation. In the year 1909, on the day of Kumara Purnima the full moonday of autumn, a festival day for the Oriyas, a small 'open air minor school' which later became a High School, was set up at Satyavadi in Puri district on the suggestion of M.S. Rao amongst splendid scenic beauties of the Churiana trees imparting charm and fragrance to the young boys to keep their minds afresh all the time.[114] This school was the product of lofty idealism of young intellectuals who were convinced that much of the evil could be eradicated through proper development and training of the young. They envisaged a school where the boys should, along with their studies, be taught the essence of life which would make them fullerman, courageous, confident and ready to work for the upliftment of their brethren. These young intellectuals had before them the images of Eton, Harrow, Rugby and the Fergusson of Pune.[115] Gopabandhu was the brain behind the school. He was greatly influenced by the personality of Harihar Das whom he had never seen.[116] Harihar Das who died as early as 1872 had recommended a new life of education as a panacea for all types of malfunctioning of the society. He was the founder of the Sanskrit and Oriya, himself learning Greek and English from him.[117]

The influence of the Brahmo Samaj and the Arya Samaj on Gopabandhu planted in him the same spirit and dynamism as was there in Raja Rammohun Roy and Swami Dayananda Saraswati- in accepting the western secularism and learning and reforming Hinduism from within.[118] Gopabandhu was also deeply impressed by the preachings of this Samaj and often quoted them in his speeches and writings.[119]

The method of education adopted in the Satyavadi School was based on the Indian tradition of spiritual foundation but was influenced by the western progressive ideas. It taught the students the importance of discipline, high moral character and simplicity bordering on austerity in their daily life. This relationship, the school contemplated, must not only be amicable, it must be as close and deep as that between the members of a single family. In the weekends, the students used to have elocution, essay and other literary competitions; discussions on history and heritage; recitations and similar activities. The boys were brought up in the midst of true Oriya traditions; traditional Oriya festivals were observed and typical Oriya food was always on the menu, Oriya scriptures were read.[120] The teachers and students worked in perfect unison even outside the class rooms and their work ranged from gardening to cremation of dead bodies during floods and epidemics.

The teachers working there had come and joined the organisation voluntarily knowing fully well that this was almost a missionary work that entailed much hardship and sacrifice. The remuneration was rather meagre and was meant to cover only their basic requirements. However, a sense of dedication sustained the enthusiasm of these young people. The five close associates of Satyavadi, famous in Orissa as 'Pancha Sakha' were Gopabandhu Das, Nilakantha Das, Acharya Harihar Das, Godavaris Misra and Krupasindhu Misra.

During the non-cooperation movement, Gopabandhu was imprisoned from 24 January 1923 to 26 June 1924. In the jail, his famous literary creations like 'Bandira Atmakatha' and 'Karakavita' came out which have become famous both for their sympathetic tone towards the countrymen as for their literary qualities. After his release from jail, he devoted his time and energy to the Congress and social work. He was also closely associated with the Servants of India Society and was its Vice-President in 1928.[121] He edited newspapers like 'Samaj' and 'Satyavadi' through which he revealed an unmatched ability as a journalist. Gopabandhu was thus a politician, an educationist, journalist, a litterateur, all blended into one but first and foremost, he was a great humanist-the authentic voice of the poor.

Gopabandhu's dream of Satyavadi might have been considered utopian but it was an exercise in the right direction- almost a fore-runner of the Santiniketan type the work of a free idealist. In the age of darkness in Orissa it acted as a beacon of light. A similar experiment was also being contemplated by Rabindranath Tagore when he opened a school at Santiniketan, Bengal, in 1911. The Satyavadi School also fostered the spirit of nationalism and patriotism among its members. One incidence clearly proves this phenomenon-Nilakantha narrated one anecdote during a vacation, Acharya Harihar Das took Nilakantha Das and Anant Misra (the future campaigner of the Oriya Movement), then the students of Ravenshaw College, Cuttack along with him to Gopabandhu's village in Suando. While sitting in a moon-lit evening on the bank of the river Bhargabi, Gopabandhu made them promise that none of them would go in for any government job, that they would instead do something about their country and the countrymen.[122]

The three personalities, Harihar, Nilakantha and Anant formed a very close group and centred their activities about Gopabandhu's ideals. They rebelled always against social taboos and class-barriers and infact, against the Brahmanic traditions, although they came from conservative Brahmin families. In the process, the Satyavadi group was victimised by the high-caste priests. A number of attempts were made to destroy it by setting fire and spreading scandalous rumours.[123] They fought against child marriage, supported female education, sympathised with the down trodden and the socially ostracised. Apart from these 'Pancha Sakha' there were other teachers too like Basudev Mohapatra, Ramachandra Rath, Haladhara Mohapatra, Madhusudan Misra, Arttatrana Das and Dhaneswar Maharana whose sacrifice and devotion was exemplary.[124]

The Satyavadi school drew attention from all quarters and its credibility as an educational institution soared up in the public eye with the growing reputation of Gopabandhu. Many boys from the outlying Oriya tracts came to study here too. His fame grew outside Orissa too. Surendranath Banerjee, on his Orissa visit in 1912 was full of praise for the school.[125] Many other dignitaries including the Bihar-Orissa Governor Sir Edward Gait and Sir Asutosh Mukherjee called at this institute.[126]

Gopabandhu and his close associates wanted the school to remain free from government control. Accordingly it never accepted any grant from official authorities. It took a long time therefore obtaining the necessary recognition from the Calcutta University which would enable its students to appear for the school final examination. The University was also empowered to provide grants for recognised high school.[127] The school gradually invited apprehensions in the Government circles. It appeared very odd to them that a group of highly educated persons who could get any lucrative job, were able to express this temptation and instead preferred to be associated with a school, where they had to settle down to a pittance. The refusal of the management of the school to any Government help further precipitated their suspicion of them. They apprehended that perhaps it was a centre for disseminating ideas of freedom struggle. They even suspected that the students and teachers were hiding lethal weapons in the school. They decided therefore to appoint plain-clothed detectives, masquerading them as relations of some student, inside the hostel and kept the school under constant surveillance.[128]

The school managed only with donations. After nine years of quiet and sustained dedication, disquieting signs showed up at Satyavadi, a clash of personalities became evident. However, Satyavadi was converted into a 'national school' by Gopabandhu after the call for non-cooperation was given. In the first ten years of its existence Satyavadi school had wielded influence which was far too deep to be blotted out of memory. In its own way it contributed a great deal to the cause of nationalism. The teachers of Satyavadi were great crusaders.

Nilakantha Das, a scholar and close associate of Gopabandhu, made outstanding contributions in the field of literature. His essays like 'mo nisa', 'niti o prakriti', 'pratibha puja o pratima puja'echoed his rebellious voice against the social setup. He laid bare the superstitions that had polluted the entire social atmosphere and had emasculated the people of Orissa and laid stress on a fresh and free national life.

Godavaris Misra, a friend of Gopabandhu and a distinguished educationist was a poet and journalist of high calibre. The anthologies of 'kalika kisalaya' were the products of his student life.[129] He also wrote many poems that reflected his rare sensibility while he roved round the outlying Oriya speaking areas campaigning for amalgamation.[130] He has left behind a considerable mass of prose writings also in the form of short stories, essays, and adapted novels. All that he wrote, breathes warm patriotism.[131]

The emergence of a middle-class elite or intellectuals or a bourgeoisie has always acted as a factor in the growth of nationalist consciousness in modern times. This class has the ability to lead the mass and propagate an ideal transcending the boundaries of their class interest. They have always played a distinct role in arousing social, cultural and political consciousness. Orissa was no exception to this general trend.

In Orissa too, the responsibility of arousing the mass consciousness to the dangers posed to their language in the coastal districts and subsequently in Sambalpur was taken up by these intellectuals. In the beginning of the 20th century, they endeavoured to enrich their literature and through it to increase public awareness so as to guard against a future threat to their language or to their culture. In this attempt many borrowed liberally from the western ideas that spoke of freedom of thought from superstition and blind belief and equality of men in society. It was hoped by them that only when the Oriyas were united under a common fold of language and culture and in fact were inspired by a sense of belonging would their political union come about. To sum up, it must be said that intellect for intellect's sake was not the motto that ran through the minds of these intellectuals. They identified their task as something more down-to-earth that of constantly illuminating for their brethren the right directions in all spheres of life so that Oriyas and Orissa could appear distinct to others.

Thus, the gradual spread of education ushered in a new age in Orissa. Although the number of advocated persons in Orissa was small, yet this enlightened group took the lead for progress of the nation in all fields. The establishment of press, circulation of Vernacular and English newspapers, publication of books, periodicals and journals and above all, the establishment of several social, cultural, educational and political associations hastened the process of awakening. The language controversy opened the eyes of the people and widened their mental, moral and intellectual outlook. A common language and literature played no less significant a role to resuscitate socio-political consciousness in different parts of Orissa. The discovery of Orissa's efflorescent past glory brought pride and self-confidence in the mind of the people. These factors developed socio-political consciousness among the educated Oriyas with considerable significance for the future. M.S. Das a brilliant lawyer with great political foresight provided leadership to the elite and stimulated people's interest in and enthusiasm for political and national activities.

He was the moving spirit in public life and the symbol of a new awakening of the people of Orissa in the last two decades of the 19th century.

Before analysing the nature of the genesis of nationalistic and popular movements in Orissa, one may fruitfully draw parallel with other such contemporary movements in India. Bengal whose nationalism is never questioned also nurtured a regional identity based on language. If the anti-partition agitation was nationalist then there is no harm in terming the Orissa movement for a separate province as nationalist. A striking feature of anti-partition movement was the failure of Bengal leadership to demand separation of Bihar and Orissa and Assam from Bengal in lieu of division of Bengali speaking people. Right from Surendra Nath Banerjee to Aurobindo Ghosh none demanded separation of Orissa from Bengal. Thus it was natural that the Oriya leadership considered the Bengal Congress to be unsympathetic to the aspirations of the Oriyas.

Hence, significantly the study of a detailed regional nationalism of the Oriyas can not achieve its objectives if it gets a stepmotherly treatment. Rather, a true and objective appraisal of the situation can be made only when one is assured of various other important regional nationalisms possessed, so that the peculiarities of each may be brought to the focus and in this background, the characteristic features of the Oriya nationalism may be well assessed. Taking the whole gamut of this above proposition an attempt has been made to analyse the development of nationalistic feelings in some regions in the British India.

The most evident pertinent regional nationalism earmarked in the British India was that of Bengal. It was pertinent because at one time, the Indian nationalism virtually identified itself with that of Bengal.[132] Bengal's nationalistic agitation did not seek a separate province for the Bengali- speaking people; indeed it was opposed to carving out the separate administrative unit of Bihar and Orissa from the Bengal Presidency in 1912. The partition of Bengal in 1905 stormed into action the Bengali nationalism. The partition brought out the sympathy of leaders from all over India and Indian National Congress condemned vehemently the step taken by the Government. However, it did not take much time for the Bangalees to be reunited and this came as an angel's boon for Bengali nationalism in particular and the linguistic nationalism in general. Though again the province in 1947 was partitioned with India achieving its freedom, still it can be asserted that at no stage did the currents of Bengal nationalism run counter to the mainstream of Indian nationalism.

The nationalistic struggle of Andhras seems to have been caused by several factors. The entire Telugu-speaking population was coming under the jurisdiction of the Modern Presidency during the British rule and the Andhras felt desperate at the Tamilians' lion's share in matters relating to education, service and commerce.[133] This depressed sentiments of the Telugus set in motion a nationalism based on the language and their feelings gathered momentum in the late 19th century when the flow of Western ideas and education started coming in.[134] With the growth and development of the Vernacular literature they felt increasingly conscious of their distinctiveness. This again got an impetus when an all-India cry during the Swadeshi movement in 1903 was raised against the injustice done to the Bengali-speaking population. The separation of Bihar and Orissa from the Bengal Province in 1912 offered an instinct to the Andhra nationalism to seek a separate identity for itself.[135] Though the Andhra leaders were championing their individual cause, they never abstained themselves from the workings of the Indian Congress movement. Rather they appealed to the Congress to grant them a separate provincial circle. The Andhra Mahasabha, essentially a nationalist organisation of the Andhras, was subordinate to their provincial Congress circle.[136] The leaders of Andhras favoured that the general administrative units of India be mapped out on the basis of language[137] and expected to gain consequently such reorganisation. The formation of the provinces of Orissa and Sind in 1936 provided the leaders of Andhra nationalism with an opportunity to substantiate their claim further. It was finally advocated that if two deficit provinces could be constituted, there should be no economic barrier to the formation of a much wealthier Andhra Province.[138] And the struggle of the Andhras was crowned with success when they were awarded a separate province-the first to be formed on linguistic basis in free India in 1956.

Similarly in Bihar the nationalistic struggle championing the cause of the local people happens to have grown out of a sense being discriminated against in the fields of education, commerce and service. Such sentiments were but a natural comprehension to the prevailing advantageous position that the Bengali community found themselves in throughout the Presidency as a result of their earlier assimilation with British system of education and administration. The nationalism among the middle class Biharis is reported to have sprouted as early as 1871 when the census figures brought to the limelight their backwardness.[139] At the outset the leaders attached themselves to the task of getting the grievances redressed in the existing administrative setup and anticipating this a Himalayan task in the midst of the intermediary rulers started demanding a separate province for them in the subsequent stages.[140] The strategy, they thought appropriate for achieving their goal, was one of keeping the British overlords sympathetically disposed towards their cause. To materialise this objective they found it unjustifiable to involve themselves in the anti-partition movement in 1905.[141] However, after 1912, when their purpose was achieved, Bihar did not hesitate to join the Indian national movement against the British.[142]

Regional sub-nationalism[143] based on language was in evidence in many other provinces too and infact led to the formation of several new provinces such as Karnataka, Kerala, Gujrat and Maharashtra. However, the case of the Punjabi Suba movement and the ultimate constitution of a separate province of the Punjab in 1966 presents interesting points for analysis while examining the characteristic features of various sub-nationalisms. It is pointed out that the Punjabis did not suffer any serious handicap in the miscegeneous province with the Hindi-speaking people as partners. But gradually religious and linguistic emotions were whipped up by the political parties. The Government felt it unsound to see communal troubles between Hindus and Sikhs flare up in a border state. Consequently they agreed to constitute two provinces. Some point out that the granting of the claim for the Punjabi Suba "is a reward to the Sikhs for their courageous and brave contribution during the 22nd fateful days of Indo-Pakistan conflict in September 1965".[144]

The Oriya nationalistic struggle when observed in the background of the other regional movements presents many an important distinctive feature. The land of Orissa did not come under the British sway all at a time. Instead, it was a piecemeal conquest of the Britishers at different times during which different portions were annexed and scattered among various administrative units. Thus the entire politico-administrative set-up of the land went through a complete structural disintegration. Significantly, however, the administrative fragmentation could not snap the thread of cultural affinity which ran through these areas and which had once bound the people of this land together.[145]

However, when the All India Congress gave indications of dealing favourably with the issue of linguistic provinces, they were divided into two camps : one remaining pro-British referred to as the moderates and the other, the extremists, aligning themselves with the Congress.

Finally, the fulfillment of the nationalistic aspiration, in this region in 1936 heralded a process which is rather contemporary in scope. It was perhaps more a fortuitous happening than anythingelse that the chain reaction resulting in the formation of distinct linguistic regions was to begin with Orissa.

The formation of Orissa also coincided with the carving out of a Muslim province, Sindh- thus giving rise to the doubt whether a separate Orissa was not created only to appease the Hindus,[146] whether the creation of Orissa played any significant role in the future division on linguistic basis or in the Hindu- Muslim relation during the subsequent years, are however issues which again are beyond the scope of the present work.

The struggle of the Oriyas to achieve for themselves a political identity makes an interesting reading in the context of Indian nationalism. The nineteenth century Europe, not withstanding the distance, was sending the forces of nationalism to Asia and Africa. In India the English brought with them the enlightenment of the west and inspired the Indians to imbibe the spirit of nationalism. The formation of the Congress in 1885 provided them with a platform in due course, to mobilize their human resources and express this spirit with force.[147]

There is dearth of examples in history where such attempts have been made which have caused complex problems. The union of Belgium with Holland under the House of Orange was a case in point which resulted in failure. Though there were one million Belgians more than the Dutch, the quality of administrative and government representation was looked upon as an injustice. The Belgian governing class was comparatively small in number and in the Flemish countryside in particular, hardly anybody could read or write.[148] As a result Belgium could not produce efficient literates to take up more important jobs in comparison to the Dutch. Thus the Belgo-Dutch relationship was at once poisoned by the disproportion in the number of the Civil Servants coming from the two regions. The Belgians felt desperate and utterly complained against the new regime. The idea of amalgamation with the people of a different and dominant race quickly tended to kindle their nationalistic feelings. The diplomat La Moussaye summarized the position as one, in which "the Belgian hates the Dutchman and the latter despises the former and consider himself greatly superior".[149] The situation turned worse when William the King ordered Dutch to serve as the only administrative language throughout the country. The Belgians were not prepared to sacrifice their language and lose their distinct identity; thus the trouble precipitated.

In India, the condition of the Oriyas was in many ways similar to that of the Belgians. In the three administrative units where Oriyas were scattered, they were forced to learn different languages, as they formed minority groups everywhere. The custom and tradition of other groups were being forced on them. Even in the mainland they had to wage a bitter struggle for their existence as a separate homogenous group. Their struggle might have been deemed in the twilight had there not been a set of circumstances that contributed to the growth of nationalism which ultimately changed its fate.

The analysis of genesis would remain incomplete without the economic scenario of Orissa. The British adopted a land/tenurial system to secure maximisation of revenue for the government. Short-term land settlements became the main instrument for increasing the revenue. They created a number of intermediaries including the zamindars and reduced the cultivators to tenants at will. Even in permanently settled areas land revenue increased disproportionately to the income of the people. After the great famine of 1866 little respite was provided partly out of sympathy for misery of the people, but mostly as a result of changed revenue policy. In the early years of industrialisation the English realised the need for creating a surplus in the hands of the peasants to facilitate greater purchasing capacity for their industrial product. As late as 1897 and 1927 new settlements were introduced. There was very little nearly no commercialisation of agriculture in Orissa.The land under cultivation remained constant around 50% throughout the first two decades of 20th century. Though Orissa participated in the cotton boom, it was only a temporary phase. The development of transport was equally negligible.

One imp tant reason for the slow growth of national consciousness in Orissa was the lack of good communication in the province. Even after the famine of 1866 things did not prosper much. The Bengal Government did not consider the construction of railways in Orissa feasible due to enormous cost of bridging a number of rivers in the coastal region. There was no good harbour also in the long sea coast of Orissa. The seaports of Balasore, Dhamra, Puri etc. had considerably declined due to several factors.[150] Hence the Government decided to construct a Coast Canal connecting the river Hooghly with the river Matai near Dhamra in the Balasore district. It was a step to secure the province against famine. The Coast Canal was opened for traffic in 1886.[151] The people had to agitate for a long time for the construction of the railways in Orissa and it was not until the end of the 19th century that the railways were completed connecting Calcutta with Puri through Balasore and Cuttack. The rail link was fully completed for passenger traffic in December 1900 and incidentally the first important visitor was Lord Curzon, the Governor-General himself who toured Puri, Bhubaneswar and Cuttack etc. in the second week of December 1900. He was the first Viceroy to visit Orissa.

The irrigation was introduced in Orissa after 1866. However the high cost prevented water being utilised by the poor farmers of Orissa. There was no appreciable impact of irrigation. As a whole the economic impact of British rule in Orissa did not materially transform the economy of Orissa or the life of the people. Only limited and half-hearted attempts were made for development of various sectors, the process was too slow. Changes did occur, yet the impact was not substantial. No economic transformation took place between 1866 to 1936.[152]

As the theoretical discussion has already been summarised the conclusion of the present chapter is confined to only the genesis of the new awakening in Orissa. Like the Indian scenario the contact with west, spread of education, development of press and communication, growth of political associations and the emergence of educated elite class contributed to the genesis of the nationalist awakening in Orissa. Growth of political consciousness can also be attributed to the discovery of Orissa's past glory and culture. However, notwithstanding the similarity there was a difference of emphasis between the national and Orissan scene. The economic component particularly the backwardness of Orissa due to the policy of total negligence and apathy aptly resulting in the 1866 famine not only claimed one-third population of Orissa Division but also created a consciousness unparallel. Similarly, the linguistic component of the genesis was predominant. It was not a mere question of imposing English or Bengàli but a positive assertion of Oriya language and its identity. The distribution of Oriyas under three presidencies was not all that unique for the English had never created administrative units on the basis of language. Yet the linguistic component of the awakening in Orissa was unique in India. Further, the role of rajas and maharajas, the feudal elements in the awakening and the nationalist struggle was outstanding.

References

1. *Oxford Illustrated Dictionary* : 545
2. Garner's definition as quoted by E. Asirvatham, *Political Theory* : 26
3. Lipson; *The Great Issues of Politics* : 339
4. E. Asirvatham, *Political Theory* : 574
5. *Ibid* : 580
6. *Ibid* : 573
7. *Ibid* : 574
8. *Oxford Dictionary* : 545
9. Hugh-Seton Watson, *Nationalism and Communalism* : 3-4
10. Ramsay Muir, *Nationalism and Internationalism* : 71
11. An Indian has his allegiance to India as a geographical unit. He still owes his allegiance to his village or city or his province to which he belongs.
12. Scotland as a part of Great Britain is a pointer in this direction. The case of Hawaii, ruled long by America finally led to its own identification and further paved the way for its assimilation with America. And so far India is concerned, she might have been divided into several nationalities instead of one had there been no a Mughal or a British rule abreast.
13. W. Ebenstein, *Political Thought* : 635 E. Asirvatham : 587-88
14. W.A. Dunning, *Political Theories* : 294-95
15. *Ibid* : 297
16. *Ibid.*
17. *Ibid* : 298
18. Hallowell, *Political Thought* : 569-71.
19. R.N. Tagore, *Gitanjali* : 35
20. The political philosophy of the moderates has already been noted earlier in this chapter.
21. Whose ideas have been specified earlier.
22. H.K. Mahtab, *Freedom Movement in Orissa* : 93-95 P. Mukherjee, *Orissa Famine of 1866* : 70-71
23. C.E. Buckland, *Bengal under the Lt. Governor* : 332
24. Nivedita Mohanty, *Oriya Nationalism* : 18
25. C.E. Buckland, *op.cit.* : 332
26. *British Parliamentary Papers,* Public No. 99
27. *Ibid,* Vol. LI
28. *Ibid,* Vol. LII

29. K.M. Patra, *Orissa Under the Company* : 321-22
30. *Orissa District Gazetteer,* Sambalpur :448
31. T.E. Ravenshaw, Letter No. 99 : 4.5.1868
32. Utkal Dipika (UD), 25 Jan 1868
33. P. Mukherjee, *History of Orissa* : 448
34. UD, 20 October 1875
35. H.K. Mahtab, *op.cit.* : 112
36. UD, 8 March 1870
37. F.M. Senapati, *Granthavali* : 28
38. Mahtab, *op.cit.* : 117
39. UD, 25 Jan 1868
40. *Ibid,* 18 April 1868
41. *Ibid,* 5 Sept 1868
42. *Ibid,* 13 Mar 1868
43. *Ibid.*
44. *Ibid.*
45. S. Mohanty, *Satabdira Surya* : 409
46. UD, 20 July/ 14 Aug/ 25 Sept 1869
47. GRPI, 1869-70 : 63-65
48. H. Kohn, *Idea of Nationalism* : 31
49. Nivedita Mohanty, *op.cit.* : 23
50. *Ibid.*
    G.P. Bhattacharjee, *Renaissance in Bangladesh* : 57-82
51. A. de Mecos, *History of the Belgians* : 268
52. *Sambad Vahika,* 30 Nov 1872
53. P. Kar, Congress and Orissa : 15-16
54. N. Samantray, *Oriya Literature* : 175-80
55. K.M. Patra, *Orissa State Legislature* : 6
56. Nivedita Mohanty : 24
57. *Ibid* : 25
58. GRPI, 1858-59 : 330
59. UD, 25 Apr 1868
60. S. Mishra, *History and Culture of Orissa* : 702
61. N. Samantray, *op.cit.* : 191-92
    K.M. Patra, *Orissa State Legislature* : 7

62. UD, 24 July 1869
63. Ibid, 19 June 1869
64. Ibid, 11 July 1874
65. Ibid, 23 July/ 17 Oct 1870
66. Ibid, 19 Oct 1870
67. Ibid, 26 June 1868
68. Ibid, 30 June 1878
69. Ibid, 10 Oct 1879
70. Ibid, 8 July 1882
71. Ibid, 9 Sept 1882
72. S.N. Das, *Desaprana* : 63
73. M. Rath, *Karmayogi* : 79
74. B.L. Grover, *Modern Indian History* : 395
75. Ibid : 394
76. UD, 26 May 1883
77. Ibid, 29 Sept 1883
78. P. Sitaramayya, *Indian National Congress* : 11
79. UD, 25 Dec 1886
80. Ibid.
81. K.M. Patra, *Orissa State Legislature* : 10
82. P.K. Nayak, *Biswanath Das* : 26
83. *Two Bachelors of Arts* : 22
84. *UD*, 24 Oct 1888
85. *Ibid*, 21 Oct 1869
86. *Ibid*, 26 Mar 1870
87. *Ibid*, 30 Apr 1870
88. F.M. Senapati, *op.cit.* : 53-54
89. Ibid, 53-55
90. M. Mansingh, *Fakir Mohan* : 20
    Ibid, *The Land of Jagannath* : 206-13
91. P. Mukherjee, *History of Orissa* : 423
92. *Two Bachelors of Arts* : 22-23
93. *Ibid* : 25
94. UD, 16 Nov 1901
95. S.N. Das, *Desaprana* : 152-154

96. UD, 14 Sept 1901
97. S.N. Das, op.cit. : 24
98. UD, 1 Jan 1903
99. *Two Bachelors of Arts* : 24
100. G.A. Grierson, *Linguistic Survey* : 370
101. UD, 22 Oct 1870
102. Home Public Proceedings, File No. 135-136, Jan'1904
103. *Two Bachelors of Arts* : 23-24
104. *Ibid* : 25
105. N. Samantray, *op.cit.* : 300-305
106. *Ibid* : 362
107. *Ibid* : 369
108. *Ibid* : 376
109. *Ibid* : 379
110. Sambalpur Hitaisini (SH), 6 Feb 1875
111. M.Mansingh, Oriya Literature : 202
112. *Ibid* : 197
113. *Ibid* : 210-11
114. Nivedita Mohanty, *op.cit.* : 86-87
115. N.Das, *Nilakantha* : 59
116. *Ibid* : 7-8
117. Nivedita Mohanty : 86
118. Andrews and Mukherjee, *Rise of Congress* : 7-13
119. *Ibid.*
120. C.S. Mishra, *Satyavadire* : 143
121. R.N. Rath, *Pt. Gopabandhu* : 19
122. N. Das, op.cit. : 19-21
123. N. Satpathy, *He Sathi He Sarathi* : 87
124. Gopinath Mohanty, *Utkalamani* : 25
125. UD, 9 Jan 1912
126. G. Mishra, *Arddha Satabdira Odisa* : 181
127. N. Mohanty : 91
128. G. Mishra : 225
129. Ibid : 148
130. J. Mohapatra, *Pandit Godavaris* : 31

131. M. Mansingh, *Oriya Literature* : 242-43
132. K. Singh, *Indian Nationalism* : 64
133. K.V. Rao Narayana, *Andhra Pradesh* : 23
134. Ibid : 8
135. Ibid : 29
136. Ibid : 128
137. Ibid : 313
138. Ibid : 128
139. V.C.P. Choudhury, *Modern Bihar* : 24
140. Ibid
141. Ibid : 91
142. Ibid : 8
143. Contributory share nationalism of various states to the mainstream of Indian nationalism.
144. K.B. Kamath, *Linguistic Vivisection* : 28
145. Nivedita : XV
146. Ibid : XVI
147. Ibid : 15
148. Ibid : 16
149. A.de Mecos : 262
150. K.M. Patra, *Orissa State Legislature* : 6
151. P. Mukherjee, *History of Orissa* : 475-78
152. Bishnu Charan Biswal, *Some Aspects of Orissan Economy* : 437-76

2

THE MOVEMENT FOR A SEPARATE PROVINCE OF ORISSA

With the growth of consciousness of separate identity, fostered by the development in literature, press, education, political associations and emergence of an elite class, the movement for formation of a separate province for the Oriyas scattered over various administrative units of British India gathered momentum in the last two decades of the 19th century.

During the British rule, the Oriya speaking country was balkanised, Ganjam and Koraput were under the Madras Presidency; Cuttack, Puri and Balasore were merged with Bengal and Sambalpur with the Central Provinces. The Oriya-speaking Feudatory states were also divided and kept under the administration of different stages. In view of these difficulties, the Oriyas were oppressed and exploited by the dominant linguistic group of the administrative unit and by the alien rulers. They faced identity crisis and the language and literature of the Oriyas faced the danger of extinction. Thus the Oriyas remained isolated and alienated and led a miserable life due to the apathy and indifference of the rulers and the dominant linguistic groups in the respective states.

The 'Utkal Union Conference' (Utkal Sammilani) provided the people with platform to put forth their desire and aspiration for a separate province, it was very much dynamic in arousing responses from various groups in the society that strengthened the nationalistic movement.

Utkal Union Conference (UUC)

The Oriyas suffered from the injustice of dismemberment for nearly a century since the British occupation of Orissa in 1803. Naturally, the enlightened Oriyas confronted this problem in the second half of the 19th century, and demanded the amalgamation of the Oriya-speaking tracts under one administration. A sustained struggle continued for many years to safeguard the interests of Oriya language till 1903 when Madhusudan Das thought of organising the Utkal Union Conference to spearhead the movement for formation of a separate province.

It is interesting to note that the earliest ideas of a separate province are reflected in British official records. After the Orissa Famine, Stafford Northcote, the Secretary of State for India suggested that as the outlying portions of the Bengal Presidency received no proper attention, Assam and possibly Orissa should be separated from Bengal.[1] But it led to no tangible result. Some years later, Raja Baikuntha Nath De of Balasore and Bichitranand Das of Cuttack submitted the first memorial to the Government for the union of all scattered Oriya-speaking tracts under the single Government.[2] Since then, continuous discussion on the question of the amalgamation of the Oriya-populated areas[3] continued in the urban centres of Orissa, such as Cuttack, Puri, Balasore, Berhampur and Parlakhemindi.

In the 70's of the 19th century the Oriyas of the Ganjam district were carrying on agitation for the recognition of Oriya as a subject of study in the Madras University and as a court language in the same district. The issue of unification of Oriya-speaking areas was kept in the background.

Madhusudan Das, the architect of the Oriya nationalist movement in the 20th century, had keenly observed the Sambalpur agitation and the developments in Orissa and was strengthened in his belief that only a well organised joint endeavour with a greater thrust could carry the aspirations of the Oriya people to fulfillment. This desire to have an Oriya organisation which would be sort of National Assembly to the Oriyas was primarily motivated by a feeling of estrangement with Bengal that was deepening everyday. In 1902 when Oriya was introduced as a separate language in the Calcutta University the Bengalis raised strong protests,[4] which disappointed the Oriyas. They became further disenchanted when Sir S.N. Banerjea, the great nationalist leader of Bengal, requested M.S. Das to include Orissa under the Bengal Provincial Congress Committee which had recently been formed by him.[5] M.S. Das could not agree to such a proposal for he had started aspiring for a separate organisation for Orissa. This episode proved to be turning point. Had they formed a separate Congress Committee for Orissa, the movement for a separate province in Orissa would have converged into the congress led nationalist movement. This had to wait till 1920.

During the later half of 1902 the Oriyas of Ganjam submitted a memorial to Lord Curzon, the then Governor General in which they stated that they were, as dissociated from the Oriya- speaking people as a limb separated from the body and they prayed, that the Government of India will be graciously pleased "to bring together the scattered divisions inhabited by Oriya-speaking people i.e. Ganjam in Madras, Sambalpur in Central Province and Oriya in Bengal under the Government of Bengal or under any one Government and one University."[6]

In January 1903 M.S Das convened an informal gathering at his residence of a large number of celebrities in Orissa including the feudatory chiefs who had earlier assembled at Cuttack for a grand court (Darbar)[7]. It was an instant success in the sense that the participants truly exchanged views on various problems affecting natural Orissa and expressed the desire to meet often, atleast once a year.

In the same year a small band of enthusiasts gathered in the town of Rambha in Ganjam under the beneficent of Raja of Khallikote and resolved to establish the 'Ganjam Jatiya Samiti' (Ganjam National Conference) whose first sitting was proposed to be held in the Town of Berhampur in the ensuing Easter.[8] So, a meeting of the Conference was held at Berhampur on the 11th and 12th April 1903 under the Presidentship of Babu Syamasundar Rajguru. The people of Ganjam were greatly enthused when they saw in their midst the well known intellectuals like M.S Das, Nanda Kishore Bal, Gopal Chandra Praharaj and Krishna Prasad Chodhury from Cuttack; Fakir Mohan Senapati from Balasore; Ram Chandra Das, Gopabandhu Das, Baksi Lokanath Bidyadhar Mohapatra, Pt. Basudev Kavyatirtha and Raghunath Rao from Puri.[9] The Conference discussed the imparting of education in Ganjam both in vernacular and in English medium and chalked out plans for opening libraries as well as for writing Oriya-text books. It also exhibited an urge for the development of modern and ancient Oriya literature. In addition, unanimous desire was expressed for the amalgamation of Oriya-speaking tracts under a common administration.[10] There was a general willingness to hold similar sittings every year.

In the same month M.S. Das presided over a meeting of the Orissa Association which was attended by the Kanika Chief, G.H. Howell, some English ladies, Gokulanand Choudhury, Brajasundar Das, Gopal Chandra Praharaj, Janakinath Bose and Ramasankar Roy, among others.[11] In this meeting there was a general discussion on the re-union of the Oriya-speaking tracts. It was decided to send an appeal to the Governor-General for uniting all the Oriya tracts and placing them under a Chief Commissionership like Assam.

This Chief Commissionership, it was further agreed, should be connected with the Calcutta High Court and the Calcutta University.

M.S. Das noticed in these meetings and other similar conferences, a basic identity with his views but he was doubtful if these congregations, so narrow in their scope would be able to translate his blue-print of ideas into a concrete shape. He had actually envisaged a much wider form embracing a large number of motivated people.

A meeting of some prominent people of Orissa was held at 9 A.M. on the 25th October 1903[12] in the Kanika Rajbati under the Presidentship of the Raja of Keonjhar. Mr. Das convened the meeting for consideration of steps to be taken for holding a conference of all Oriya-speaking areas at Cuttack in December. He also very much appreciated the idea of representatives of Oriya people of different Oriya-speaking areas meeting together each year for exchange of ideas and for discussion on matters of common interest. So, he proposed holding a conference during the ensuing Christmas vacation to which the representatives from outlying Oriya-speaking areas were to be invited. December 30 and 31 were the dates chosen. An Executive Committee was constituted to carry on preparatory work for the meeting. That was how Utkal Union Conference was born and was christened in December 1903.

Finally, on 30 December 1903, the Utkal Union Conference (UUC) met in due solemnity at Cuttack. It was presided over by Maharaja Sriram Chandra Bhanjadeo and was attended by a number of ruling princes, zamindars and Government servants from Balasore, Cuttack and Puri.[13] Utkal Union Conference as the name implies was to bring in its fold all the Oriyas in Orissa as well as those that were tagged on to other provinces. It included the non-Oriya people who had settled in Orissa generations ago, and also the recent settlers who had identified their interests with that of Orissa. In that sense it was truly a conference of the 'Utkaliyas'. It did not maintain any list of its membership and was open to everyone who came under one of the above categories. The Oriyas everywhere wanted to come closer and know each other[14] and the UUC was to provide a platform for this rendezvous. The delegates from the outlying tracts numbered 335. There were 10 delegates from Midnapur, 25 from Sambalpur and 300 from Ganjam.[15] It was a proof of the nascent spirit of national consciousness in the outlying tracts.

It was decided to make the functional structure of the UUC federal in character.[16] An executive committee was contemplated for working out broad programmes and each district was to have a committee of its own. Each village was to send delegates to the sub-divisional committee which in turn, was to elect representatives for the district committees, and from each district committee, delegates were to attend the Union Conference. In this way, thought M.S. Das the ideas could percolate to the remotest village.

The proceedings of the Conference were conducted in Oriya. The exhibition was inaugurated by K.G. Gupta, Commissioner of Orissa. In his address the President elaborated the objects of the Conference in three main points :(1) to inculcate unity among the Oriya-speaking people, (2) to develop industrial potentiality of Orissa and (3) to spread education, general, technical and female. In his inspiring address, he also referred to the necessity of social reform, promotion of agriculture, livestock and exploitation of national resources.[17] Quoting the popular sloka of the Ramayana, 'Janani Janmabhumischa Swargadapi gariyasi', he concluded his talk invoking the blessings of God for the success of the Conference.[18]

The Maharaja addressed the delegates as 'Brothers'. It was an unprecedented gesture on the part of a feudatory Chief, Sriram Chandra's address at once electrified the audience and thereby helped to generate "national consciousness among his compatriots".[19] There is no doubt that this Conference quickened the pace of political awakening among the Oriyas wherever they lived. It inaugurated a new era of hope and understanding among the people.

The main purpose of the Conference was to spearhead the 'Oriya Movement' for the amalgamation of the outlying Oriya tracts under one Government. It discussed many socio-cultural and political problems relating to the Oriyas and adopted six resolutions. It extended its sincere gratitude to Lord Curzon, Governor-General of India for his proposal to unit the Oriya-speaking tracts outlined in the famous Risley circular. Gratitude was also expressed to Andrew Fraser, Lt. Governor of Bengal for reinstating Oriya as the court language in Sambalpur. Other resolutions related to educating public opinion, introduction of social reforms,[20] improvement of the Oriya literature and language,[21] agricultural and utilisation of its natural products.[22] It was also resolved to emphasize the necessity of fostering and strengthening friendly relations between the Oriyas and the neighbouring peoples.[23] A number of Committees for implementing the resolutions were formed and they were to send their reports to the second session of the Conference.

Depicting the picture of this conference the Amrit Bazar Patrika wrote :

"The most striking of these is that, this is the first time, that a long number of Indian Chiefs, Rajas, Zamindars and the gentry of an Indian province were found assembled together for the purpose of improving their material condition by mutual help. In Orissa, the provinces were brought together with the aristocracy, the gentry and the poor. Not only do the princes and the people in the Province speak the same language, but they are all bound by the same ties of region, customs, usages and associations. The whole movement was thus actuated by one feeling of nationality, its main object being to unite all the Oriya- speaking peoples into one race".[24]

It cannot, however, be denied that the presence of the zamindars, rajas and maharajas made the conference more respectable. They were attracted to the Oriya Movement being actuated by a strong feeling of nationality and by the great personality of M.S. Das who undoubtedly, ushered into existence of the Utkal Union Conference.

The UUC was a socio-political organisation peculiar to the existing condition of Orissa in the beginning of the twentieth century. It enthused the princes, zamindars and the educated class. It was truly a representative national forum embodying the hopes and aspirations of the people. With its foundations, an unprecedented atmosphere of unity, cooperation and understanding prevailed among the Oriyas and the domiciled Bengalis.[25] Madhusudan had given a call to the Oriyas to join this conference which he discussed as the "ocean of nation's life" in his famous poem 'Sammilani'.[26]

It may be argued that the Conference did not come up from any narrow provincial feeling. It was a broad-based organisation which aimed at putting pressure on all concerned for the political unification, industrial progress and economic development of Orissa. In his speeches, he categorically made it clear that the UUC should not be considered as step-mother of the National Congress. Its aim, he said was the promotion of the Oriyas' interests. Its main purpose was to awaken the Oriyas to fight for their cause, so that they would place themselves in advancing upsurge of political life. Its success was noticed by Sri Aurobindo, who wrote, "It is for instance a cause of gratification that Orissa is beginning to feel its separate consciousness."[27]

Mr. H.H. Risley, Home Secretary to the Government of India, in his Letter No. 3678 dated the 3rd December, 1903 to the Home Secretary to the Government of Bengal proposed transfer of Oriya-speaking areas under the administration of Central Province and Madras to the jurisdiction of the Government of Bengal so as to compensate Bengal for the loss of Dacca, Rajsahi, Chittagong and Assam according to Lord Curzon's famous scheme of partition of Bengal of 1905. Mr. Risley thought that the proposal would solve the question of amalgamation of Oriya-speaking areas and relieve both Central Province and Madras Government of troubles of language agitation.

This letter brought the problem of unification of Oriya-speaking tracts into the limelight of public attention in Orissa as also in other outlying Oriya-speaking areas. This time the leaders took up the problem quite seriously and proceeded in an organised and constitutional way. A Conference was set up with representatives from all Oriya-speaking areas. The agitation for unification of all Oriya-speaking tracts was, thus, started from 1903. Though it did not produce immediate result, it made a lasting impression on the authorities who could no longer evade the problem.[28]

In the letter of Mr. Risley referred above, it was suggested that all outlying Oriya-speaking tracts under the administration of Central Province and of Madras were to be amalgamated with Orissa and placed under the Bengal administration. It was further stated in the said letter that it would relieve both the Central Provinces and Madras of troublesome excrescence upon their administrative system and it would result in handling over Oriya problem to one Provincial Government only on a scale and with a unity that would admit of its being treated with consistency and efficiency.[29] The details of the proposal contained in Mr. Risley's letter were published in the 'Utkal Dipika' in Oriya.

This happy news caused a wave of enthusiasm among the people of Orissa and those in the outlying tracts. They very well knew that idle complacency was not only useless but positively harmful to the attainment of aspiration of the Oriyas which after much struggle had taken a concrete shape. All knew that a perfect organisation, strenuous agitation and coordination of all activities in different areas were the needs of the movement. So the leaders lost no time in taking steps for preparing the field of the purpose.

Lord Curzon's proposal for the partition of Bengal caused a wave of deep resentment in Bengal. But while the proposal embodied in Risley's circular was quite welcome to the people of Orissa to whom it meant attainment of their cherished ambition, it was a serious blow to the unity of Bengal. The whole political atmosphere of Bengal was surcharged with explosive emotion when the 19th session of Congress was held at Madras on the 30th December, 1903 under the Presidentship of Lalmohan Ghose. The following resolution on the subject of partition of Bengal was passed.

"The Congress views with deep concern the present policy of the Government of India in breaking up territorial divisions which have been of long standing and are closely united by ethnological, linguistic, social and administrative relations and the Congress deprecates the separation from Bengal and Dacca, Rajsahi and Chittagong Divisions and also separation of the District of Ganjam and Agency tracts of Ganjam and Vizagpatam from Madras Presidency".[30]

The main idea was to pass a resolution deprecating the scheme of partition of Bengal. But the last portion of the resolution relating to the Ganjam district and the Vizagpatam Agency was added superfluously at the instance and pressure of the Telugu delegate. V. Krishnaswami Iyer, a Tamil delegate questioned the propriety of addition of the portion of the resolution relating to the Ganjam district and the Vizag Agency to the question of partition of Bengal and moved an amendment to delete that portion, but the amendment was lost.[31]

While the resolution was being moved in the Congress, the UUC was passing a resolution on integration of Oriya-speaking areas for all-round development of Orissa. No representative of Orissa could attend that session of the Congress, consequently, the resolution was passed almost unopposed excepting for the objection raised by V.Krishnaswami Iyer.

This action of the Congress was resented by the people of the Oriya-speaking areas and led to the alienation of their sympathy for the Congress. The Oriyas, then became determined to fight out their own case without the help of the Congress. In consequence, the politicians of Orissa devoted themselves solely to the problem of unification of the Oriya-speaking areas under one administration from 1904. Orissa remained quite aloof from the Congress activities for a period of about

18 years till 1920, when one neighbouring Bengal and other parts of India were witnessing Swadeshi Movement and its aftermath. The political leaders of Orissa, though were no less nationalist than any of their contemporaries, remained apathetic to the Swadeshi movement, 1903-1908, as they thought it to be basically a movement of Bengalis for the maintenance of their hegemony over a vast area in Eastern and North-Eastern India. (The details of the influence of the Swadeshi movement of Orissa will be discussed in the next chapter). Perhaps this would explain the indifference of people of Orissa to the said agitation though their participation in later movements like 1920-22, 1930-34 and 1942 was massive and drew national attention.

Workings of the UUC

The maiden session of the Conference was held 30 and 31 of December 1903 at the Idga field at Cuttack following a month of meticulous preparation. It was inaugurated amidst an air of mutual affection and understanding of the Oriya from all over who had come with great expectations. The session was attended by five Oriya chiefs and the delegates from the outlying tracts alone numbered 335.[32] There were many resolutions passed and decisions arrived at in this session. It was agreed that the Conference would meet annually. Pink turban was adopted as a symbol of the Oriyas. Also a few patriotic songs were chosen to be sung at the beginning of every UUC session. The conference asked for fostering brotherhood among themselves and agreed to make proper arguments so that deserving students could be sent abroad for receiving higher education and be provided with other facilities. A number of committees were formed to undertake social reform work, protect and develop the handicrafts industry and also to encourage literary and cultural activities. The executive committee was entrusted with the charge of maintaining the finance, the main source of which was personal donations.[33]

People were greatly impressed by the organising ability of M.S. Das.[34] It was also a novel experience for the common people of the feudatory areas to attend the session on an equal footing along with their rulers and it was reassuring to see all the aristocratic and leading Oriyas taking part in the organisation as also in the deliberations. Emotion and sense of oneness must have risen to great heights when people reportedly collected handfuls of earth from the meeting ground and preserved it with them as something holy and auspicious.

Soon after, the activities began proliferating through branch associations numbering 381 in 1904 organised by 15 competent paid propagandists.[35] Madhusudan made extensive tours in different parts of Orissa, addressed the local branches and, thus, maintained regular communications between the centre and the units. The following shows the figure of the branches.[36]

Year (1904)

Place	*No. of Branches*
Cuttack	170
Puri	109
Feudatory States	44
Balasore	24
Ganjam	23
Sambalpur	05
Calcutta	04
Midnapur	02
Total	381

The second session of the Conference was held at Cuttack on 28 and 29 December 1904 under the Presidentship of Madan Mohan Singhdeo, Raja of Dharakote. Maharaja Dhanurjay Narayan Bhanjdeo of Keonjhar state was the Chairman, Reception Committee. About 2,000 people attended this session.[37] In this address, the President referred to the unification of the Oriya-speaking tracts, promotion of the Oriya language and literature, female education, social reforms, development of industries and the formation of branches.[38] The resolution of Sailabala Das to start a Girls' High School at Cuttack was adopted. The Conference pressed for a scholarship for B.Sc. classes to be instituted in the memory of Samanta Chandrasekhar. The 'Young Utkal' Association which was formed simultaneously with the UUC for the students was declared a part of the Conference too.[39]

In the meantime, much propaganda work was going on in different parts of Orissa. In villages, the branch associations were working with tremendous enthusiasm. There was for instance, a meeting on 9th October 1905 in Chanahatta village organised by the Secretary of the Chanahatta

UUC, Lakshmidhar Pattanaik. This was very widely attended by common people and landlords alike. It was decided here that a number of committees should be formed, each one comprising three important members of a village. This would be done to ensure that indigenous articles were used and that every family should pay atleast a 'pice' per month as donation. Attention should be drawn towards growing cotton that was to be purchased by M.S. Das' industries. Instances like this were to be found in every village during that time.[40]

The Government of India's response to the demands of the Oriyas was apathetic in the beginning. But having received the memorials of Raja Baikuntha Nath De of Balasore,[41] Chandra Sekhar Behera of Sambalpur,[42] Harihar Tripathy of Ganjam[43] and Madhusudan and Gouri Shankar of Cuttack[44] for the union of all Oriya- speaking tracts under one administration, Herbert Risley, Secretary to the Government of India, Home Department gave some attention to the problem of Orissa when he prepared a scheme on territorial redistribution. The Risley proposal has been discussed earlier.

The merger of Sambalpur with Orissa on 16 October 1905 strengthened the nascent unity of the people. It was followed by several meetings in Ganjam where the prospect of the union of outlying tracts was the main issue of discussion. Propaganda work was activised by press and circulation of pamphlets and brochures like, 'Jatiya Sangita' published by Raja Harihar Mardaraj Deo. Some pamphlets vividly depicted the evils of dismemberment of Orissa into three parts where the Oriyas formed a minority. Damodar Kar and Sashi Bhusan Ray were sent to Sambalpur to felicitate the chiefs, zamindars and leaders of that area for the active part they played in the merger of Sambalpur with Orissa.[45] Sambalpur's return greatly encouraged the people and they hoped that, Ganjam, Singhbhum and Midnapur would soon follow suit.

The third session of the conference was held at Balasore on 13 and 14 April 1906 and was presided over by the Raja of Talcher. Raja Baikuntha Nath De was the Chairman, Reception Committee.[46] The Conference published a bulletin known as the Journal of Utkal Sammmilani in order to popularise its activities. But unfortunately it went into oblivion just after two issues.[47] They dealt with many aspects of the history of Orissa. The Conference also adopted swadeshi on principle.[48] Political as well as ideological questions, then, crept into the programme of the Conference. Deliberations reiterated the need for the development of agriculture and cottage industry. It was thought practical to educate and train up the children of weavers and farmers. Importance was also attached for the setting up of an Engineering school in orissa.[49]

The fourth session which was held the same year in December at Berhampur in Ganjam was quite significant in that it was the first time that UUC meeting was held in one of the outlying areas. As was expected, it generated great excitement among the people of Ganjam and needless to say, it contributed to the intensification of activities of the amalgamation movement in South Orissa. This session was presided over by Raja of Kanika.[50] Stress was laid for female education and on educational development of Ganjam in general. Also gratitude was expressed to the Madras Government for providing concessions in matter of Oriya education in Madras.

The credit for its success goes, to a large extent, to Raja Harihar Mardaraj Deo of Khallikote. The Oriyas of Ganjam expected justice and fairplay from the new Governor of Madras. The devoted workers turned their attention to keep the movement alive. In the pages of the Prajabandhu, Nilamani Vidyaratna urged the people to maintain solidarity of the Oriyas. His younger brother Damodar Kaviratna edited another weekly, named 'Utkalabasini' in which he gave a call to the Oriyas of Ganjam to rise up to the occasion.[51] Chintamani Mohanty gave further momentum to the amalgamation movement by editing another weekly, the 'Ganjam Hitavadini'.[52] These three editors kept the flame of the nascent Oriya nationalism burning in Ganjam and the neighbouring Oriya speaking tracts.

In 1908 two sessions were held,[53] one in April at Puri and the other in December at Cuttack. In both these sessions emphasis was once more laid on female education. It was also decided to keep aside some funds of the conference for educational purposes. The office bearers of Central and District Committees were mainly nominated in this session.

The seventh session[54] was held at Cuttack in December 1910 where special gratitude was rendered to Mr. Ravenshaw who had sent Rs. 1000 for the education of the Oriya children. District Committees were organised at Cuttack, Puri and Balasore.

The creation of the new Province of Bihar and Orissa in 1912 generated mixed feelings. It aimed at satisfying the Biharis, but there was no justification to attach Orissa to the new province as an appendix.

The Oriyas had nothing in common with the Biharis. Taking part in the debate in the House of Lords in June 1912, Lord Curzon who was a party to the territorial organisation, said, "They want the reunion of the Oriya-speaking people. They want to remain under Calcutta to which they have been attached so long. Were the Orissans an agitating people, which they are not, they would soon make their protest hea: 1".[55]

The Oriya weeklies bitterly criticised the decision of the Government in forming the new Province. Protest meetings were held in different places of Orissa. It was also demanded that Puri should be made the summer capital of the new province.[56] The Utkal Dipika remarked that the creation of the new province was a 'political carthquakc'[57] or 'the birth of twins'.[58] Before the creation of the province the Government never took into consideration the popular sentiments in Orissa. It was created in order to provide a sea-board to Bihar. In the words of Curzon the interests of the Oriyas "have been sacrificed without compunction".[59]

The pan-Oriya movement in Ganjam became very intense. The UUC continued its insistent agitation for the merger of Ganjam with Orissa. On 24 January 1912, a memorial was submitted to Lord Hardinge demanding the transfer of Ganjam and the Agency tracts to Orissa.[60] But the Government considered the transfer of these linguistically homogenous areas neither desirable nor necessary.[61] The UUC, however, recorded its 'respectful and loyal protest' against the non-inclusion of Ganjam. The Berhampur session, 1912 recorded its emphatic protest against the conversion of the Oriya-training School at Berhampur into Telugu[62] and urged the authorities to move Oriya a subject for the Vidwan title examination in the Madras University.[63]

The eighth session was held at Berhampur in April 1912.[64] This session was doubly important-first, it was meeting in an outlying Oriya tract, after a lapse of six years; second, it was the first session of the Bihar Orissa province was announced. The all Orissa meeting at Ganjam apparently intensified the union movement in that region and the feed-back of the movement perhaps engendered a natural sympathy of the Oriya leaders towards that place. It must be mentioned that while not a single session had been held either in Singhbhum or Midnapur, UUC was meeting for the second time in Ganjam. As Bihar and Orissa Province was carved out of the Bengal Presidency without the amalgamation of Ganjam, it was felt by its people that yet another opportunity for their re-union with Orissa had been lost. It also created great disappointment in the rest of Orissa. In Ganjam and Koraput meetings were held in different areas like Khallikote, Rambha, Biruli, Dharkote, Puttugram, Jeypore, Badakhemindi and in other places.[65] It was emphasized in this session that the union of Ganjam and other tracts with Orissa be insisted upon under the same principle guiding the Bengal re-union. It thanked Lord Curzon and Mac Callen Scott for having suggested the union of Oriya-speaking areas in British Parliament.[66] The most unique feature that this session hinted out was the adoption of political propaganda in its agenda.[67] Such a step was clearly a sequel to the creation of Bihar-Orissa Province without the reunion of Oriya-tracts. It was the general feeling that Orissa was being used for the political advantage of Bihar as it had been used for Bengal.

The ninth session was held at Puri in December 1913 under M.S. Das' Presidentship[68] which dealt with the problem of amalgamation of Oriya tracts, and introduction of Oriya in Schools, courts and offices in those tracts. It put forward the demand for an Engineering School in Orissa. Deep appreciation was expressed for Satyavadi School, an open air institution which had been opened at Satyavadi in Puri in 1909.[69]

The next session was held at Parlakhemindi in December 1914 under the Presidentship of Vikram Deo Verma, the Jeypore Chief which proved to be a milestone in the Oriya movement. The young and promising Raja Krushna Chandra Gajapati of Parlakhemindi became an exponent of the Utkal Union movement. Never before did any Raja of an estate in the outlying tracts take so much initiative to safeguard the interests of the Oriyas and fight for their cause as Gajapati Krushna Chandra. Mr. Vikram Deo Verma earnestly appealed to the gathering that intense campaigning should be started in the outlying Oriya-speaking areas and that agitation must begin in every village, every city and indeed every house. He fully appreciated Grierson's division of actual Orissa on the basis of language.[70]

In the same session, Harihar Panda a leading personality from southern Orissa delivered a moving speech in which he decried the timidity of the Government in officially recognising Oriya only in one division out of four in the district of Ganjam. He highlighted in favour of Government attempts for establishing a large number of elementary and secondary schools in the Oriya-speaking tracts and pleaded for better transport facilities for connecting different outlying areas with the main Orissa.[71] Its resolutions included the amalgamation of the Oriya areas, use of Oriya in courts and Offices in the different outlying tracts. A remarkable decision taken here was to sponsor one doctor Rammurti Patnaik with the monthly allowance of Rs. 300/- to treat the wounded soldiers of the war.[72]

A large number of common people attended this session. The representatives who came from Banpur, Khallikote, Athgarh, Dharakote, Badakimedi, Sankimedi, Delang, Nuagada, and Nimapada comprised, not only the chiefs but also people of humbler origin. M.S. Das despite the demise of his brother the previous day, attended the same.[73] The session appointed Ananta Mishra as the 'roving missionary' to carry on propaganda work throughout Orissa.[74] He moved by train, in bus, in carts and very frequently on foot for the campaign. He started sending his reports of the daily tour and meetings which were published from time to time in the newspaper, Asa, edited by Sashibhusan Rath.[75] His meetings influenced the people to a large extent in actively participating in the Oriya agitation programme. He was alone in this endeavour and eventhough his dedication for work was of the highest order, the lone endeavour was but a drop in the ocean. The UUC ultimately paid the price for this lack of farsightedness.

The eleventh session which was held in Sambalpur in December 1915 emphasized mostly the earlier demands like facilities for Oriya education in outlying tracts, declaration of Oriya as a court language in Singhbhum, Phuljhar, Chandrapur, Padmapur and a separate University for all Oriya tracts.[76] It also put up a case for including an Oriya representative in the Imperial Council. A little embarrassment however cropped up from the use of the word 'Oriya', for the domiciled Bengalis, who had been associated with the Conference took offence.[77] After much argument, it was decided to use the word "Orissa-inhabitants". M.S. Das could not attend the session as he had gone over to preside over the All-India Christian Conference at Allahabad.[78]

The twelfth session was held in December 1916 at Balasore which was presided over by the Raja of Manjusha.[79] This was the first session where the deliberations centred not only around the union of all the Oriya - speaking tracts, but also the question of putting them into a separate administrative unit as well.[80] It also demanded that the Jeypore Agency in Madras be made a separate district and Oriya be introduced here. It pleaded for an Oriya member in the Parliament. A demand was also raised for the teaching of Oriya in Patna University and for the introduction of Oriya in the courts in Singhbhum and Ganjam. The agenda also included the claim for setting up of an Engineering School, the opening of M.A. and B.L. classes in Ravenshaw College, the starting of a Sanskrit College in Puri, the beginning of a project of a port in Orissa and the revival of the salt manufacture industry.[81]

Regarding the union of the Oriya-speaking tracts throughout the year, a Committee consisting of seven members was formed by this session. The Utkal Union Committee consisted of M.S. Das, Harihar Panda, Braja Sundar Das, Gopabandhu Das, Sudam Charan Nayak and the Rajas of Kanika and Sheragad (Ganjam).[82] The August Declaration of E.S. Montague, Secretary of State for India in the House of Commons on 20 August 1917 that "the policy of his Majesty's Govt...... is the gradual development of self governing institutions with a view to the progressive realisation of responsible Government in India as an integral part of the British empire" had stimulated the interests of this Committee. It prepared an address with a memorandum of arguments and a statement and map of the Oriya tracts. Its members hoped that Montague's liberal outlook would redress the long standing grievances of the Oriyas. They waited in deputation on Montague and Lord Chelmsford, Governor-General of India at Calcutta on 11 December 1917. The memorialists said that "the Oriya-speaking tracts outlined by Dr. Grierson in the Linguistic Survey of India, Vol.V, be brought together under one separate administration of the type which Bihar and Orissa now has".[83]

In support of these demands mass meetings were held at different places of Orissa. All efforts were made to convince the British authorities for giving special attention to the Orissa problem. Montague was convinced that least regard was paid to the culture, language and interests of the Oriyas in the creation of the Bihar and Orissa province. He was impressed by the arguments for the amalgamation of the Oriya tracts. So, the Joint Report on Indian Constitutional Reforms recommended "In Orissa and Bihar, at all events, it seems to us that the possibility of instituting sub-provinces need not be excluded from consideration at an early date".[84]

Agitation for the amalgamation of the Oriya-speaking areas of Singhbhum, Seraikella and Kharaswan became very powerful under the leadership of B.N. Misra, bar-at law, an inhabitant of Singhbhum and Pandit Krishna Chandra Acharya, a Sirastadar of the Kharaswan estate. Both of them opposed the introduction of Hindi in those areas. An association called the "Udita Club" was formed in the Saraikella estate for the restoration of Oriya.[85] Under the caption "Neglected Singhbhum", written by B.N. Misra, an appeal was made to the Government for the same.[86] Pandit Acharya wrote several letters through newspapers inviting

Oriyas of other Oriya-speaking areas to visit Singhbhum, Saraikella and Kharaswan for pro-Oriya propaganda.[87] A petition, dated 21 January 1916, was submitted by the rulers, land-lords and the common people of Singhbhum to Sir Edward Albert Gait, Lieutenant - Governor of the Bihar and Orissa Province, for the restoration of the Oriya language.[88]

During this time, proposals for constitutional reforms of the country were being discussed both in India and in England. In 1917 Mr. Curtis, a member of the 'Round-Table Group' in London, had suggested to divide India into small provincial states.[89] In case of Orissa, he suggested the amalgamation of the Oriya-speaking areas under a separate provincial administration. Regarding Bihar and Orissa province, he wrote, "The defect of the present areas is that they are too mechanical. The province of Bihar and Orissa for instance, combines communities with an almost cynical disregard of the differences between them. The plan suggested will remedy these unnatural unions. This particular province would fall naturally into three provincial states - Bihar with its population of 24,000,000 and Orissa and Chot Nagpur with 5,000,000 apiece. But Orissa itself ought to be increased by the inclusion of those people and race who inhabit the northern extremity of Madras and Central Provinces".[90] He continued, "One part of the Oriya-people is included in Madras and another in the Central Provinces. Naturally they desire a union with Orissa which will bring together in one self-governing state some, 10,000,000 Oriya-speaking people".[91] Although this scheme encouraged the Oriya-speaking people, the Montague-Chelmsford Report disappointed them.

In July 1917 M.S. Montague, then Under Secretary of State for India, in a debate on Mesopotamia Commission drew a picture of a federated India in the House of Commons in the following terms" I see the great self-governing dominions and provinces of India organised and coordinated with the great principalities, the existing principalities and perhaps new ones-not one great Home Rule Country, but a series of self-governing provinces and principalities.[92] The declaration was followed by his appointment as the Secretary of State for India and in August 1917 he announced the progressive realisation of Responsible Government in India. He visited India and consulted various opinions not only on the subject of Responsible Government but questions vitally affecting the political well-being of the communities inhabiting the land.

A meeting attended by more than five hundred people was held in the Cuttack Municipality ground with Madhusudan Das in chair. A special attraction of this meeting was that people of all classes including the rajas, maharajas, poor and rich from the Oriya-speaking areas attended it. It was decided there to submit a memorandum to M.S. Montague for amalgamation of all the Oriya-speaking areas under one administration.[93] Meetings were also held at Puri, Dharakote, Rambha and other Oriya-speaking areas for the same purpose.[94] In some meetings resolutions were passed demanding a separate province for Orissa.[95] At last, an address was prepared with all facts and figures. The demand included the formation of a united Orissa with Orissa Division including the feudatory states, Singhbhum, Saraikella and Kharaswan in the Chhotnagpur Division, the Ganjam plains and agency tracts (excepting Chicacole area) and the Vizagpatam agency in the Madras Government, Padmapur-Chandrapur, Phuljhar and Khariar Zamindaries and the states of Bastar, Sarangarh, Raipur, Udaipur and Jashpur in the Central Provinces, Contai- subdivision, Keshpur, Danton, Gopiballabhapur, Jhargram and Narayangarh thanas in the Midnapur district of Bengal.[96] The area of the proposed province was calculated to be 88,057 sq. miles and the population about 14,996,566.[97]

On 11 December 1917, the Oriyas waited on deputation to Montague and Lord Chelmsford the Governor-General, at Calcutta under M.S. Das and the Raja of Kanika, the then Finance Member of the Bihar and Orissa Province.[98]

During that time public meetings were held in different places demanding the union of the Oriya-speaking areas. In December 1917, a meeting held at Calcutta was attended by seven hundred Oriyas. The Amrit Bazar Patrika commented, "It was a mass meeting in every sense unprecedented in the history of the Oriyas of Calcutta, the special feature being the active and enthusiastic support with which the labouring classes carried the resolution for the amalgamation of the Oriya-speaking tracts".[99] Other meetings were held at Cuttack, Puri, Balasore, Berhampur etc. "The Oriya", a weekly English paper was published under the UUC to educate the public. The Oriyas were very much encouraged by a resolution moved in the Imperial Council in 6 February 1918 by B.N. Sarma of the Telugu country regarding the distribution of the provinces on the linguistic basis, although the resolution was at last negatived.[100]

The UUC held its 13th annual session on 30 and 31 March 1918 at Cuttack with Fakir Mohan Senapati, the father of modern Oriya literature in chair.[101] A Standing Council of 65 members from Oriya-speaking areas was constituted with the Raja of Kanika as its President and M.S. Das as Secretary to create public opinion. A band of 52 national service volunteers was taken in and a National Fund was raised according to the decision of the Council.[102]

In this session discussions related to the revival of Salt industry, introduction of Oriya as the court language in the Oriya areas of Singhbhum and Central Province. It demanded again that two Oriyas be taken as members of the Imperial Council and one in the Provincial Executive Council. The Domiciled Bengali Association, consisting of those who were considered "in every sense indigenous to the province," was incorporated in the UUC.

The presence of the great writer who had produced masterpieces rendered the atmosphere a special charm and splendour. In an eloquent speech he brought out the significance of the mother tongue and pointed out that "clothing some other nation's language as your own would kill the spontaneity of your tongue and brain".[103] In this session, there was a misunderstanding between M.S. Das and some student-groups who refused to work as volunteers. M.S. Das there upon invited the Satyavadi boys to come to the rescue of the UUC and they readily obliged. The dedication and discipline of the Satyavadi boys impressed the public and the organisers alike. Gopabandhu Das, the founder of the Satyavadi School who had already come in to the political limelight in Orissa and outside delivered a speech supporting the process of amalgamation and received a lot of appreciation for the excellent training imparted to his students.[104] He refuted the allegation that the Oriya agitation was confined only to M.S. Das and his group. The fact was, he pointed out that there had been meetings and organisations in every place, in every village and practically in all outlying areas. People from even the lowest strata of the society were accepted into the fold.[105]

All this however did not cool down some of the critics of the grand old leader, M.S. Das. As Secretary for this session, M.S. Das was selecting speakers for various occasions and seemed to have omitted some names from Ganjam, perhaps inadvertently. This act infuriated quite a few delegates and generated some ill-feeling. M.S. Das appeared very much pained at this intolerance and subsequently wrote a letter to 'Asa' saying apologetically, ".....I have been grieved to learn that some errors and omission in the selection of speakers to move and support the several resolutions adopted by the UUC on 31st March have given offence to some brethren of Ganjam whose hearty cooperation we need to give effect to the resolutions ..... I am very sorry for what has occurred. I hope my brethren who have been offended will pardon me. .... ".[106] This episode was only symptomatic of a decline in the unchallenged leadership of M.S. Das. Hereafter, his activities were to be restricted to a good deal and he appeared to be losing ground in the UUC to some younger members.

The Mont-Ford Reforms, however, disappointed the Oriyas. Therefore, a special session of the UUC was convened at Cuttack in 21-22 September 1918 which was presided over by M.S. Das. It adopted two resolutions and pointed out that "unless a separate Province under a Governor-General and a Legislative Assembly .....be given to the united Oriya-speaking tracts the legislative aspirations of the people cannot be fulfilled".[107]

The question of constituting a sub-province for Orissa was pursued both in the Bihar and Orissa Legislative Council and the Indian Legislative Council. Sachchidananda Sinha moved a resolution for this in the Indian Legislative Council on 20 February 1920.[108] He was warmly supported by Surendra Nath Banerjee.[109] The Government of India pointed out that the possibility of creating Orissa as a sub-province would be considered only after the introduction of the reform scheme. This session was firm in its demand that the Oriya linguistic union was essential for the undertaking of any reform.

On the eve of Montague's visit, steps were taken by UUC in 1917 to publish a paper in order to carry on propaganda work throughout Orissa. It did not have any journal by that time. The bulletin that came out in 1907 was stopped after its two issues. So the necessity was felt for starting a paper. On 5th December 1917, with the donations of some persons, came out the long awaited paper, 'The Oriya' in English under the editorship of M.S. Das.[110] Utkal Dipika commended the paper and requested the public to patronise it."[111]

However, towards the end of 1918, M.S. Das announced his retirement from UUC and also from the editorship of 'The Oriya' because of his utter physical exhaustion.[112] Soon after, Braja Sundar Das, the closest follower of M.S. Das and the Secretary of the UUC also resigned.[113] As reasons for his stepping down from the editorship of the paper, Das cited the lack of promised financial help.[114] His dissociation from the UUC, came as a great surprise to the common people. Utkal Dipika wrote in its editorial,"The Grand Old Man has laid down his arms. The young veteran to whom Orissa owes the special meeting of the Utkal Conference has laid aside his portfolio and 'The Oriya' is now to go rudderless ...."[115] 'The Oriya' was given the start with all the effusion of national spirit and enthusiasm as if without it, Orissa would go to the limbo of vanity. The open criticism of M.S. Das' decision by an important paper of the time, which had once been a great supporter of him showed that there was shift in the emphasis of the movement.

In the 14th session held at Cuttack on April 1919 Gopabandhu Das, a young leader from Puri district was the President and M.S. Das was present there.[116] The latter was requested to make speech. In his speech he poured forth his patriotic feelings. At the same time he did not keep it a secret that he was extremely hurt by the open campaign directed against him. He highlighted the difficulties he faced while forming the UUC brick by brick at the initial stage and added that his exit from the UUC was perhaps for the good of the organisation itself; as he was an aristocratic, immodest and whimsical person to some people.[117]

Gopabandhu in his reply paid rich tributes to him and pointed out that history would certainly recognize contribution of M.S. Das towards the Oriya nationalism as a great act. It was he, Gopabandhu added, who first nurtured the idea of national union, and felt sad that M.S. Das was being criticised by some young people.[118]

This session passed some resolutions relating to the amalgamation of the Oriya tracts into a single province and the declarations of Oriya as a court language in the outlying tracts. Gopabandhu had already been associated with the Indian National Congress and in this meeting he indicated sufficiently that his interest also lay in the wider sphere of the all-India problem.[119]

The next session (15th) held at Puri in December the same year in which a lawyer from Sambalpur Chandrasekhar Behera for the first time presided.[120] It was decided here to form an Oriya preservation fund. Consequently a Committee often was constituted consisting of influential persons from different places, with Gopabandhu Das as the Secretary whose office, it was decided, to be maintained at Chakradharpur in the Singhbhum district. Anant Misra and Sashi Bhusun Rath were entrusted with the duty to campaign on behalf of the fund. Bhagabat Prasad Mohapatra from Balasore, Chandrasekhar Behera from Sambalpur, Someswar Singh of Madhya Pradesh, Krushna Chandra Acharya and Kanhu Kishore Pani of Singhbhum were its members.[121] This session attempted to draw UUC closer to the All-India Congress. Gopabandhu had already explained to the people in the preceding session the significance of a broader concept of nationalism which would envelop the whole of India. Mr. Behera pointed out that, when the neighbours of Orissa had taken a longer leap under the British administration Oriyas were still stagnating.[122] Utkal Union Conference had been created primarily to uplift the condition of the Oriyas. Now the time had come when the Conference should join shoulders with the All-India Congress and present the Orissan problem on their platform through regular representations during Congress session.[123]

Mr. Behera also demanded the system of separate electorate for the Oriyas in the Imperial Legislative Council and the Legislative Councils of Bengal, Central Provinces and Madras. This provision he insisted, to continue until they were placed together under one administration.[124] When Sir Ali Imam, the Indian Member of the Bihar and Orissa Executive Council had accepted a service in Hyderabad State, the Oriyas demanded to take one Oriya member in his place, so that he would fight for the amalgamation of the Oriya-speaking areas.[125] It was generally felt in Orissa that the Act of 1919 would not help the Oriyas as they were scattered in different provinces.[126]

The Oriyas of Ganjam district demanded to get atleast five seats in proportion to their total number and pleaded for the reservation of seats for the Oriyas.[127] A public meeting was held at Berhampur on 28 January 1920 on behalf of the Ganjam District Oriya Association with the Maharaja of Parlakhemindi on chair. It demanded administrative union of the Oriya tracts or creating a sub-province for Orissa with its adjoining Oriya tracts. At the same time it demanded more seats for the Oriyas in the Madras Legislative Council. It was decided in the meeting to send a deputation to the Governor of Madras to redress their grievances.[128] The 'Aska Oriya Samaj' held a meeting at Aska on 15 February 1920 to the same effect.[129] The 'Utkal Hitaisini Samaj' of Parlakhemindi organised a public meeting at Parlakhemindi and passed resolutions for the union of the Oriya tracts and reservation of seats for the Oriyas.[130] On 27 November 1922, the Governor received a deputation from the Ganjam district which demanded that the ultimate desire of the Oriyas was to form a separate province. But the immediate need was to amalgamate all the Oriya-speaking areas under any provincial administration. But the Governor in reply pointed out that the Telugus of Ganjam would face the same difficulties like the Oriyas after the amalgamation of the Oriya-speaking areas of Ganjam.[131] This point was also raised by Mr. Jogeya, a Telugu gentleman, in the newspaper.[132]

During this period the Telugus made counter organisation to oppose the amalgamation of Ganjam with Orissa. Besides the 'Ganjam Defence League', they formed another organisation, called the 'Andhra Business People's Association'. Its aim was to form a separate Andhra Province with Ganjam as a part of it.[133] A Telugu deputation on behalf of the 'Ganjam Defence League' met the Governor and opposed the amalgamation of Ganjam with Orissa. They pleaded that Ganjam had deeper relation with Madras than Orissa.[134]

However, the Ganjam Oriya District Association met again and again to work out details of the movement to achieve amalgamation. Representatives to this meeting came from Aska, Russelkonda, Khallikote, Parla and eminent Oriyas from outside Ganjam like M.S. Das, Gopabandhu Das, Jagabandhu Singh, Biswanath Das and Bichitrananda Das who took leading role in the deliberations.[135] A resolution was passed on 8th May, 1920 making plans for the union of the Oriya-speaking tracts and an appeal was sent out to UUC to hold a special session in Ganjam for this purpose.[136]

Thus from 1903 to 1920 the Oriya Movement was very active under the aegis of the Utkal Union Conference and Orissa politics was almost solely confined to agitation for unification of Oriya-speaking tracts. The UUC had mobilised the public opinion more effectively by holding annual conferences and meetings in different parts of the Oriya-speaking areas. It had moved the authorities towards the Oriya cause through resolutions, representations and deputations. At the same time it had counter-acted the reaction of the neighbouring provinces. But the creation of the new province of Bihar and Orissa in 1912 and the Reform Act of 1919 did not satisfy the minimum demands of the Oriyas. Moreover, with the appearance of Mahatma Gandhi in Indian politics, the atmosphere was surcharged with a new zeal and enthusiasm of National Movement which swept away all local politics and merged there with the broad current of National struggle. Orissa, too was enthused with the new spirit of Indian nationalism and made preparation for contributing her due share to the National struggle. Now leadership in politics emerged and the older group of leaders who had steered the course of Orissa politics for long eighteen years, however, continued their agitation for a separate province until their object was achieved in 1936.

Response from Press and Public Individuals

Probably the most significant contribution of the UUC was the mass consciousness it generated in the society and in its trail public activities proliferated in several areas assuming diverse shapes.

Newspapers

Since the late 19th century a number of celebrated scholars and litterateurs had been meeting frequently at Cuttack for literary discussions. In January 1897, they brought out a literary magazir e,'Utkal Sahitya' under the editorship of Biswanath Kar.[137] They also formed the 'Cuttack Library Association' on 7 May 1903[138] which continues till today and functions as an important forum for the men of letters and social workers. It also preserves a large mass of valuable documents of the 19th and 20th centuries.

In 1905, the 'Star of Utkal' an English weekly came out from Cuttack which was edited by Kshirod Chandra Ray.[139] It dealt very candidly with the Oriya national agitation and other allied problems. But it went out of favour with the Government for the frankness of its views and was banned. It was however revived in 1922 under Lakshminarayan Sahu's editorship.

The same year, Brajasunder Das brought out a literary monthly named 'Mukura' which encouraged nationalistic literature. The young intellectuals who later constituted the 'Satyavadi Era' started their literary career through this magazine.[140]

Newspapers and magazines gradually started appearing in great numbers. 'Chitrotpala' 'Madhukosa', 'Rashmi' and 'Young Utkal' came out in quick succession in 1907.[141] The Oriyas began to feel the urge to ventilate their feeling through their writings, which were purported to preserve and advance their national life. In 1913, Gopabandhu Das brought out a journal called 'Satyavadi' which expressed his views on Oriya nationalism. In 1919 he founded the weekly 'Samaj' which served as a vehicle for his political ideas. The journalistic language, for the first time, started drawing heavily on the reservoir of colloquial words used by common Oriyas. The weekly became extremely popular and received wide circulation. All his papers were printed by the press at Satyavadi. After his death in 1928, this press was shifted to Puri and finally to Cuttack where it still runs successfully and the paper 'Samaj' continues today as the premier daily of Orissa.

'Asa', edited by Sashi Bhusan Rath which made its maiden appearance in Ganjam in 1913, was the most important weekly after 'Utkal Dipika'. It acted as a successful communication link between southern Orissa and the mainland. It was a powerful Oriya nationalist newspaper which supported the UUC activities, encouraged the Satyavadi group and invited articles from them. However, later on, the paper failed to subscribe to the views of Satyavadi when the school set up by Gopabandhu was converted into a national school. 'Utkal Dipika', 'Samaj' and 'Asa' were the significant trio dealing with Oriya nationalism. After 1920, 'Samaj' became the voice of the Congress organisation in Orissa and criticised the so-called 'Moderates' who would still maintain a soft, conciliatory policy towards the British Government. 'Asa' was 'pro-moderate' for a long time and later on expressed a desire for a rapport between the two groups.'Utkal Dipika', the oldest of the group, maintained an even tone with a pragmatic approach in the context of Oriya nationalism. All these three in due course became dailies.

In 1924, 'Prajatantra' came out with Harekrushna Mahtab as the editor. It was a political weekly from Balasore and assumed great importance in a short period after it had joined the Oriya issue of amalgamation and separation. The paper advocated the Oriya movement through the Congress organisation. Newspaper started appearing too from the feudatory states. In 1923, 'Gadajata basini' was published from Talcher.[142] It also centred its attention around the Oriya nationalism with special reference to the problems relating to the feudatory and hill states.

With the advent of Civil Disobedience in 1930, there was again a glut in newspapers and pamphlets pouring forth from various camps in Orissa. 'Satya-Samachara' under the joint editorship of Brajasundar Das and Gopal Chandra Praharaj appeared in 1930.[143] It desperately wanted the Oriya movement to intensify its activities disregarding the Congress idealism. It therefore ventilated all its criticism of the Congress in the most vociferous manner. The paper appealed to the people to turn their faith towards UUC again which had lost its vitality since 1920. Some of the views expressed under the columns of the paper had highlighted the uniqueness of Oriya nationalism. During the same period, many other papers like 'Samskara', 'Svarajya', 'Yugavina', 'Yugabartha', 'Nababharata', 'Banabina', 'Odia Siksya Darpana' also appeared on the scene although their impact was not felt.[144]

Most of these magazines and newspapers that took birth during the first two decades of the 20th century did not always deal with the

Oriya political problem directly. They focussed on the socio-economic and educational issues and through them intended to foster the nationalist spirit.

Students

A number of educational institutions sprouted around the second half of the 19th century and young men joined them in large numbers. Their financial condition did not always allow them to go to the cities for receiving education. Schools in the neighbourhood naturally opened before them new horizons now. But their experience in the schools was not entirely satisfactory because they had to learn an alien language and their teachers were all outsiders speaking different tongues and they were often made targets of ridicule by non-Oriya students. M.S. Das elaborates in his unfinished autobiography the humiliations he suffered at the hands of the yellow non-Oriya students at Cuttack-the heart of Orissa, because according to the Oriya tradition he was putting on dhoti and sporting a pigtail.[145]

By the end of the 19th century, when it had already been realised that the Oriya problem was unique in character, the students were beginning to forge a solidarity. The connotation of the word nationalism and its implementation in Western Europe, added a new dimension to their imagination. Many dismembered states of Europe succeeded in unifying and freeing themselves. As they read these stories and discussed them, they felt inspired. The Congress too created an atmosphere of enthusiasm; young boys in schools and colleges were full of excitement with the hope of associating themselves in the national struggle through the Congress. The youth activities in other provinces of India who had been exposed to Western education earlier, also started inspiring the Oriya students.

The emergence of M.S. Das marked a unique watershed in the history of the Oriya movement through the students. He formed the 'Orissa Graduate and Undergraduate Association' on March 17, 1888[146] which aimed at spreading education in Orissa and held discussions on the socio-economic aspects of the country. And with the formation of the UUC in 1903, the people found a common instrument with the help of which the movement could be shaped and directed. As a supporting organisation it was thought proper to encourage the students to form an association, through which their energies could be mobilised. It is believed that this idea was mooted by Miss Sailabala (the adopted daughter of M.S. Das).[147] On 18 July 1904, the Young Utkal Association was formed at Cuttack with 100 students as its members[148] which aimed at fostering socio-economic and cultural development of Orissa.

The organisation started functioning in a very well- organised way. It also did a good deal of social service during the time of calamitous flood, drought and epidemic. Godavaris Misra says in his autobiography that, around 1908, this association used to have two sittings-the secret sessions were held in the backyard of Brajasundar Das' residence where revolutionary poems were recited in Oriya and Bengali by Godavaris and Subodh Hazra; the open sittings at Gopabandhu's place in the normal school lane, where the young members practised physical training.[149] In one of its meetings in 1912 held to welcome the Matriculate-examinees, M.S. Das who was then its President suggested that the students should spend some time with the villagers and should get acquainted with their problems. Social service should constitute one important purpose in student life apart from studies.[150]

Gradually a general consciousness among the students was generated which did not remain confined to main Orissa but spread among the Oriya students studying elsewhere too including in the feudatory states for example, in Mayurbhanj, an association of the students was organised in the Baripada High School and it functioned quite well for some time.[151] The Oriya students, studying abroad came forward to give financial help. A letter was sent by Mr. B. Das from Glasgow, England, to R.S. Ray, the President of the Utkal Sahitya Samaj where he wrote that on behalf of the Oriya Students, he was enclosing a postal order of seven shillings to Madhusudan Rao Memorial Fund.[152]

House No. 9 of Panchanan Ghosh Lane in Calcutta served for a long time as a lodging house (mess) for all the Oriya students in Calcutta. It became the nucleus of student activities.[153] Here they deliberated on the growing problems relating to Orissa and the Oriyas. A number of Oriya students studying at Calcutta hardly spoke in Oriya in public places for fear of being ridiculed. There were thousands of Oriya workers and a good number of wealthy families who preferred to adopt the Bengali culture and language to avoid humiliation. This made the Oriya students quite conscious of the tragic situation of the Oriyas and they decided to remedy it. For instance, they decided, in the face of embarrassing experiences, to put on pink turbans which M.S. Das had introduced in the UUC as the symbol of the Oriyas.[154]

But in course of time, the activities of the students lapsed into a low key. This was primarily because no sustained effort was made to keep it alive. Most of the founder-members of the students association had also finished their education and the in-coming members did not find much interest in it. Criticisers also surfaced about the activities of the 'Young Utkal Association'. However, within a decade of its emergence the Association became virtually defunct.

Subsequently, a new "Students' Conference" was constituted which aimed at creating a strong and healthy social atmosphere, fostering a spirit of solidarity amongst the Orissa students and making them sympathetic, useful and influential citizens of the rising Orissa.[155]

After a few years of active existence, this organisation also faded. In March 1918, when the UUC arranged its annual meeting with Fakir Mohan Senapati as its President friction between the UUC and the students came to the limelight. The students who had earlier decided under their leader Jadumani Mangaraj to be volunteers at the session refused to do so.[156] This group of students thought that the refusal of Mr. Debiprasad Sarbadhikari, the Calcutta University Vice-Chancellor, to preside over the Students' Conference (which annually sat along with the UUC) was made at the instruction of M.S. Das. This resulted in a great deal of bitterness and the students were divided into two camps.[157]

In order to resolve the crisis, a meeting of the students was convened on 8 March 1919 Cuttack Town Hall with Kalpataru Das in the chair.[158] After long deliberations, it was agreed to sink all differences and that there would be only one "Utkal Students' Association" under the Chairmanship of Prof. Jogesh Chandra Roy. It was decided further that this committee would frame the constitution and prepare the agenda for the students.

This Students' Association started enlarging its sphere of activity by opening branch associations in different districts. Healthy competition in various fields was encouraged among students at the conferences of different districts and they were urged to fight casteism and such other social evils.[159] By 1927, however, the authorities banned the students' organisations in all colleges in Orissa except in Ravenshaw College. This subdued the students' organisations considerably.

Indeed, this organisation contributed in many ways towards the Oriya national movement. The creation of the UUC was a trumpet call to all factions in the society and the students could not naturally sit idle; they too volunteered to contribute their mite for the cause.

Women

A rise in the consciousness among the people in Orissa also brought in a change in the life style of its women. Gradually their attention was shifted to the virtues of education. Female education was very much highlighted and much initiatives were taken for the development of Girls' School in various districts. By 1895, there were 5 girls studying even in the Cuttack Medical School.[160] Many educated and progressive ladies also tried to help house-wives and girls for getting trained in various vocations. Smt. Reba Ray (niece of the poet Madhusudan Rao) brought out a magazine for women called 'Asa' in the late 19th century. She set up one ideal girls' school at her own residence at Kaligali, Cuttack, where various types of vocational training like sewing, music and cooking were imparted. Text book education for such training was given through both Bengali and Oriya.[161]

Progress in education opened up a new vision for the Oriya women. Even then, it was not easy for women to ignore the age- old social taboos and go in for higher education. But a wind of change blowing already in other progressive provinces was being awaited eagerly.[162] Different social organisations also took interest in pushing forward the cause of women's education. The Orissa Association bore the expenses for Nirmala Bala Das and Narmada Kar for studying B.A. at Calcutta University.[163] Birupakshya Kar during his visit to Japan, America and England studied the educational pattern there and put forward many suggestions for the development of various education programmes including that of female education.[164] By 1918 many people had started writing books on the education of women. Many women themselves started writing on the problems of their education and social development. One Oriya monthly called 'Siksya Darpana' edited by Smt. Basant Ku. Dei, created excitement in the ladies' circles all over Orissa.[165] The educational progress of women received much encouragement from the UUC which stressed female education almost in every session. Woman was never treated as an object of dependant cult, rather she was given all sorts of facilities for higher education so that she would rise above the petty parochial thoughts, superstitious social taboos and demand her own entity in the society, strive for it and challenge the oppressors and exploiters of the society.

This generated an increasing consciousness among the Oriya women. During the World War I, women appealed the Oriya youth to join the army if the nation desired.[166] Many women participated actively in Gandhiji's popular movements which shall be discussed in the next chapter.

The women of Orissa thus became active participants in the Oriya movement as it grew in intensity and the activities of the Congress organisation also started engaging their keen attention.

Backward Castes and the Tribal People

The UUC programmes for the removal of social exploitation and economic disparity and their stress on the spread of education among all classes including women and the backward classes had an impact on all concerned. Its federal structure also facilitated the spread of such ideas to the villages. Newspapers started coming in, people showed interest in the political discussions, and their children started going to schools. All this opened up a new vista of progress for all classes in the villages. The downtroddens particularly started pondering over their states in the social set-up and would not accept their exploitation and ostracism as a freak of destiny.

A letter which appeared in an important newspaper would reveal how the self-consciousness, perhaps the most significant character of nationalism, had taken roots in the backward society. The letter written by one Ramachandra Das from Cuttack, read ".... In the modern Hindu Society eventhough the Kantha (Bauri, one of the scheduled castes) belongs to a lower strata, it is very much a part of the Hindu system of law; marriages are conducted according to the regulations of the sastra or Hindu scriptures. Bibhuti Bhanja's book of 'Ganesh bibhuti' shows that the Bauris are children of Visvamitra, they are devotees of Vishnu. It is only since the time of Prataprudra that their social position has been brought down. I cannot comprehend why they should be considered as untouchables to-day".[167] Such a defiant attitude drew strength from the spread of education.

During the First World War when tremendous amount of manpower was required for taking up various jobs, many tribal folks from different feudatory states were called upon by the military to work as 'Coolies'. They were despatched to as far as Mesopotamia without of course any prior intimation or their consent. But this information leaked out. Consequently, the tribals in Mayurbhanj rebelled and refused to go.[168]

By 1920, the untouchables had formed their own association called "The National Conference of the Scheduled Castes'.[169] In one of their sessions at Mundalo village in Salepur, around 100 people from different groups of 'Dhobi', 'Pan', 'Kandara', 'Bauri' were present. Through its resolutions it pressed for separate schools for the untouchables with the help of special grants as were provided to the girls' schools. It also urged that free schooling be provided for all untouchables and demanded special favour and award of scholarships.[170]

Many smaller associations came into existence which met more often and discussed their development. They were elated whenever the slightest attention was paid to their upliftment. A news item in the Utkal Dipika carried a report from a person belonging to one of the scheduled castes that ".... it is quite encouraging to learn of the decision taken of Government to send Sridhar Samal as the representative of the scheduled caste who happens to be our first graduate ....".[171]

The educated class too took increasing interest in the amelioration of their condition. Satyavadi School had a special wing for the untouchables called 'Kadua Ashram' founded by Gopabandhu Das.[172] He collected the untouchable boys wherever he went and got them admitted into this school. The strength of the students here grew in number and some of them rose to important positions in their later life. The students organisations often included the problems of the scheduled castes in their agenda and help was extended whenever sought.[173] This indicates how in the wake of the UUC the nationalistic spirit was shaking every brick in the social structure that had been lying inert since long. It were these tribals who played a very decisive role in the amalgamation issue by foiling the attempts of Oriya leaders to unite Singhbhum with Orissa.

UUC Versus Congress

Before discussing the participation of the Oriya delegates in the Congress sessions between 1903-1919, it may be noted here that Madhusudan's relations with the Congress had not been entirely disrupted although he did not regularly attend its sessions. He dissociated himself from it not for ever. He was one of the Vice-Chairmen of the Reception Committee of the 27th session of the Congress at Bankipore (Bihar) in 1912.[174] In January 1915, S.N. Banerjee visited Cuttack. A large meeting was organised in the Town Hall in honour of Banerjee which was presided over by Madhusudan Das.[175] Brajasundar Das, Biswanath Kar and Gopabandhu Das spoke on the occasion. Banerjee had a soft corner for the Oriya problems. The Oriyas, it appears were never indifferent to the Congress activities.

Very often, through his speeches, writings and correspondences, Madhusudan had explained the relation of the Utkal Union Conference with the Congress. Once he said : "Mother-Utkal is not separate from the Mother-India. The former is neither the step- mother nor enemy of the latter. The UUC which consists of the Oriyas, Bangalis, Telugus and Rajputs is a part of Indian nationalism".[176] Most of the active members of the Conference were delegates to the Congress sessions year after year, but the political ambition of the Oriyas, Madhusudan said, was the amalgamation of the Oriya-speaking tracts under one administration.[177] He had many lofty ideas. In course of his talks and conversations with the students, he was able to awaken the youth. He wanted to inculcate the ideas of patriotism and nationalism in the hearts of the students. Under his able leadership, the conference became a nursery for leadership in Orissa.

Madhusudan sacrificed his life for the cause of the country. The foremost aim of his life was to uplift his province and his nation. Noted for his political sagacity and independence of thought, he believed that in the uplift of the Oriya nation lay the progress of India. He belonged to the old school of politicians like, Surendra Nath Banerjee, Gopal Krishna Gokhale and Dadabhai Naoroji, but he sincerely believed that the unification of the Oriya tracts could not be achieved by National Congress. Hence the necessity of a provincial organisation to fight for the cause of the Oriyas. This enlightened Oriya nationalism, he said, was not opposed to Indian nationalism. A greater Orissa as a distinct political unit, he believed, would give further momentum to Indian nationalism. Shyama Prasad Mukherjee, therefore, pointed out" Madhusudan was a mighty Indian first and everythingelse afterwards".[178] So Madhusudan believed that only when the Oriyas would be united as a homogeneous nation, they would forget their feelings or inferiority and take far greater interest in Congress activities.

In the 19th session of the Indian National Congress which was held in the last week of December 1930 in Madras, Bhagabat Prasad Mohapatra and J. Ghosal of the National Society, Balasore and Harimohan Raychoudhury, Ram Sankar Ray and Janakinath Bose of the Utkal Sabha, Cuttack participated.[179] Even after the formation of the UUC, Orissa never forgot to send her delegate to the Congress sessions. A host of new delegates like, H.M. Raychoudhury, Gopi Mohan Ray and Radhashyam

Das attended the next Congress session at Bombay (1904) with the old ones.[180] Year after year, more and more Oriyas participated in the Congress session.[181] As a result, the number of persons taking part in Congress activities gradually increased and a strong public opinion was built up in Orissa.

In the Bankipore session of the Congress in 1912, excluding the dignity that M.S. Das was one of the Vice-Chairman of the Reception Committee, some students of Ravenshaw College, Cuttack participated and proceeded to work with the students of Patna College as volunteers.[182] The Lucknow Session of the Congress (1916) which stands unique and unparallel in the history of the Freedom Movement in India because of its two most significant features-first, the union between Moderates and Extremists who had been fighting tooth and nail since the Surat Session (1907) and second, the unity between the Indian National Congress and All-India Muslim League was attended by a large number of Oriya delegates. This Congress had elected M.S. Das as a member of AICC.[183] After two years, Gopabandhu Das was elected to this position from Orissa.[184] The emergence of Gopabandhu Das gave a totally unexpected turn to the Congress activities in Orissa.

As a student in Calcutta, Gopabandhu had been inspired by the nationalistic fervour of the Swasdeshi Movement, and the resolution of national education passed in the Calcutta Congress (1906).[185] In order to implement this programme, he established the Satyavadi Vana Vidyalaya at Sakshigopal. After returning from the Lucknow Session of the Congress, he completely plunged into the Congress organisation and made an all-out endeavour to give a new life to it in Orissa.[186] The year 1917 saw the emergence of Gopabandhu as a new leader who played an important role in moulding the character of the Congress organisation in Orissa. He nurtured the Congress in Orissa, the seeds of which were sown long ago. He started a systematic campaign to propagate Congress ideas in Orissa and advocated that the UUC should become a part of the Indian National Congress.

Gopabandhu made an extensive tour. In the meetings, he preached that "the conference has attained majority and its isolated existence in national life is no longer possible".[187] Elsewhere he propagated that the Indian National Movement was forging ahead and its reactions were felt in Orissa ... If Orissa did not join the mainstream of the Indian National Congress, it might be, she might lose her identity altogether.[188]

In order to broadcast the message of the Congress Gopabandhu published an Oriya weekly, 'The Samaj' whose first issue came out on Dussehra, 4 October 1919.[189] Thereafter, it became the mouthpiece of the Congress movement in Orissa. It helped Gopabandhu to activise propaganda through press and public meetings, because, his idea was to transform the purely constitutional progress of the UUC into an activist movement with the programme of direct action.

The special session[190] of the National Conference in Calcutta on 4 September 1920 took a firm pledge to attain Swarajya or self-government.[191] and adopted the policy of progressive non-violent non-cooperation[192] inaugurated by M.K. Gandhi. Gopabandhu was elected as a member of AICC and he whole heartedly supported Gandhiji's stand on non-cooperation and decided to launch its programme in Orissa.[193] Other nationalists of Orissa also highly appreciated this programme. The 'Utkal Dipika', which always professed moderate views also changed its voice and reported, "The mahamantra of Non-Cooperation has been accepted universally, not generally. The Mahatma has given the mantra".[194]

The Nagpur session of the Congress (1920) gave sanction to the Non-Cooperation Resolution. Here Gopabandhu succeeded in persuading Gandhi to adopt the principle of the formation of linguistic Congress provinces.[195] The UUC also aimed at the unification of the Oriya-speaking tracts on the basis of language. Sri Gopabandhu thought, there was no bar for the conference to accept the Congress programme and its method of agitation. He was of the opinion that the formation of the Orissa province should be preceded by the organisation of Utkal Pradesh Congress Committee. From there Gopabandhu came straight to Chakradharpur, an important town in Singhbhum to attend a memorable meeting, the 16th session of the UUC to be held on 30 December 1920.[196]

By that time a Provincial Congress Committee had already been set up in Orissa in the beginning of 1920 with the efforts of Gopabandhu. He himself was the president of it and Sayed Ekram Rosul was the Vice-President. Bhagirathi Mahapatra, a legal practitioner gave up his profession to take over the Secretaryship.[197]

Jagabandhu Singh, the president-designate for the session came by the Bombay Mail straight from the Nagpur Congress and reached Chakradharpur on 29th morning. On his arrival, cheers went up in the name of India and Orissa, and he was accorded a great ovation.[198] Here

Gopabandhu and his supporters succeeded in adopting two resolutions. He moved the first resolution "that the aims and objectives of the Indian National Congress be accepted as those of the UUC in addition to the accepted objectives of the Conference". Supported by Chandra Sekhar Behera, it was adopted by a vote of 127 against 17.[199] Krushna Chandra Acharya moved the second resolution: "that this conference wholeheartedly endorses the resolution of the Indian National Congress (INC) recommending the creation of linguistic provinces". Supported by Nilakantha Das, it was also adopted.[200]

The Chakradharpur session marked a triumph of the nationalists under the leadership of Gopabandhu over the Moderates. Henceforth the aim of the UUC would be 'Swarajya'[201] in addition to its accepted objectives. The conference adopted the programme of the Congress in principle, but it did not merge with the National Congress. It continued to meet from time to time demanding the formation of Orissa into a new Province.

Movement From 1920 to 1936

Since the Mont-Ford report did not highlight the problem of an amalgamation, the Oriyas continued the movement and the question of amalgamation was taken up for discussion from time to time in the Central and the Provincial Legislatures. On 20 February 1920 S.N. Sinha moved a resolution in the Imperial Council which read : "This recommends to the Governor-General-in Council that a mixed committee of non-officials be appointed to formulate a scheme for the amalgamation of the Oriya-speaking tracts at present administered or controlled by the Governments of Madras, Bengal and the Central Provinces with the existing Orissa Division of the Province of Bihar and Orissa".[202] He did not make any special reference to the possibility of a sub-province. This motion was supported by S.N. Banerjee, Sir Dinshaw E. Wacha and Sri Kamini Kumar Chanda.[203] But B.N. Sarma, a representative from Madras, opposed this resolution. While advocating a linguistic distribution of provinces he suggested that instead of forming a block of the Oriya-speaking tracts as a part and parcel of the proper Bihar and Orissa Province, a separate province for the Oriyas should be created.[204]

Sir William Vincent, the Home Member, speaking on behalf of the Government sympathised with the Oriyas. But he expressed his inability to take any step to change the provincial boundaries before the reformed provincial councils came into being. However, in concluding his speech he gave the Council the following assurance."I am quite prepared, however, if I can secure the sanction of His Excellency-in-Council to this course, to have a full investigation of the facts to ascertain the views of the Local Governments and prepare such materials for the use of the new governments as may assist them in arriving at a joint decision in this matter".[205] On reviving this assurance, Mr. Sinha withdrew his resolution.

On 21 Sept. 1912, the following regulation was noted by A.B. Latthe in the Indian Legislative Assembly for reorganization of provinces on linguistic basis. "This Assembly recommends to the Governor-General-in-Council that he may be pleased to undertake the task of reconstituting the provinces of India in consultation with the various local Governments and with a view to facilitating the constitutional development of the Provinces".[206] Regarding Oriya-speaking people he stated, "A more striking example of this class of division of people between the various provinces is that of the Uriyas".[207] Rai G.C. Nag Bahadur in an amendment demanded to take steps in that direction after ascertaining the wishes of the people of the areas through various local Governments.[208] Braja Sundar Das, an Oriya member, supported the resolution. In reply Sir William Vincent referred to the report of the Joint Select Committee and expressed the non-feasibility of the task of reconstituting Provincial boundaries unless it came up from the local Governments concerned.[209]

In the very year resolutions were tabled in the Legislative Councils of Bihar-Orissa and Madras to effect unification of the Oriya-speaking areas and bringing them under one administration. On 25 November 1921, Biswanath Kar moved one resolution where he emphasized more on the amalgamation of the Oriya-speaking areas than on a separate Orissa Province.[210] Among other Ganesh Dutta Singh and Rai Bahadur Dvarikanath from Bihar gave strong support to this resolution with deep sympathy for the Oriyas.[211] In their reply, the Government accepted the spirit of the resolution and further wanted a consensus of the people of the outlying Oriya-speaking tracts whether they were willing to be merged with their counter-parts in Bihar and Orissa.[212] With a view to the ultimate formation of a separate Orissa province, in the same year Shashibhusan Rath moved a resolution in the Madras Legislative Council to transfer the Oriya-speaking areas of Madras to the Bihar and Orissa Province.[213] This resolution was, however, disallowed by the Governor under Rule 22(1) of the Madras Legislative Council Rules.

The Government of India drew the attention of the Governments of Bengal, Bihar and Orissa, Madras and the Central Provinces and directed them to ascertain the wishes of the people affected by the proposal. The replies of the Provincial Governments which were received during 1922 were as follow : The Government of Madras opposed the transfer of Oriya-speaking areas on the plea that such transfer involved administrative and financial complications. They further pointed out that the Telugu inhabitants of that area and the Raja of Jeypore opposed the proposed transfer.[214] The Government of Bengal reported the unwillingness of the Oriyas in Midnapore for a separation from Bengal since they had already adopted Bengali.[215] The Government of the Central Provinces opposed the transfer of the Oriya-speaking areas under their jurisdiction excepting Khariar only which according to them, contained majority of Oriyas.[216] The Government of Bihar and Orissa reported that in the Orissa Division educated opinion was in favour of union of the Oriya-speaking tracts. But they did not recommend the inclusion of Singhbhum on the ground that majority of the people were in favour of the transfer.[217] These replies did not satisfy the Government of India. So the Government of India, through their independent agency. sought to further ascertain the popular opinion of the outlying Oriya tracts. They proposed to depute two officers to these areas for inquiry.[218]

A meeting was held at Vizagpatam on behalf of the 'Utkal Samaj' on 8 April 1927 insisted on the formation of provinces on the linguistic basis. In one of the resolutions, the Government of India was requested not to appoint a Commission consisting only of two officers, but to appoint instead a Commission of inquiry consisting both of official and non-official members according to the recommendation of the Selbourne Commission.[219] Same leaders of Madras and Bengal supported the issue. P.C. Chatterjee, a Bengali leader, started the issue of the Oriyas as 'legitimate, fair and most frank'.[220] Again, Suba Rao, the Secretary of the Indian National Congress supported the transfer of the Oriya-speaking areas of Madras to Orissa.[221]

In 1924, the 'Reforms Enquiry Committee' (Muddiman Committee) came to India to review the situation. M.S. Das, ex- Minister of Bihar and Orissa, in a note dated 6 June 1924 to the Committee pointed out the Oriya disabilities in the most unequivocal terms. He pointed out that the Oriyas were very much ill- treated by the Biharis who did not like the Oriyas to develop capacity for shouldering responsibilities. The Oriyas had no voice as the Biharis formed majority in the Council. He strongly advocated for the appointment of separate minister who would remain in charge of all the transferred subjects relating to Orissa.[222] But the Government negating the provision of a separate minister highlighted the provision of a Deputy Governor for the purpose.[223] But the Muddiman Committee did not even favour the appointment of Deputy Governors.[224]

On 27th November, 1922 the Oriya District Association's representatives including Sashi Bhusan Rath, Biswanath Das, Mandhata Gorachand Patnaik, L.N. Deo met the Governor of Madras and requested him to recommend the constitution of a separate Orissa Province under a Governor. However, they maintained that as a prelude to this end, the amalgamation of the Oriya-tracts should promptly be carried out under any of the administration.[225] When the Raja of Jeypore, Sri Vikram Dev Verma published a printed memorandum "A note on the Oriya-speaking tracts of Madras", Sri Biswanath Das wrote its foreword and powerfully argued that the entire Ganjam district and Zamindari of Jeypore excepting the taluk of Sikakol should join with a separate Orissa Province.

The Orissa leaders were divided over the question of their participation in the Orissa amalgamation movement.[226] While Madhusudan Das, Krushna Chandra Gajapati and their followers were in favour of the formation of Orissa Province even before the achievement of independence, other leaders like H.K. Mahtab, N.K. Choudhury and Nityananda Kanungo, demanded that their first priority was the liberation of India. But Congress leaders, like Gopabandhu Das, Nilakantha Das, Biswanath Das, Niranjan Patnaik and Dibakar Patnaik served as a bridge between the National liberation struggle and Orissa amalgamation movement. The Patrapur session of Utkal District Committee in 1924 permitted Biswanath Das, Sashi Bhusan Rath and Dibakar Patnaik to extend all kinds of support to K.C. Gajapati who at that time attempted to inject new dynamism to the UUC which had become ineffective after the Chakradharpur session on 1920 when it was converted into a forum of Indian National Congress. It was made broad-based, to represent the cause of the proposed province before the newly constituted Phillip-Duff Committee set up to examine the Southern boundary between the proposed province and Madras.

When Gandhiji announced the programme of his maiden visit to Orissa in 1921, people felt enlightened because apart from his principles of non-cooperation his favourable views on the formation of linguistic provinces were also known. Gandhi wrote in 'Navajiban', "people want to make provinces on the linguistic basis, of course public opinion might not be correct always, but if there is no harm done in working according to this opinion, is it not advisable to do so ? Because sooner or later, provinces will be made on the basis of the language. And the sooner it is, the better".[227] Gandhiji made an extensive tour over Cuttack, Puri, Bhadrak and Ganjam.[228] On his return from the tour of Orissa, Gandhiji wrote in 'Young India' (dt. April 1920) and through this article brought to notice, the sad political situation in Orissa. A book entitled, "Orissa movement' was presented to him and he seemed to have agreed in principle, with the view points expressed here when he argued in favour of a separate province for Orissa.[229] Gandhi's considerate and sympathetic views on the Orissa problem proved beyond doubt his genuine concern for the people of this region. He also made it known that Orissa's feeble voice was getting drowned in the presence of more influential members inside the Congress and hinted that the minority opinions should not be ignored. The people of Orissa realized that through Gandhiji, their cause could be projected into the all-India scene.[230]

When Gandhi made his tour to Berhampur, the Oriya-speaking and Telugu-speaking Congress leaders of Ganjam took a decision to settle the problem in his presence. Although they decided to write leaders like Gopabandhu Das and Konda Venkatappiah, the latter remained absent when Gandhiji arrived at Berhampur on 29 March 1921. Gandhiji stayed in the official residence of Madhusudan Panigrahi presently known as 'Madhu Mandir' and listened to both the parties. While appreciating the gravity of the problem he declared in the public meeting : "Before the sun rises tomorrow, the Telugu-Orissa boundary disputes should be settled. The stronger Telugus must yield to the weaker Oriyas".[231] The responsibility of organising meeting and mobilizing people at various meetings in the district addressed by Gandhiji was given to Biswanath Das, Niranjan Patnaik and Sashibhusan Rath. After the departure of Gandhiji, the Congress leaders of Ganjam invited leaders like Pattavi Sitaramayya, T. Prakasam, Gopabandhu Das and Nilakantha Das with the approval of Indian National Congress to meet at Berhampur on 28 September 1921 in the presence of Dr. Munje of Maharashtra for the purpose of finding out an amicable solution to the problem. Being mobilized by Biswanath Das, Ram Chandra Mardaraj, Sashibhusan Rath and Lingaraj Panigrahi, lakhs of Oriya-speaking people gathered at Berhampur to press their demand for a separate province.

Being astonished by the enthusiastic presence of the masses, the Andhra leaders decided to confine their discussion to the representative level without inviting the masses for recording their views. Dr. Munje was therefore, forced to adjourn the meeting to a future date. The Secretary of the Indian National Congress then appointed C. Rajagopalachari as an arbitrator to be assisted by both the Andhra and Utkal Congress leaders and asked him to submit its report by 31st March, 1924. The problem why the Andhra leaders non-cooperated one after the other Oriyas was a tricky one. They thought that any decision going against Andhras might dampen the freedom struggle there. But the resignation of C. Rajagopalachari from assignment and indifference of Sitaramayya and Prakasam made the committee virtually defunct. Later on Rajendra Prasad was also requested to act as the arbitrator, but he too denied. Thus the non-cooperation of the top Congress leaders created temporary frustration among the Congress workers of Ganjam. They therefore, decided at the Patrapur Session of the District Congress Committee to extend all kinds of support to K.C. Gajapati during the visit of Phillip-Duff Committee.

After the release of Pt. Gopabandhu Das from jail in July 1924, Utkal Pradesh Congress Committee (UPCC) organised the Utkal Provincial Conference which was held at Cuttack on 28th July 1924 with Gopabandhu Choudhury as Chairman of the Reception Committee where a resolution authorising the Committee to place the question of amalgamation of Oriya-speaking tracts before Mahatma Gandhi was passed. But as Gandhi was very much pre-occupied at that time he could not take up the question.

Biswanath Das organised the Oriyas of Ganjam and Koraput for putting pressure on the government for their merger with Orissa. As a result of the persistent demand of the Oriyas under the Madras Presidency for their merger with Orissa, the Phillip- Duff Committee was appointed to ascertain the opinion of the Oriya-speaking people of the Madras Presidency on the question of their merger with Orissa.[232] The Committee consisted of C.L. Phillip, I.C.S., then Political Agent in the Orissa Feudatory States and A.C. Duff, I. C.S. then Collector of Vizagpatam, as the nominee of the Madras Government.

The appointment of the Phillip-Duff Committee generated excitement all over Orissa. The Oriya leaders in Orissa thought it wise to start some propaganda work in the interior areas so as to acquaint the illiterate people with the nature of the interview of this Enquiry Committee. Even a questionnaire containing possible questions from the committee was prepared and the campaigners tried to explain to the people the mode of answering the questions.[233]

This Committee began in October 1924 and submitted its report on 26 December of the same year. The Committee was the first of its kind at the Government level, which recommended for the creation of provinces on linguistic basis. While recognizing the legitimate demand of the Oriyas of Ganjam and Koraput, the Committee observed in 'Paragraph 12' of its report that, ".... Our enquiry has shown that there is a genuine long-standing and deep-seated desire on the part of the educated Oriya-speaking tracts of Madras for amalgamation".[234] The Committee was of the opinion that Oriya-speaking areas of Madras Presidency including Ganjam and Vizagpatam Agency should be merged with Orissa. It also recommended that Manjusa, Tarala, Tekkali, Jalantar, Bodarsingh and Parlakhemindi estates of Ganjam District and Jeypore estate should form parts of Orissa except Chicacole and Narasenapeta taluks where the Oriyas were in minority.[235] .

At Aska, Surada, Dharakote, Sergada, Bodagada, the Malukdari villages round Aska, Ghumsur, Chhatrapur, the estates of Khallikote and Atagada, and the small estates of Biridi, Huma and Pulur, the Committee met rallies and received deputations and address in favour of amalgamation.[236] This success was an outcome of the unity that was established between the Congress and the UUC leaders. Earlier alongwith the Congress and the UUC the Congress leaders like Biswanath Das, Sashibhusan Rath, Lingaraj Panigrahi, Madhusudan Panigrahi and Harihar Panda had started creating mass awareness and persuaded people to speak out their minds before the Phillip-Duff Committee during their visit to Berhampur, Parlakhemindi, Jeypore, Khallikote, Russelkonda (Bhanjanagar) and Rambha. A book entitled 'Oriya movement' written by Niranjan Patnaik and Chakrapani Pradhan was widely circulated among the intellectuals to get a glimpse of the agony of the Oriyas during the British rule. Thousands of resolutions and memoranda had been submitted to the Committee to make them realize the aspirations of Oriyas.

On the basis of the recommendations of the Phillip-Duff Committee, Pt. Nilakantha Das moved a resolution in February 1927 in the Bihar and Orissa Legislative Assembly for the creation of a separate Orissa state and it was approved in principle by the Assembly. This was also viewed sympathetically by the Government at the centre. According to the direction of the Government of India, the Bihar and Orissa Government on March 1927 appointed Rai Sahib U.N. Sen, their Financial Advisor, to investigate into the financial implications of the amalgamation of the proposed ten taluks of the Ganjam district of Madras.[237] The report of the annual income and expenditure in thousands of the Ganjam district submitted by U.S. Sen contained the facts that the annual receipt from the predominating Oriya-speaking tracts was thousand Rs. 2,506 while the annual expenditure was thousand Rs.3,642.[238] He calculated that the deficit would be to the tone of 11 lakhs and 36 thousands. The Bihar and Orissa Government reported the findings of their financial inquiries to the Government of India and mentioned that owing to financial deficit they did not argue for the transfer of the ten taluks of the Ganjam district to Orissa. The Government of India did not proceed further. The matter was left to Provincial Governments.[239]

Biswanath Das, Member of the Legislative Council published 'The Fallacy of a Deficit' and criticised Rai Sahib Sen's Report. According to him, neither the treasury figures nor the standard figures were based on a correct understanding of the facts. The report had excluded the Oriya speaking areas of the Jeypore Agency and the revenue taluks and sub-taluks of Chicacole, Narasenapeta, Tekkali, Parlakhemindi, Somapeta and others. It was pointed out that the revenue in thousands of the district would be 4,039 instead of 3,863. That reduced the deficit as a whole from 651 thousand to 475 since the expenditure incurred was thousand 4,514. Finally according to Sri Das, Rai Sahib Sen had underestimated the expenditure on those five taluks which he had excluded as non-Oriya tracts. Pointing out how Mr. Sen applied a most right and parsimonious scrutiny to income and was as liberal as possible with expenditure, Biswanath Das tried to prove through facts and figures that there would be a surplus of four lakhs instead of deficit as shown by Mr. Sen.[240]

At that time the All Party Conference appointed a Committee with Pandit Motilal Nehru as its Chairman on the redistribution of the provinces. The Committee recommended for the redistribution of the provinces on the basis of the wishes of the people and the linguistic unity of the area concerned. It also advocated taking into consideration the geographical, economic and historical factors.[241] In the Committee, Subhas Chandra Bose insisted on the formation of a separate Orissa province provided such a province was financially solvent.[242] On 30 Aug 1928, the All-Parties Conference met at Lucknow and approved the report of the Nehru Committee.[243] A resolution was passed demanding the creation of Sind as a new province. It was also received to create a separate Orissa province after amalgamating all the Oriya-speaking areas provided Orissa 'bears the financial burden which is incidental to separation.[244] This decision insisting on the financial pre-condition was very much resented in Orissa. The Utkal All Parties Conference sent a memorandum for the creation of the new Orissa province to the All Parties National

Convention which was held in Calcutta on 22 December 1928.[245] On 29 December 1927, the Governor of Bihar and Orissa visited Sambalpur where he received a memorandum supporting amalgamation. In reply, he exposed the difficulties involved in that issue and disclosed that nothing could be done before the Parliamentary Commission (Simon Commission) which was coming to India for administrative organisation had conducted the final inquiry.[246] There after, the Orissa leaders wanted for the report of the Simon Commission.

The British Government appointed a Statutory Commission in 1928 under the Chairmanship of Sir John Simon to report on the working of the reforms in India. As all the seven members of the Commission were Englishmen, the Congress resoluted to boycott it. By the time Simon Commission visited India in 1928 the atmosphere was quite tense on account of national agitation. The Congress boycotted the Commission. On the arrival of the Commission, 'Hartals' were organised all over the country and slogans of 'Simon go back' rented the air. The case of Orissa was presented before the Commission by the UUC with regard to the claim of the people of Orissa.

On 14 December 1928, the Oriya deputation met the Simon Commission in Patna and demanded a separate Orissa province.[247] But a member of the Central Committee suggested alternative methods of administration of a sub-province under a Deputy Governor. But all the members of the Orissa Committee rejected it and submitted a demand for a separate province.[248] On 30 May 1928 the Madras Presidency Oriya Association submitted its memorandum to the Simon Commission.[249] On 23 Feb 1929 a deputation of the said association waited on the Commission and insisted on a separate province.[250] Countless memorandums and telegrams reached the Commission from all parts of Orissa.

As regards the province of Bihar and Orissa, the Simon Commission mentioned that it was the most artificial and defective unit of all the provinces of India. This province comprised three areas which widely differed in physical features, racial traits, linguistic characteristics and cultural traditions.[251] Regarding the Madras Presidency, the Commission stated that there were many Oriya-speaking areas in it which were mostly found in the north-east of the province. Hence, they recommended division of the province on the basis of language.[252] The Commission agreed tentatively with the Nehru Report for the redistribution of Provinces on linguistic pattern. The Commission was generally against redrawing the map of India; but they made particular deviation with regards to Sind and

Orissa, and recommended special consideration. The Report said, "Bihar and Orissa is a glaring example of the artificial connection of areas which are not naturally related".[253] Therefore, the Commission, in cooperation with the Indian Central Committee and the Bihar and Orissa Committee, appointed a sub-committee to have a detailed investigation.

A Sub-committee under the chairmanship of Mr. C.R. Attlee was formed with Suhrawardy of the Indian Central Committee, the Raja of Kanika and Rai Bahadur Laxmidhar Mahanti of the Bihar and Orissa Provincial Committee. As regards the demands of the amalgamation of the Oriya-speaking areas and the creation of a separate Orissa province, the Sub-committee stated, "The grievance was well-founded, the demand substantially supported by the people, and the Oriya came deserving of sympathy".[254] It recommended creation of a separate Orissa province consisting of Orissa Division, Angul, feudatory states of Orissa, some portions of Mohanpur and Gopiballabhapur under the Bengal Presidency, Khariar estate under the Central Provinces and the Ganjam district under the Madras Presidency. It did not recommend the inclusion of other Oriya-speaking areas including Singhbhum and the Jeypore Agency in various grounds.[255]

The cordiality extended by the Oriya leaders to the Simon Commission, irrespective of party and ideological considerations evoked criticism in the Congress Organisation. In 1928, at the Calcutta Session of the Congress, the then president Motilal Nehru made certain critical remarks about the Orissa Congress for cooperating with the Simon Commission, against the directive issued by the Congress Working Committee. The Oriyas declared that the formation of a separate province was a question of life and death for the Oriyas. The remarks of the Congress President injured the sentiments of the Oriyas. The Orissa Congress delegation under the leadership of Biswanath Das, Pandit Nilakantha Das, Rajkrishna Bose and Niranjan Patnaik took strong exception to the uncharitable remarks from the chair and staged a walk out in protest.[256]

The report of the Simon Commission led to the summoning of the Round Table Conference in London in 1930. Three Round Table Conferences were held in 1930, 1931 and 1932 to decide the future of the new constitution of India. Orissa question was discussed in the very first conference. The Raja of Parlakhemindi, Krushna Chandra Gajapati, an Oriya delegate to the conference, tried his best to impress all the delegates for the creation of new Orissa province. The financial prospects of the Oriya speaking tracts as assessed by Biswanath Das strengthened the hands of K.C. Gajapati who convinced the members of the First Round Table Conference at London headed by Sir William Jowett, the Minister of State, Sir Samuel Hoare and the Parliament Members of England of the financial viability of the proposed province. He circulated a pamphlet, "The Oriyas, their Needs and Reasons for a separate province".[257] He presented valid arguments in favour of a new Orissa province. The Raja stated in that connection, that the ideal of All India Federation was meaningless to the Oriyas unless they got a separate province. The Secretary of State for India announced at the end of the First Round Table Conference that Orissa would be made a separate province. The efforts of the Oriya delegates bore fruits ; before the Third Round Table Conference ended, the Orissa Boundary Committee was appointed to review the boundary lines of the proposed Orissa province.[258]

The Government of India agreed with the suggestions of the Simon Commission and appointed a Boundary Commission of Orissa with S.P. O'Donnell as the Chairman. Other members of the Committee were T.R. Phookan, H.M. Mehta, Raja of Parlakhemindi, Sachidananda Sinha and Rai Bahadur C.V.S. Narasingha Raju Guru.[259] The terms of this Committee were to examine and report on the financial and other consequences of setting up a separate administration for Orissa and make recommendations regarding the adjustment of boundaries.

The O'Donnell Committee held its first meeting at Patna on 7 November 1931. The investigation was completed by 14 January 1932 and the report was signed on 19 April 1932.[260] The Congress decision was to emphasise the linguistic aspect of the problem and on that basis they outlined the territories to be claimed.[261] After considering all aspects of the problem, the Committee proposed that the province of Orissa should include "the Orissa Division, Angul, the Khariar Zamindari of the Raipur district, and the greater part of the Ganjam district and the Vizagpatam Agency tracts". It would have an area of approximately 33,000 sq. miles and a population of about 8,277,000.[262]

The O'Donnell Committee Report had a mixed reception in Orissa. The exclusion of certain Oriya speaking territories from the boundary of the province evoked strong reaction.[263] A special session of the UUC met on 21 August 1932 at Berhampur under the presidency of Lakshmidhar Mahanti, the Deputy President of the Legislative Council of Bihar and Orissa. The Conference urged upon the Government to constitute the separate province at an early date. It was also decided to send a deputation under the leadership of the Raja of Parlakhemindi to the Viceroy to acquaint him with the Orissa cause in its proper perspective.[264]

Soon after the Conference, the matter was brought to the Legislative Council of Bihar & Orissa in the form of a resolution moved by Lakshmidhar Mahanti on 2 September 1932 which read : "This Council recommends to Government that they be pleased to move the Government of India to constitute immediately a separate Orissa Province".[265] The resolution was widely supported and was carried without any division on 3 September 1932.

The recommendation of the O'Donnell Committee for the creation of the Orissa Province was opposed by the Telugus. They supported the merger of the Ganjam district with the proposed Andhra Province. They held a meeting at Berhampur on 6 May 1932 with Bhupati Raju Sitaram Raju in chair to criticise the Report of the Committee. It was also decided to send a deputation to Delhi and Madras to represent their claims.[266] A group of Telugus went to meet the Viceroy under the leadership of the Raja of Bobbil on 21 October 1932 to oppose the recommendation of the O'Donnell Committee and the creation of the Orissa Province.[267] The Telugus organised a meeting at Berhampur on 11 November 1931 to raise subscription to meet the expenditure of Varahgiri Jogeya, a Telugu pleader, who was to go to England to represent their grievances. He went to England and pleaded against the transfer of Berhampur town and other taluks to Orissa.[268] A Telugu Professor Dr. Sesagiri Rao suggested to form a separate Kaling Province consisting of the districts of Vizagpatam and Ganjam and the Telugu and Oriya speaking areas of the Central Provinces.[269] On the other hand, a group of Telugus demanded merger of Parlakhemindi and other zamindaris of the southern extremity of the Ganjam district with the proposed Orissa Province. They apprehended that in the events of inclusion of only Berhampur and Chhatrapur in Orissa the Telugus would be minority and hence would suffer.[270]

At the same time the Bengalis made attempts to include some Oriya-speaking areas in Bengal. It was found that when the Oriyas of Singhbhum, Manbhum, Saraikella, Kharaswan and Jharkhand areas of Chhotnagpur Division had been trying to merge these areas with Orissa the Bengalis too made parallel claims to add these very areas to Bengal.[271] A meeting of the Bengalis was held at Jamshedpur on 1 July 1931 with Nagendranath Rakhit in chair and demanded the merger of the aforesaid areas with Bengal. It was also resolved to submit this matter to the Viceroy.[272]

Consequent upon the discussion at the Round Table Conferences, the British Government was set for the reform of the Indian constitution, the draft proposals of which were embodied in the "White Paper" published on 17 March 1933 that proposed to create two new provinces, Sind and Orissa.[273] But the proposal regarding the boundary of Orissa as contained in the Government of India notification on the "White Paper" was far from being satisfactory. The "White Paper" proposed that the then Governors' Provinces should retain the boundaries which had existed at that time, with such alterations as the establishment of Sind and Orissa might involve.[274] It accepted the recommendations of the O'Donnell Committee with certain modifications. It excluded the Vizagpatam Agency and the Parlakhemindi Estates and Jalantar in the Ganjam Agency from the proposed Orissa Province.[275]

The special session of the UUC was held at Cuttack on 12 February 1933 with Sri Sailendra Narayan Bhanj Deo of Kanika as Secretary and Mr. Bhubanananda Das as President. The Raja of Madhupur, Raja Bahadur of Khallikote, Maharaja of Parlakhemindi and Mr. M.S. Das took leading part in the deliberations of the conference. The Committee passed a resolution expressing dissatisfaction at the proposed exclusion of the Parlakhemindi and Jeypore estates from the proposed province of Orissa and urging the inclusion of the said tracts and also of Singhbhum in Orissa.

Another special Conference was held at Jeypore with Mr. Biswanath Das as President in June, 1933 which reiterated in demand about inclusion of Jeypore in the proposed province of Orissa.

However, the Raja of Parlakhemindi decided to divide his estate and to bring a portion of it including the town of Parlakhemindi to the new province. His decision was emphatically placed before the Secretary of State. The UUC which met at Cuttack on 11 February 1934 under the presidency of Madhu Sudan Panigrahi of Ganjam, passed a few resolutions on the matter and they were duly forwarded to the Reforms Office. The conference decided to press for the inclusion of the following areas : (1) The Jeypore Agency (2) North-eastern parts of Parlakhemindi (3) The Parlakhemindi estate (Maliahs) (4) Western portion of Mandasa and Jalantar estates and (5) The entire Zamindari of Budarsingh. For this purpose they authorised the Raja of Parlakhemindi to represent before the British Parliament during the discussion of the Government of India Bill.[276]

Before departing for London, the Raja of Parlakhemindi in a Memorial to the Government of Madras, appealed them to support the inclusion of his estate to Orissa.[277] In England, the Raja approached the Secretary of State to transfer atleast a portion of his estate including the Parlakhemindi town to Orissa. His arguments could not convince the Secretary who asked the Viceroy of India for his views on this matter.[278] But the Viceroy strongly opposed the transfer both of Jeypore and Parlakhemindi to Orissa.[279]

In spite of such categorical objections of the Government of India, the long and insistent demands of the people of Orissa ably represented by the Raja of Parla had finally borne some fruits. The Joint Committee on Indian Constitutional Reforms in their report in November 1934, added to the Province as defined in the White Paper (a) that portion of the Jeypore estate which the Orissa Committee of 1932 recommended for transfer to Orissa, (b) the Parlakhemindi and Jalantar Maliahs (estates), and (c) a small portion of the Parlakhemindi estate, including Parlakhemindi town. The total area of the new province of Orissa was thus raised from 21,545 to 32,695 sq. miles.[280] In spite of financial difficulties to be faced by the new province, it was said : "A separate Province of Orissa would, however, be perhaps the most homogenous province in the whole of British India, both racially and linguistically; the communal difficulty is practically non-existent; and its claim appears to have the sympathy and support of all parties in India... In these circumstances we recommended that a new Province of Orissa be constituted".[281] Thus the Joint Parliamentary Committee gave the final shape to the new Province of Orissa which emerged as one of the eleven provinces of British India by the Act of 1935.

The Joint Parliamentary Committee under the chairmanship of Lord Linlithgow had submitted its report in November 1934. It has accepted the White Paper proposals in general but in some details it was even considered to be a more retrograde measure. Therefore, it was condemned by almost all sections of public opinion in India. The Congress asked the people to reject it outright. The Muslim League and the National Liberal Federation also could not accept its proposals. However, the Government brought the matter to the legislatures for discussion in order to ascertain their views. In the Legislative Council of Bihar and Orissa, the Finance Member, N.N. Sinha, moved the resolution on 15 January 1935 for bringing into consideration the Report of the Joint Committee on Indian Constitutional Reform.[282]

Soon Mr. Sachidananda Sinha, the leader of the Constitutional Nationalist Party, moved an amendment on a similar line to his criticism on the White Paper. He characterised the scheme, as a whole, as "highly unsatis-factory, grossly inadequate to meet popular aspirations and hedged round by unnecessary and undesirable safeguards betraying a deep distrust of Indian capacity and character".[283]

The next amendment was moved by Nikunja Kishore Das, a member from Orissa.To him the constitution recommended by its Joint Parliamentary Committee was "unsatisfactory" as it did not fulfil the aspirations of the Indians. But at the same time he suggested that it should work in a friendly spirit. He supported the contentions of the authors of the Report that "the success of a constitution depends far more upon the manner and spirit in which it is worked than on its formal provisions".[284] To him and also to other members of Orissa, the report had a peculiar significance in as much as it gave them separate identity. Even though, as it was believed, the delimitation of the boundaries still left much to be desired, yet he expressed the feelings of the people of Orissa in the following lines: "We are glad at the prospect that half a century of agitation and representation has at last borne some fruit and that most of us speaking the same language and inheriting the same culture will, after all these sorrowful years of separation, be united under one administration and minister to our own problems of flood and famine".[285]

Two more amendments were moved thereafter, one by Srikrishna Prasad and another by Muhammed Yunus. The former criticised the Report saying that any Act of Parliament based on such an anti-national scheme will be unacceptance to the people of india", while the latter observed that the omission of the expression 'Dominion Status' from the report was unfortunate. However, he desired to work it in a spirit of cooperation and goodwill.

The recommendations of the Joint Parliamentary Committee were accepted by the House of Commons. It was decided to introduce a bill on the general lines of the report. Accordingly, the Government of India Bill was prepared and the provision for the creation of a separate Orissa province and the boundaries recommended by the Joint Parliamentary Committee for the said province were enlisted in the Bill. An amendment was moved by Colonel Wedgwood to the Bill. He said that the population in Orissa was perhaps 16,000,000 out of whom nearly half were aboriginal tribes. He referred to the descriptions of Orissa as having been the scene of the "Jungle Book"written by Rudyard Kipling and alluded to the various tribes. He suggested that these people for their backwardness required direct administration.That the rest of Orissa on the south had been cut off from the province of Madras on the linguistic ground was tenable to Wedgwood. He further added that half of the province was tangled jungle, and on the coast there was a Hindu Oriya population which had hitherto been attached to Madras or Bihar. As far as he saw it, there was absolutely no need of a new Orissa province.[286]

Major Attlee refused to accept Wedgwood's interpretations of the geography,the population, the finance and the opinion of the inhabitants of Orissa.Attlee agreed that Oriya-speaking people were settled in different province; neither they had any common interest with those areas nor had they similarity with the people there of. They were made to live there as small minority and hence had no chance for self-government and self- expression, particularly when the province was vast like Madras. Attlee admitted that the number of the tribal people was very large but they were vivisected into sections allotted to different provinces. For their future development, as Attlee argued, these people should come together to Orissa under special administration. On the question of financial deficit, he said that it was an extremely fallacious argument.Of course, Orissa was a deficit area at that time, but at the same time there were many such deficit areas as well.[287] He admitted that the new arrangement might have involved increase in cost. But he was confident that given a chance to run their own show, the people of Orissa would pay increased taxes far more willingly than they would if they were merely part of such heterogenous province as Bihar and Orissa.[288]

G. Nicholson, in the course of his discussion, praised Attlee as the father of Orissa, and God-father of the new Orissa province. He behaved that there had been a real popular demand in Orissa for a separate province to preserve the national culture and language. Of course, he had his reservations regarding a perfect homogeneity under the new system considering the existence of as many as six languages - Oriya, Bengali, Urdu, Khond, Sanskrit and English.[289]

Sir Reginald Craddock took up the cause of the opposition and jeered that it was ridiculous to turn an area which had been run by a Commissioner into a Governor's province. He thought it to be the most extravagant step which would incur a perpetual deficit of 30 lakhs of rupees a year. According to him, the union of the Oriya-speaking areas would not be congenial. Craddock was critical over the financial estimates of the new province in which there was no provision for a University or a High Court. It was no logic in having a separate province, felt he, if the Oriyas would have to depend on other provinces for their academic and judiciary needs.[290]

Craddock accused the Government of setting up a province for 6,000,000 Oriyas. The number of Telugus, he argued, was 18,000,000 and so they could as well demand a new province. Similarly demands might be made to transfer Malbar from Tamil areas and the Hindi-speaking districts of the Central Provinces from the Marathi-speaking districts. Citing the demands of the Oriyas, he opined, that "It is contradictory in terms, and entirely illogical. For administrative reasons this scheme is sheer folly, for financial reasons it is extravagant, and for political reasons it is mostly make-belief".[291]

R.A. Butler, the Under Secretary of States for India, did his best to answer some of the points raised by the mover of the amendment and those who had intervened in the discussion. As regards the boundaries of the new province, Butler said that the boundaries decided by the Joint Committee for the proposed new province of Orissa would not be changed.[292]

The Govt. of India Bill, based on the report of the Joint Parliamentary Committee, was introduced in the Parliament on 1 February 1935 and received the royal assent on 4 August 1935. According to Section 289 of the Government of India Act, 1935, new provinces of Sind and Orissa were created. Section 289(1-b) of the Act contained the following: "Orissa and such other areas in the province of Bihar and Orissa as may be specified in the Order of His Majesty shall be separated from that province, and such areas as may be the specified in the said Order shall be separated from the Presidency of Madras and the Central Provinces respectively, and Orissa and the other areas so separated shall together form a Governor's province to be known as the Province of Orissa".[293]

In the meantime, the British authorities had published the draft Orders in Council regarding the constitution of the provinces of Sind and Orissa. It was released both in England and in Orissa on 21 January 1936.[294] His Majesty issued the order on 3 March 1936 which was entitled" The Govt. of India (constitution of Orissa) Order, 1936". The members from Orissa attended the Legislative Council of Bihar and

Orissa for the last time on 28 March 1936. On that day the Council gave them a touching farewell.[295]

The new province of Orissa was inaugurated on 1 April 1936. The province comprised an area of 32,695 square miles with a population of 8,043,681 drawn from three provinces as stated below.[296]

Name of the province	*Area*	*Population*
Madras (approximate)	17,400	2,552,874
Central Provinces	1,589	184,665
Bihar & Orissa	13,706	5,306,142
Total :	32,695	8,043,681

On that historic occasion, His Majesty the King, Edward VIII and the Governor General, Marquess of Linlithgow sent warm messages of greetings to the people.[297] Thus ended the long- cherished drama and Orissa entered into a new phase of her history.

Reserving the discussion on the nature of the movement to a subsequent chapter, a limited conclusion may be attempted here. The linguistic movement demanding formation of a separate province was definitely nationalist. Broad features of nationalism viewed in global perspective include linguistic identity. The feeling of oneness based on linguistic identity was nationalist too. This does not erase the contradiction in the Indian context. If one takes rather a narrow view, of considering all movements devoted to the freedom of India to be only nationalist in Indian context than terming the Orissa movement nationalist will call for a different debate. This aspect will be taken up later. As a whole, the movement proceeded on two fronts-one, consisted of representations, appeals etc. to the government, the other included formation of associations, holding of meetings and positive defence of Oriya identity. The leadership principally came from the feudal class and the rising educated elite. This movement ushered in the freedom struggle in Orissa and ultimately merged with the latter.

References

1. Home Public Proceedings, 10 Jan 1868, F.No. 38,
   Also UD, 27 Feb 1875
2. UD, 27 Feb 1875

3. Ibid, 5 July 1875
4. N.K.Das, Utkalgauraba: 50
5. Ibid.
6. Two Bachelors of Arts: 24
7. UD, 10 Jan 1903
8. Two Bachelors : 24-25
9. S.N.Das, Desaprana : 170-71
10. Ibid.
11. UD , 25 Apr 1903
12. S.N Das, op.cit. : 186
13. UD, 2 Jan 1904
14. Proceedings of UUC (PUS), 1903-1915
15. B. Mohapatra, Odia Andolanara Itihasa : 61-65
16. PUS, 1903-1915
17. UD, 2 Jan 1904
18. B. Mohapatra : 83
19. M. Mansingh, The Land of Jagannath : 196
20. Resolution IV
21. Resolution V
22. Resolution VI
23. Resolution III
24. *Amrita Bazar Patrika* (A B P), 9 Jan 1904
25. P.Kar, *Congress and Orissa* : 54
26. N.K. Das, *Madhubabunka Odia Gita* : 91
27. Vande Mataram, 17 Dec 1907 : 645
28. P.K. Nayak, *Biswanath Das* : 31
29. Two Bachelors : 29
30. Ibid : 30-31
31. Ibid.
32. Ibid : 329
33. PUS, 1903-1915
34. S.N. Das, op.cit. : 199

35. Two Bachelors : 196
36. Ibid.
37. Ibid : 330
38. UD, 31 Dec 1904
39. Two Bachelors : 330
40. UD, 18 Nov 1905
41. Home Public, Part 'B' Proceedings, No 16-162, Dec 1903
42. Ibid, part 'A', Proceedings, No. 155-167, Feb 1905
43. Ibid, No. 149-160, Dec 1903
44. Ibid, No. 155-167, Feb 1905
45. UD, 29 Sept 1905.
46. Ibid, 14 and 21 Apr 1906
47. Two Bachelors : 331
48. UD, 21 Apr 1906
49. Ibid.
50. PUS, 1903-1915
51. B. Mohapatra : 129
52. Ibid.
53. Two Bachelors : 332-33
54. Ibid.
55. Quoted in the report, ISC, Vol. IV : 538
56. UD, 24 Apr 1912
57. Ibid, 20 July 1912
58. Ibid, 27 July 1912
59. Report, ISC, iv : 538
60. The memorial contained the signatures of 621 persons including those of the rajas, land- holders, merchants and general public of the district of Ganjam. (Home Pub. 'B' Progs, No. 75- 78, Jan 1912.
61. Home Pub., G.O. No. 994 22 May 1916
62. UD, 13 Apr 1912
63. Ibid.
64. Two Bachelors : 332-33
65. UD, 13 Jan/20 Jan/ 10 Feb 1912

66. British Parliamentary Papers, 1912
67. PUS, 1903-1915
68. Two Bachelors : 334
69. Ibid.
70. PUS, 1903-1915
71. Ibid.
72. Two Bachelors : 334
73. Ibid.
74. UD, 22 Feb 1915
75. Asha (AA), 22 Mar/22 Apr 1915
76. Two Bachelors : 335
77. AA, 16 Jan 1916
78. Ibid.
79. Two Bachelors : 335
80. AA, 27 Nov 1916
81. Two Bachelors : 335-36
82. Ibid : 46
83. UD, 20 Oct/ 10 Nov 1917
84. Montague Chelmsford Report : 119
85. AA, 1 Dec 1913
86. Ibid.
87. Ibid, 17 Aug 1914
88. Ibid, 7 Feb 1916 UD, 4 May 1916
89. AA, 25 Feb 1918
    UD, 7 Oct 1918
90. UD, 7 Oct 1918
91. Ibid.
92. Two Bachelors : 45
93. UD, 20 Oct 1917
94. AA, 19 Nov 1917
95. Ibid, 12 Nov 1917
96. ISC, Vol. IV : 565

97. Ibid.
98. Two Bachelors : 47
99. Ibid.
100. AA, 18 Feb 1918
101. Ibid, 18 Mar 1918
102. Two Bachelors: 48
103. AA, 1 Apr 1918
104. S.N.Das, Desaprana: 410
105. AA, 8 Apr 1918
106. UD, 15 Apr 1918
107. Two Bachelors : 50-51
108. Home Public Proceedings No. 203-203A, May 1920
109. Progs. of Indian Legislative Council (ILC), 1919-20 : 831
110. UD, 22 Sept 1917
111. Ibid, 18 Dec 1917
112. Ibid, 5 Oct 1919
113. Ibid.
114. Ibid.
115. Ibid, 5 Jan 1919
116. Two Bachelors : 337
117. AA, 28 Apr 1919
118. Ibid.
119. Ibid.
120. Samaj (SJ), 13 Dec 1919
121. AA, 12 Jan 1920
122. Ibid, 5 Jan 1920
123. SJ, 13 Dec 1919
124. AA, 12 Jan 1920
125. UD, 14 June 1919
126. Ibid, 20 Dec 1919
127. AA, 2 Feb 1920
128. Ibid, 26 Jan & 2 Feb 1920

129. Ibid, 25 Feb 1920
130. Ibid, 2 Mar 1920
131. Ibid, 14 Dec 1922
132. Ibid, 22 Dec 1924
133. Ibid, 26 Sept 1921
134. Ibid, 4 Dec 1922
135. Ibid, 10 May 1920
136. Ibid, 15 May 1920
137. C.Mohapatra, *Odisara Patra Patrika* : 69
138. UD, 16 May 1903
139. C.Mohapatra :17
140. Ibid.
141. Ibid.
142. N.Mohanty, Oriya Nationalism : 69
143. Ibid.
144. C.Mohapatra : 17
145. N.K.Das,Madhusudan's Immortal Works : 3
146. S.N.Das, Desaprana: 86
147. UD, 14 Jan 1905
148. Ibid.
149. S.N.Das: 214
150. Ibid: 320-21
151. UD, 16 Mar 1912
152. Ibid, 22 Mar 1912
153. G. Mishra, *Arddha Satabdira Odisa*: 149-157
154. Ibid.
155. AA, 28 Feb 1916
156. S.N Das: 406-07
157. Ibid.
158. UD, 22 Mar 1919
159. N.Mohanty, *op.cit.*: 80
160. *Sambalpur Hitaisini* (SH), 15 Mar 1895

161. UD,7 Jan 1905
162. *Ibid*, 27 June 1915
163. *Ibid,* 13 July 1912
164. AA,19 June 1916
165. UD, 27 May 1919
166. *Ibid,* 28 June 1917
167. *Ibid.*
168. *Ibid,* 26 May 1917
169. SJ, 17 Apr 1920
170. *Ibid.*
171. UD, 12 Feb 1927
172. Gopinath Mohanty , *Utkalamani* :30-31
173. Prajatantra (PA), 18 Feb 1925
174. Progs. of INC (Micro) reel No.4 :123
175. UD, 9 Jan 1915
176. N.K Das, *Madhubabunka Gita* : 9-10
177. Ibid.
178. Sailabala Das, *Life of M.S.Das* :9
179. Progs of INC (MICRO) 1903, Reel No. 3, Bombay Session, 1904
180. Ibid.
181. Ibid, *Benaras Session,* 1905
182. UD, 18 Jan 1913
183. Progs of INC (MICRO) 1916, Reel No. 5
184. Ibid (1918)
185. Ibid (1906)
186. H.K. Mahtab, *Dasha Barshara Odisha*: 5
187. S.C.Dash, *Pt. Gopabandhu*: 86
188. *Ibid.*
189. SJ, 4 Oct 1919
190. Progs of INC (MICRO) Reel No.6
191. UD,11 Nov 1920
192. Ibid, Also P. Sitaramayya, *History of the Congress*: 202-03

193. UD, 11 Sept 1920
194. Ibid, 18 & 25 Sept 1920
195. P. Sitaramayya, *op.cit.*: 209
196. UD, 7 Jan 1921
197. H.K. Mahtab: *Odisha Itihasa*: 504
198. UD, 7 Jan 1921
199. *Utkal Sevak,* 6 Jan 1920
200. *Ibid.*, Also SJ, 8 Jan 1920
201. *Utkal Sevak,* 27 Jan 1921
202. *Imperial Legislative Council (ILC), Progs.*, 1919 1920 : 828
203. Ibid : 835-37
204. Ibid : 840-41
205. Ibid : 839
206. ILA, Debates, Vol.II, Sept 1921 : 711
207. Ibid.
208. Ibid : 717
209. Ibid : 725
210. BOLC Debates, 1921 : 165
211. Ibid : 190
212. Ibid : 163-65
213. AA, 31 Oct 1921
214. ISC, Vol. IV : 542-43
215. Ibid : Ibid : 545-46
216. Ibid : 545
217. Ibid : 544-45
218. AA, 11 Feb 1924
219. Ibid, 21 Apr 1924
220. Ibid, 17 Mar 1924
221. Ibid, 27 Oct 1924
222. ISC, Vol. XVI, Memorandum on behalf of the people of Orissa : 391-92.
223. Ibid.
224. Report of the Reforms Enquiry Committee, 1924 (Calcutta, 1929) : 180.

225. AA, 4 Dec 1922
226. P.K. Nayak, Biswanath Das : 38
227. AA, 7 June 1920
228. H.K. Mahtab, *Gandhiji O' Odisha* : 13-16
229. Ibid : 21-22
230. PA , 27 Feb 1924
231. Prahallad Panda, *Souvenir on Biswanath Das* : 23
232. Phillip-Duff Committee : 1 (Resolution by the Govt. of India, Home Deptt., No. F 669/22- Public dated Simla 1 Oct 1924).
233. UD, 8 Nov 1924
234. ISC Report, Vol. IV : 583-602
235. AA, 3 Nov 1924
236. Phillip-Duff Committee, para-8 : 10
237. AA, 11 Apr 1927
238. ISC, Vol. XVI, An Addendum to Oriya Memorandum : 395
239. S.C. Patra, *Formation of Orissa Province* : 174
240. ISC, Vol. XIV : 398-402
241. The Nehru Report (Redistribution of Provinces) : 61
242. Ibid : 63-64
243. UD, 1 Sept 1928
244. AA, 3 Sept 1928 and 20 Aug 1920
245. UD, 29 Dec 1928
246. AA, 23 Jan 1928
247. ISC, Vol. XVI : 428
248. Ibid : 402

Also Sj, 19 Dec 1928

249. ISC, Vol. XVII : 236-47
250. Ibid : 247-50
251. Ibid, Vol. I : 68-69
252. Ibid : 55-56
253. Ibid, Vol. II : 312
254. Ibid : 50

255. Ibid : 51
256. UD, 3 May 1930
257. Indian Round Table Conference, 1931 : 211-17
258. BOLC Progs, 1932 : 333
259. ABP, 19 Sept 1931
260. Report on the Orissa Boundary Committee (ROBC) 1932 : 1
261. SJ, 18 Nov 1931
262. ROBC : 34
263. UD, 11 June 1932
264. Ibid, 27 Aug 1932
265. BOLC Progs, 1932 : 307
266. AA, 1 May 1932
267. Ibid, 24 Oct 1932 and UD, 19 Nov 1932
268. UD, 19 Nov 1932
269. AA, 1 May 1934
270. Ibid, 27 Mar 1933
271. Ibid, 2 Mar 1931
272. Ibid, 6 July 1931
273. Proposals for Indian Constitutional Reform (ICR). 1933 : 44
274. Joint Committee on ICR Progs, 1933-34 : 70
275. Proposals for ICR : 44
276. Reforms Office, F.No. 47/1/34-R and K.W. National Archives of India (NAI) (New Delhi), Secretary to UUC Committee to Reforms Commissioner, 24 Feb 1934
277. Ibid, Memorial to the Govt. of Madras, 23 Feb 1934
278. Ibid, Telegram from Secretary of State to the Viceroy, No. 1687, 5 July 1934.
279. Ibid, Telegram to the Secretary of State from the Viceroy No. 1555, 17 July 1934.
280. Joint Committee on ICR, 1934 : 36
281. Ibid : 35
282. BOLC Progs, 1935 : 68
283. Ibid : 86

284. Ibid : 87-90

285. Ibid : 94

286. PD Commons, 1934-35 : 478

287. *Ibid* : 480

288. *Ibid* : 481

289. *Ibid* : 482

290. *Ibid* : 485

291. *Ibid.*

292. *Ibid* : 3

293. Govt. of India Act, 1935, Section 289 : 182-83

294. Reforms Office, F.No. 46/36, NAI (New Delhi)

295. BOLC Progs,1936 : 1471-72

296. Govt. of Orissa at work, work of the Congress Ministry, 1938 : 1

297. Reforms Office, F.No. 46/36 (New Delhi)

3

THE NATIONALIST MOVEMENT

The World War I changed the perspective of the nationalist freedom movement in India. The birth of the Communist Russia, the economic depression of the twenties and the rising Afro-Asian nationalist movements effected the English thinking on India. The repressive Rowlatt Act passed by the British Government, the Jalianwallabagh Massacre, the Muslim awakening in the wake of the dismemberment of Turkey and the anti-Caliphate English policy and the emergence of Mahatma Gandhi– the foremost charismatic cult figure of India's freedom movement, had changed the Indian scenario. Mahatma Gandhi returned to India in 1915, his unique political methods and his ability to identify himself with the common man not just the educated middle class gave the nationalist movement a wider political and mass base. The age of moderate constitutional Congress agitationist and at the Nationalist Congress faction was over, Pherozeshah Mehta, S.N. Banerjea, B.G. Tilak, Aurobindo Ghosh were no longer active. Gandhi gradually emerged as the undisputed leader of the Congress. These changes also forced some rethinking amongst the ranks and file of Orissan movement. The Utkal Union Conference which was committed to the cause of formation of Orissa as a separate province was now equally concerned with the question of national freedom. The former was no longer opposed to the latter, nor the latter excluded the former. The Congress even accepted the linguistic basis for formation of states. In other words the contradiction between the two had collapsed and there was a convergence of both the nationalist movements.

In 1920 there were two lines of thinking in Orissa. On one hand, Madhusudan Das and his followers believed in achieving the goal of the unification of Oriya-speaking tracts by cooperation with the British Government. On the other hand, Gopabandhu Das and his young band of followers were prone to the call of the National Congress under Gandhi's leadership. Gopabandhu had already been disillusioned with the "callousness" and "indifference" of the British Government towards the Oriyas.

The Non-Co-Operation Movement in Orissa

Eking out the vivid perception of the events and in the hope of getting unflinching support of the people, Mahatma Gandhi thought of launching Non-Cooperation as the only remedy for the Amritsar and Khilafat wrongs. "It was the clearest remedy", he exclaimed, "as it was the most effective when it was absolutely free from all violence".[1] It was launched on 1 August 1920.

The proposed departure of the Congress from the traditional constitutional path was considered an issue big enough for a special Congress.[2] The Congress workers of Orissa were unanimous in accepting the principle of Non-Cooperation. Gopabandhu Das, A.V. Thakkar (a social activist of Servants of India Society working in Orissa) and Jagabandhu Singh as delegates and Krupasindhu Mishra, Nilakantha Das and Harekrushna Mahtab as observers attended the special Congress in Calcutta on 4 September 1920.[3] It took a firm pledge for the attainment of Swaraj and adopted the policy of progressive non-violent Non-Cooperation.

Gopabandhu returned from the Calcutta Session of the Congress, being committed to the idea of Non-Cooperation and made extensive tours in the province amidst scenes of great enthusiasm . On 30 October 1920, he wrote in the Samaj about the powerful impact of the Non-Cooperation movement upon the students and lawyers in different parts of the country and mentioned the names of nine persons who had decided to boycott the legislatures. The Utkal Dipika wrote, "Mahatma Gandhi now stands higher and higher having scored a triumph which was seldom attained by any Indian politician".[4]

The regular session of the Congress was held at Nagpur on 26 December 1920 under the presidency of C. Vijiaraghabachariar. As many as 27 delegates from Orissa including Gopabandhu Das, Jagabandhu Singh and Mukunda Prasad Das attended the session.[5] The Nagpur Congress marked a new era in the history of the freedom movement in India. Gandhi's clarion call awakened the entire country with patriotic fervour the like of which the country had never before seen. In Orissa leadership passed from moderate leaders like M.S. Das for whom the Orissa question was supreme to Gandhians like Gopabandhu Das for whom the question of national independence was more important, atleast not the least.

Soon after the Nagpur Congress, the meeting of Utkal Union Conference (UUC) was held at Chakradharpur from 30 December 1920 to 1 January 1921. After this Chakradharpur session, it was the Congress not the UUC which dominated the political scene in Orissa. Those who subscribed to the Congress ideology and programme withdrew from the UUC and tried to work simultaneously for the cause of Indian nationalism and amalgamation of Oriya tracts through the Congress. The UUC which hereafter failed to hold its annual sessions regularly remained in the hands of the moderates who believed in the cooperation with the Government. The moderates' acceptance of the Government of India Act, 1919 was criticised by the Congressmen, especially by the young elements. Criticising Madhusudan's acceptance of ministry in the Government of Bihar and Orissa in January 1921, the Bharati Mandira (a reading club established by some of the students of Ravenshaw College like H.K. Mahtab, Jadumani Mangaraj and Bhagirathi Mahapatra in Cuttack to discuss the political, national, local and international matters)[6] circulated a leaflet titled "At last Mr. Das, a Government servant drawing Rs. 60,000- from Malaria of Balasore, famine of Puri and floods of Cuttack".[7] Such criticism of Madhusudan may be derogatory but it reflected the sense of frustration and desperation of the younger generation. Actually he entered into the legislature and accepted the ministry not out of avarice for money and power but because like Gokhale he believed in the attainment of Swaraj or self-government by entering into legislature.

Soon after, the Utkal Pradesh Congress Committee (UPCC) was formed in the last week of February 1921 according to new rules and the following office bearers took charge of the organisation: Pandit Gopabandhu Das, President, Dr. Ekram Rosul, Vice- President, Bhagirathi Mahapatra, the Secretary and Brajabandhu Das, the Joint Secretary. Besides, five members were also taken in the Executive Committee.[8] The District Congress Committees were gradually formed. Organisation of the party in different districts was entrusted to the following persons-H.K. Mahtab (Balasore), Bhagirathi Mahapatra (Cuttack Sadar), Jadumani Mangaraj (Kendrapara), Rajkrushna Bose (Jajpur), Jagabandhu Singh and Krupasindhu Mishra (Puri), Pandit Nilakantha Das (Sambalpur), Pandit Godavaris Misra (Singhbhum) and Niranjan Patnaik (Ganjam).

Gandhi had been highly impressed with the sincerity and devotion of Gopabandhu Das to national cause.[9] Gopabandhu and other Oriya leaders invited Gandhiji to Orissa to give a momentum to the Non-Cooperation Movement. Gandhi accepted the invitation and wrote to C.F.Andrews, "The poorest province will be the last to be visited".[10] The people of Orissa also had great respect for the Mahatma and received him as an incarnation of God and a "Worker of Miracles".[11] In every railway station large crowds gathered to have a glimpse of the Mahatma.

With his wife Kasturba and youngest son Devdas, Gandhi reached Cuttack in the morning of 23 March 1921.From the Cuttack railway station he was taken to the Swaraj Ashram in a procession of thousands in which there were seventy-two kirtan parties (Parties of devotional singers).[12] In the same day afternoon Gandhi addressed a small meeting of women in Binod Bihari where some women donated their ornaments to him.[13] In the evening Gandhi addressed a mammoth gathering in the Katjuri river bed to which 50,000 people attended.[14] In his speech he appealed to the people for Hindu-Muslim unity, to organise villages, enrol one lakh of Congress members, spread one lakh of charkhas and collect three lakhs of rupees for Tilak Swaraj Fund.[15] Gandhi also addressed separate meetings of Marwaris and Gujratis, Muslims, students and lawyers at Cuttack and appealed them to boycott foreign cloth and popularise spinning wheel.

From Cuttack Gandhi proceeded to Bhadrak on 25 March to fulfil the promise he had made to the large crowds in the Bhadrak Railway station. Addressing three meetings in Bhadrak he exhorted the people to boycott foreign cloth and institutions, establish national schools and arbitration courts, spread khadi, adjure alcohol and intoxicating drugs and such other things.[16]

From Bhadrak Gandhi went to Puri and on his way he visited the Satyavadi grove on 26 March where he was impressed with the educational system of the school and the simple living of its students. At the Puri railway station he was received by large enthusiastic crowds. On 27 March he addressed a large gathering in Saradhabali. In his speech Gandhi criticized the priests of the Jagannath Temple for disallowing entry to the depressed class people. The priests, he said, had become insincere and "foreign-minded" by draping the deities in the foreign cloths.[17] He suggested to the audience and to the Raja of Puri that the deities of the Jagannath temple should be draped in khadar.[18]

From Puri Gandhi went to Berhampur. After addressing there separate meetings of people and municipal councillors he proceeded to Bejwada to attend the meeting of AICC.

Gandhi's first visit to Orissa gave a tremendous impetus to the freedom movement in Orissa. As pointed out by H.K. Mahtab, Gandhi's stress on the attainment of Swaraj as the birth right of the people and denunciation of the British Government as the satanic government dispelled fear from the people's minds and roused a new spirit of self confidence.[19] And Gandhi left Orissa with an "ineffaceable" memory of her poverty. He admitted that natural calamities had made the peasants of Orissa poorer than those of Champaran of Bihar. About his tour the Government reported : "In this land (Orissa) of Hindus, Mr. Gandhi was considered as an avatar of the deity and worker of miracles."[20]

At the Belgaon Congress of 1924 he told the delegates from Orissa: " The picture of Orissa which is dancing before my eyes has convinced me that it will be Swaraj for them if we can provide food to the people of Orissa. So I would request the Congress workers of Orissa to forget their internal squabbles and work to provide food to the starving people of Orissa".[21] Later on, in December 1928 when Gopabandhu Choudhury met Gandhi at Wardha, he found that the latter's voice got chocked and his eyes became tearful while he was recalling the scenes of Orissa's poverty-stricken people.[22] Gandhi felt that Orissa's condition could be ameliorated by selfless and full-time workers with missionary zeal and spirit of dedication. Gandhi held that the remedy for Orissa's poverty lay in the promotion of the Khadi work in the villages. He exhorted the Oriya Congress workers to make Orissa "the Khadi store of India".[23] Accordingly Gopabandhu Das and other Congress leaders tried to make khadi an efficient vehicle for the economic relief of poverty and flood-stricken Orissa.[24]

The programme of the Non-cooperation movement had negative as well positive or constructive aspects. The negative aspect included.

(a)boycott of the impending elections of the legislative councils under the Government of India Act, 1919,

(b)boycott of the Government and Government aided schools and colleges,

(c)boycott of the law courts and surrendering of titles and distinctions conferred by the Government, (d)boycott of the foreign cloth,

(e) refusal to attend government darbars and other official or semi-official functions and

(f) refusal by the people to offer themselves to be employed in Mesopotamia in military sphere.

The positive aspect of the programme included-

(a)establishment of national schools and colleges

(b)use of private arbitration courts in place of Government courts,

(c) the adoption of 'Swadeshi' in a vast scale,

(d)the revival of hand spinning and hand weaving,

(e) promotion of Hindu-Muslim unity and

(f) the removal of untouchability.

As a response to the call about two-third of the students of Sambalpur Zilla School, deserted it on 3 January 1921 under the student leaders, Jagannath Misra, Laxmi Narayan Misra and Nrusingh Guru.[25] They were the first batch of students in Orissa who withdrew themselves from their educational institution. It is a matter of pride on the part of Orissa that Sambalpur became an example before Calcutta.[26] At Cuttack, students like H.K. Mahtab, Nabakrushna Choudhury, Nityananda Kanungo, Jadumani Mangaraj and many others left their studies.[27] At Balasore, Nilambar Das, Subodh Chandra De and Biswanath Hota left their schools.[28]

The movement also had its impact on the Oriya students studying outside Orissa. Ganesh Prasad Padhi, Chakradhar Panda, Madan Mohan Patnaik, Dukhishyam Misra and Binod Bihari Parida left the Patna Engineering College.[29] Bhagirathi Mishra left the Calcutta Law College.[30] Nanda Kishore Mishra and Arjun Panigrahi of Parlakhemindi left Pachiappa College, Madras.[31]

The boycott of schools and colleges was accompanied by the establishment of national schools in Orissa. In response to this call, Gopabandhu Das converted his pet institution, the Satyavadi School into the first national school in Orissa under the charges of Pandit Krupasindhu Mishra.[32] Under the leadership of Godavaris Misra the Chakradharpur High School was converted to a national school. National schools were also established at Sambalpur, Jagatsinghpur, Bhadrak, Balasore, Soro,

Berhampur and Parlakhemindi. Teaching in these schools was different from those of Government schools. To inculcate and infuse the spirit of freedom and patriotism, events of the French Revolution, Italian and German unifications and history of the Irish agitation were taught.

To supervise these schools and conduct examinations for them, a type of national university, called, Utkal Swarajya Shiksha Parishad (Orissa Council of National Education) was established. Gopabandhu Das and Nanda Kishore Das were elected as the President and the Secretary of the Institution respectively.[33]

To train the Congress workers and volunteers and guide their work centres were opened at Cuttack, Jagatsingpur, Puri, Sakshigopal, Balasore, Bhadrak and Soro. The Swaraj Ashram of Cuttack, the major centre, the headquarter of UPCC was concerned with the distribution of spinning wheels, promotion of spinning and training the workers for the propagation of the Congress programme. The Sakshigopal Ashram to which the Satyavadi School was attached was under the supervision of Gopabandhu Das. Gopabandhu Choudhury and Bhagirathi Mahapatra established 'Alakashram' which was the centre of their activities. Attached to the Alakashram was a national school where the students, besides pedagogic education, were imparted training in various handicrafts, spinning, weaving and gardening. The Swaraj Mandir of Balasore which was under the guidance of H.K. Mahtab trained workers in the propagation of Non-Cooperation programme, promotion of Khadar and establishment of Panchayats and national school.

So far as the programme of renunciation of titles and resignation from all posts held under the Government was concerned, in Orissa Gopabandhu Choudhury, then a Deputy Collector at Bargarh tendered his resignation from the Government service,[34] followed by Purna Chandra Das and Raghunath Mishra resigning from teachership and Kshetra Mohan Mohanty and Hari Charan Mohanty from clerical posts.[35] Both Pandit Nilakantha Das, Professor of Oriya and Comparative Philology, Calcutta University and Pandit Lingaraj Mishra, Professor of Sanskrit in Government college at Muzzafarpur resigned and joined the movement.[36] At Balasore and Bhadrak respectively, Surendranath Das and Md. Hanif resigned from their posts of Police Sub-Inspector and Excise Sub- Inspector and joined the Congress.[37] In Ganjam too, Sribasta Panda resigned from the post of sub-Registrar. He joined the Non-Cooperation movement along with Biswanath Das, Niranjan Patnaik, Mahendra Kumar Patnaik, Banchhanidhi Patnaik and Jaimangal Rath.[38]

In response to the call of the Congress lawyers like Bhagirathi Mahapatra at Cuttack, Jagabandhu Singh at Puri and Mahendra Nath Verma and Achyutananda Purohita at Sambalpur renounced their lucrative income in order to take part in the movement. The boycott of law courts was accompanied by the establishment of private arbitration courts for the settlement of disputes. Gour Mohan Das and Banchhanidhi Mohanty respectively were instrumental to make this programme effective at Srijang near Balasore and Bhadrak. The same courts were established at Tirtol in the Cuttack district and in other villages of the Puri district which worked with great success.[39]

The boycott of foreign goods was an important item of the Non-Cooperation programme. Gandhi stood for Swadeshi pure and simple. In his opinion, 'Swadeshi' meant the increase in the production and use of 'Khadi'. The production of 'Khadi' led to the revival of hand spinning and hand weaving for which Orissa was famous. Having obtained training, the Congress workers toured the rural areas to popularize the 'Charkha' and 'Khadi'. Hundreds of 'Charkhas' now began to boom in the Orissan houses.[40] Khadi became the symbol of unity among all Congressmen.

Gandhi encouraged the production and use of Khadi in his speeches and talks. His visit to Orissa helped popularize the use of Khadi. The All India Congress Committee which met at Bejwada on 31 March 1921 decided, at the suggestion of Gandhi to collect one crore of rupees towards the Tilak Swaraj Fund, enlist one crore of Congress workers and introduce twenty lakhs of Charkhas.[41] The quota for Orissa was to enlist 20,000 workers and raise 30,000 rupees for the Tilak Swaraj Fund. The Congress workers of Orissa worked with unflagging zeal to reach the quota. As reported in the Samaj, by 30 June 1921, the UPCC had enrolled 39,000 Congress men raised Rs. 21,000/- for the Tilak Swaraj Fund and distributed 16,000 spinning wheels in Orissa.[42] H.K. Mahtab pointed out that by 30 June 1921 only 20,000 Congressmen had been enrolled and 17,000 rupees had been raised for the purpose.[43] The reasons why the UPCC fell short of contributing its quota according to the Bejwada programme were the want of sufficient number of suitable and experienced workers and absence of Congress organisation in the Orissa princely states.[44]

On 31 July 1921, Gandhi made a great bonfire in Bombay by burning a huge stock of foreign cloth. This was followed by intense boycott of foreign cloth in Orissa in August and September. Bonfires were made at Puri on 6 August 1921. At Cuttack, bonfires and meetings were organized on 11 and 14 August respectively.[45] On 2 October 1921, the 53rd birthday of Gandhi, foreign cloths were burnt in many places.[46] On 8 september 1921, in an appeal to the people of Orissa, on the eve of Durga Puja and Kumar Purnima festivals (when people used to wear new cloths), through the Samaj, Gopabandhu requested them to wear cloths woven out of self-spun yarn instead of wearing foreign cloths. Early in September 1921, at the advice Gopabandhu, the Oriya labourers of Calcutta refused to carry the foreign cloths. In the Bara Bazar area of Calcutta, where the cloth merchants depended on the Oriya labourers, the merchants were forced by the latter not to deal with the foreign cloths upto 31 December 1921.[47] At Jaleswar (Balasore), a Marwari cloth merchant was socially boycotted for he had sold foreign cloths. He was forced by the local Congress workers to pay fine and give an undertaking promising not to sell any foreign cloth.[48]

To the effect of the implementation of the 'Khadar' programme, the district, Sambalpur stood much ahead of others under the UPCC jurisdiction. By the end of June 1921, 7000 spinning wheels were running in the Sambalpur district.[49] The success behind the Khadi movement in the district was due to the fact that the traditional spinning and weaving industry had maintained itself in spite of competition from the mill cloths and the women of Sambalpur generally wore Sambalpuri Saree. When Gandhi visited Sambalpur towards the end of 1928 before attending the Calcutta session of the Congress, he was pleased to observe a large gathering of Sambalpuri women in the indigenous handloom textiles, not observing purdah.[50] Khadi and Charkha Centres were opened in Fraser Club (Sambalpur), Bargarh, Remanda, Barpali, Jharsuguda and Talpati. Krutartha Acharya played a leading role in the development of weaving industry in Sambalpur. He applied the technique of lasting dying. He opened a cooperative store through which the weavers could sell their cloths. It is noteworthy to mention that 600 depressed class weavers of Ganda caste of Sambalpur enrolled themselves as the members of the Congress.[51]

Picketing was carried on before foreign liquor and cloth shops in towns like Balasore, Bhadrak, Cuttack, Puri, Berhampur and Sambalpur.

On 17 November 1921, the day of Prince of Wales' arrival in Bombay the people of Orissa participated in nation-wide hartal. There was complete suspension of business in Cuttack town on this occasion.[52]

The UPCC elected 127 delegates (most of whom were villagers) to attend the Ahmedabad session of the Congress in December 1921.[53] Lenders like Bhagirathi Mahapatra, Gopabandhu Choudhury, Niranjan Patnaik and Nabakrushna Choudhury had an interview with Gandhi at Ahmedabad on 30 December, 1921. Gandhi told them : " Utkal haunts me. Give the message of Charkha to every home. Make Utkal the store-house of Khadar for the rest of India. Feed the hungry men and women. This is the best political training you can give to your people."[54] This message provided a great fillip to the non-cooperators of Orissa who had been faithfully and sincerely working for the implementation of Gandhi's programme.

The Ahmedabad session of the Congress decided to launch the Civil Disobedience movement against the British Government under the leadership of Mahatma Gandhi. But after the violent attack by a mob on the police in the Chauri Chaura village of the Gorakhpur district of UP, which took place on 5 February 1922, at Gandhi's instance the Congress suspended the movement on 24 February 1922. As a result the agitational activities of the Non-Cooperation Movement virtually ended in Orissa as in the rest of the country. But the official oppression continued.

The movement did not confine itself to the urban areas only. The students who left schools and colleges in response to the call of Gandhi and the trained non-cooperators went to their respective village and propagated the non-cooperation programme. Leaders regularly organized public meetings in towns and rural areas. The Utkal Dipika and the Samaj became the mouthpiece to broadcast the message of Gandhi, Gopabandhu, the apostle of Non-cooperation in Orissa unfurled everywhere the meaning and significance of Swadeshi and Swaraj. His words fruited like magic spell reaching every nook and corner of Orissa. Apart from Puri, Cuttack, Balasore and Ganjam he toured the Singhbhum district with Godavaris Misra[55] and Sambalpur district with Nilakantha Das, Chandrasekhar Behera, Dharanidhar Misra and Ganesh Prasad Padhi.[56] He also went to Jeypore state in the Madras Presidency.

Cuttack was the cynosure of all political activities when young men from the districts flocked together and they were sent out as bands of trained volunteers to spread the message of non-cooperation in the far-flung villages. The Swaraj Ashrams in the district headquarters maintained regular communications with the villages.

The Musalmans of Orissa this time organized the Orissa Khilafat Committee at Cuttack under the chairmanship of Dr. Ekram Rosul, who was also the Vice-President of UPCC.[57] A strong unity existed among the Hindus and Muslims in Orissa. The Khilafat Committee meeting was largely attended by Hindus too.

When the Non-Cooperation Movement was gathering momentum, Gandhi's visit intensified the freedom movement in Orissa. Membership of the Congress increased rapidly when the depressed classes joined it. There was unprecedented enthusiasm in the province. Without any fear the Oriyas joined it. Mass awakening of the people made the movement a great success.

While this was the trend in other parts of Orissa, Sambalpur made history by openly challenging the Government in a perfect non-violent manner. Chandra Sekhar Behera led the Non-Cooperation movement in Sambalpur with much enthusiasm and Fakir Misra, a teacher of Sambalpur Zilla School spread the message of Swadeshi among the students.[58] Long processions were carried out by Nilakantha Das, Chandra Sekhar Behera, Laxmi Narayan Mishra, Bhagirathi Mishra and others followed by public meetings at Sambalpur, Bargarh, Jharsuguda and in important villages like Talpatia and Rampella.[59] Sambalpur also attracted the attention of Deshabandhu C.R. Das who sent observers to study how the movement spread so rapidly there.

While the Congress tried to mobilise the people for the Non-Cooperation Movement, the government tried to keep the people aloof from the movement by a policy of repression. Orders under section 144 and 108 I.P.C. were served on many leaders prohibiting them to make speeches in public meetings and enter some areas. The Government was determined to scotch the movement. The Government of Bihar and Orissa directed the district Magistrates and Sub-Divisional Officers to take all possible steps to suppress the movement and move about in the Mofussils to propagate against the movement.[60] On 8 March 1921 District Magistrate of Puri called a meeting of the zamindars, mahants and money-lenders of the Puri town and its surrounding areas to tell them what they should do to suppress the Non-Cooperation Movement.[61] On 8 May 1921 the Government officials organized a meeting at Rampella, where Shankar Prasad Mishra, a loyalist asked the people not to support the Congressmen.[62]

The Municipal Commissioners and members of district boards and the employees of the municipalities were directed by the Bihar and Orissa Government not to attend any meeting of the non-cooperators. The Government issued a circular that anybody found coercing people for boycotting foreign cloths would be tried on charge of criminal offence. In some Mofussil areas police officials told the people that those who were working on spinning wheels would pay taxes and fines. As a consequence many people began hiding spinning wheels which resulted in a reduction in the volume of production of indigenous cloths. Restrictions were imposed on meetings and processions. The students of High Schools in Puri and Khurda towns had to take permission from the police authorities even to go in processions for the immersion of the image of goddess Saraswati.[63]

The Government warned most of the leaders to refrain from speaking, waiting or circulating pamphlets against government or picket the cloth and liquor shops. But the leaders stood adamant. Rajkrushna Bose was arrested under section 108 IPC on 21 June 1921 and put to one year's imprisonment. Thus he became the first political prisoner in Orissa followed by Babaji Ramdas imprisoned for one year too. Gopabandhu Das was arrested and tried as an undertrial prisoner for publishing a news item, titled "Serious indeed if true" in his weekly Samaj, dated 13 August 1921. Finally he was honourably acquitted by the Magistrate Suresh Chandra Bose (elder brother of Subhas Chandra Bose) on 21 November 1921 and released. A huge and enthusiastic crowd waiting the judgement, welcomed Gopabandhu at Khurda, Puri and Sakshigopal on 21 and 22 November.[64] His acquittal spread like wild fire in the nook and corner of Orissa creating further zest among the non-cooperators.

To terrorize the people the police indulged in heinous work. As many as 20,000 houses were set on fire by the agents of the police. In the Cuttack town, 8,000 houses were burnt.[65] But the police accused the Congressmen of the arson. On one occasion, out of anger some people of the Cuttack town assaulted a police constable and severely wounded him. Gopabandhu Das took pity on him and according to his instruction the constable was brought to the Swaraj Ashram where he was given medical aid, food to eat and a Khadar cloth to wear. But constable brought a reverse allegation on Gopabandhu and some of his associates that they had assaulted him and compelled him to wear the Khadar. On the basis of this charge Gopabandhu Das, Bhagirathi Mahapatra, Atal Bihari Acharya and Gopabandhu Choudhury were prosecuted.[66] Many active non-cooperators - Govinda Chandra Mishra, Uma Charan Mohanty, Jadumani Mangaraj, Banchhanidhi Mohapatra and Satyavadi Nanda were arrested on various charges and imprisoned and others were prohibited from making speeches in public meetings.[67]

The official policy of repression was strongly criticized in the Bihar and Orissa Legislative Council by the non-official members who did not subscribe to the Congress principle of non-cooperation. Rai Bahadur, Harendra Narayan Ray Mahasay, a member from Orissa advised the Government "to do things with tact and discretion and not to impose restrictions on the elementary rights of citizenship".[68] Another member from Orissa, Rebati Kanta Ghose spoke out : "It was certainly the duty of the government to preserve law and order in the country but under the mask of this duty, the government should not suppress non-cooperators by repressive measures and lay violent hands on the liberty and freedom of the preachers of non-cooperation". He asked the government to evolve a new system of administration to please the mass of the people. If the government were afraid that the people no longer trusted them, it should adopt means by which trust and mutual confidence might be restored.That would not be obtained by a policy of repression and highhandedness.[69] Chaudhury Bhagabat Prasad Samantaray Mahapatra pleaded for the release of Non-cooperators like Gopabandhu Das and H.K. Mahtab from jail.[70]

Kanika Agitation

The Non-Cooperation Movement also encouraged rural peasants agitations. Peasants' resistance movement simultaneously started at Sitamarhi, Champaran, and Muzzafarpur in Bihar against the Zamindars.[71] At about the same time there occurred serious disturbances in Kanika in which some of the permanently settled estate situated both in the districts of Cuttack and Balasore.

The Raja of Kanika, Rajendra Narayan Bhanj Deo, was a man of public spirit and had distinguished himself as a leader of the Utkal Union Conference and as a member of both provincial and Central Legislative Councils. In his big estate, people suffered from under exactions of several taxes by his subordinate officials. The grievances of the disgruntled tenants were brought to the notice of the Congress leaders in Orissa during the early months of the non-cooperation movement. Dr. Atal Behari Acharya, Secretary of the District Congress Committee of Cuttack, went to Kanika to enquire into the matter. He met the Raja to inform about the complaints of the people and the Congress workers. The Raja assured him that he would look into the matter and asked the Congress leader to bring to his notice specific instances of oppressive measures of his subordinates. The Raja too agreed to introduce Charkha in the flood affected areas of his estate and panchayat system in the territories under his control.[72]

Despite such assurances, the situation deteriorated from the beginning of 1922. The Raja proposed to increase the land revenue in his estate which the people strongly resisted. Many peasants in certain areas instead of paying revenue to the Raja, deposited directly in the government treasury at Kendrapara. They demanded that the settlement, instead of being done by the Raja, should be done by the Government. But no step was taken to redress their problems. The situation albeit worsened and finally the Raja sought the help of the police contingent from Cuttack. The Raja too reported to the authorities that his tenants had been inspired by the Congressmen. The Government also believed that the Rajas tenants had been stirred up by his semi-lunatic brother, the owner of the adjoining Aul estate, who had called into his assistance the local non-cooperators, and under the guise of agrarian agitation organised a hostile conspiracy of the Kanika tenants known locally as a "meli".[73] Subsequently a few people died and several others were wounded by the police action in April 1922. With the order of firing of Srikrushna Mohapatra, the Superintendent of Police, two persons, Basu Sethi and Bisuni Madhual died which was followed by untold oppression of police such as looting of properties, setting fire to houses and molestation of women. Many preferred escape to other places to police torture.[74]

The Samaj and Utkal Dipika widely publicized the stories of oppression in Kanika. Gopabandhu Das wrote critical editorials in the Samaj, for which defamation cases were filed against him. He and Bhagirathi Mahapatra were arrested for violating the prohibitory orders to enter the Kanika estate. They were sent to Hazaribag jail, where Gopabandhu wrote 'Bandira Atmakatha' in which he depicted the repressive policy in Kanika. Banchhanidhi Mohanty composed a booklet, 'Dukhini Kanika' which was banned. Chakradhar Behera wrote 'Bandira Bilapa' citing the entire story of Kanika agitation "Efforts were made to secure the visit of Madan Mohan Malaviya to Kanika estate"[75] by Harekrushna Mahtab and Niranjan Patnaik, but they were imprisoned.

On 25 August 1922, Chaudhuri Bhagabat Prasad Mahapatra moved a resolution in the Bihar and Orissa Legislative Council for the appointment of a Committee of non-official majority to enquire into the Kanika troubles.[76] He narrated how an agrarian dispute of vast magnitude had been converted to a problem of law and order. Some members from Orissa supported the move. On behalf of the government, H. McPherson, called it as 'the most extraordinary case', but justified the action of the Raja and put the entire blame on the non-cooperators. The resolution was lost without any division.[77]

The real issue was definitely the high revenue exerted by the local ruler not the freedom of the country yet the inspiration came from the Non-Cooperation movement.

The Non-Cooperation movement offered the common people an unprecedented experience in fearlessness and defiance of the authorities. The policemen who had earlier auctioned the fear psychology of the villagers found themselves faced with a new spirit of defiance; the people had learnt not only how to escape the fear of the police, but also to insult and offend the latter.[78] In Orissa, Gandhi's ideas and messages spread to villages. Gopabandhu Das steered the movement into a mass movement. The movement made the inert masses of Orissa bold enough to challenge the Government, the exacting zamindars as well as the feudatory Chiefs. Gandhi's visit to Orissa accelerated the motion of the Congress activities and instilled a new freshet into the dynamic minds of the people. Constructive programmes in full swing continued in the various towns and rural areas of the state under the direction and inspiration of Gandhiji.

The Intermezzo (1922-29)

The withdrawal of the Non-Cooperation movement in February 1922 was followed by the arrest of Gandhiji in March and his conviction and imprisonment for six years for the crime of spreading disaffection against the Government. The result was the spread of disintegration, disorganization and demoralization in the nationalist ranks. There arose the danger of the movement lapsing into passivity. Many began to question the wisdom of the total Gandhian strategy. Others started looking for ways out of the impasse.

A new line of resistant political activity to colonial rule was now advocated by C.R. Das and Motilal Nehru. They suggested that the nationalists should end the boycott of the legislative councils, enter them, expose them as 'Sham parliaments' and as 'a mask which the bureaucracy has put on', and obstruct 'every work of the Council'.[79] This, they argued, would not be giving up non-cooperation but continuing it in a more effective form by extending it to the Councils themselves. They were called pro-changers.

Another section of the Congress, called no-changers, headed by Vallabhbhai Patel, Rajendra Prasad and C. Rajagopalachari, opposed the new proposal which was consequently defeated by 1748 to 890 votes taken in Gaya session of the Congress in December 1922. Das and Motilal resigned from their respective offices in the Congress and on 1 January 1923 announced the formation of the Congress-Khilafat Swaraj Party, better known as the Swaraj Party.

Between 1922-29, the leaders of Orissa concentrated their attention on two main issues : continuation of the Gandhian constructive programmes and the agitation for the union of the outlying Oriya-speaking tracts into a separate province. So far as the second issue is concerned, the scholar has already dealt the issue in the preceding chapter. Activities on the first issue will be discussed here.

The Gaya session of the Congress was attended by more than 200 delegates and 22 volunteers from Orissa. Almost all of them voted against the pro-changers' proposal for entry into the legislature.[80] In Orissa, at that time many Congressmen were criticizing C.R. Das and Motilal Nehru for their deviation from the Gandhian time.[81]

The Swarajists did not achieve any great success in Orissa. Some Congressmen of Orissa, such as Nanda Kishore Das, Pandit Nilakantha Das and Radharanjan Das subscribed to the pro-changers' view. In the elections of 1923, Pandit Nilakantha Das and Rudraranjan Das (representing North Balasore Constituency) were elected to the Central Legislative Assembly and Bihar and Orissa Legislative Council respectively on the tickets of pro-changers party (Swaraj Party). Two Oriya members of the Bihar and Orissa Legislative Council, Jagabandhu Singh and Godavaris Misra also supported the programme of the Swaraj Party in the legislature.

On the other hand, those Congressmen of Orissa who did not enter the legislatures did not firmly adhere to the no-changers' ideology. Though Pandit Gopabandhu Das himself did not want to enter the legislatures by others. Though Harekrushna Mahtab himself did not seek election to the legislature, he backed Radharanjan Das who was elected from the North Balasore Constituency to the Bihar and Orissa Legislature Council. The teachers of the Satyavadi National School- Krupasindhu Mishra, Lingaraj Mishra and Nanda Kishore Das campaigned whole heartedly and got him elected to the Central Legislative Assembly.

Since there did not exist any controversy between pro-changers and no-changers on the question of election to the local bodies, a number of Congressmen got themselves elected to the District Boards and Municipalities under the Bihar and Orissa Local Self-Government Act, 1923. Three Congressmen-Gopabandhu Choudhury, Banamali Das and Harekrushna Mahtab were elected as the Chairmen of Cuttack, Puri and Balasore District Boards respectively. Harekrushna Mahtab as the Chairman of the Balasore District Board convened a conference of the teachers and issued a circular directing all teachers in primary schools to wear Khadar.[82] He also took initiative to make spinning compulsory in the schools. In other places of Orissa, attempts were made to hoist the Swaraj flag on the municipal buildings. The Congressmen of Sambalpur, Puri and other places carried on similar attempts to remove untouchability and break the apathy of the people regarding the use of khadar.[83]

After the suspension of the Non-Cooperation movement, some devoted Congressmen of Orissa-Niranjan Patnaik, Gopabandhu Choudhury, Jayamangala Rath and Krupasindhu Hota diverted all their attention towards the implementation of Gandhian constructive programme. Niranjan Patnaik remained in charge of the Orissa branch of the All India Charkha, Gopabandhu Choudhury took the responsibility of Village Improvement Trust and Harekrushna Mahtab that of the propaganda work throughout Orissa. Under the scheme of Village Improvement Trust, many salaried young men were appointed to popularise the Gandhian constructive programme. Mahtab started an Oriya weekly, the Prajatantra on 2 October 1923 in the birthday of Mahatma Gandhi.

Pandit Gopabandhu Das, while going from Puri to Cuttack after arrest, on 31 May 1922, by way of giving message for the people of Orissa, told Niranjan Patnaik: "Khadar is my only message. Orissa has been chronically affected by famines. Production of khadar is the best way to alleviate the effects of famine".[84] After his release from jail in June 1924, Gopabandhu dedicated himself to two constructive works-promotion of khadar and famine relief.

At Basta the second session of the Balasore District Congress Conference was held on 22 and 23 April 1923 under the presidentship of Rajkrushna Bose, the Secretary of UPCC which was attended by nearly 8,000 people and passed resolutions for boycott of the schools and courts, establishment of Panchayats, promotion of national education and promotion of spinning and cotton cultivation.[85]

From the beginning of the Non-cooperation, Khadar programme did not run fair. Thousands of spinning wheels had been distributed among the people of Puri district without giving them proper orientation in Khadar programme. By the time Gopabandhu was released from jail, he found that spinning wheels had become rare phenomena and that khadar dressed Congress workers had changed over to mill-made cloths.[86]

An All-India Khadi Board was constituted with full powers to organize and carry on Khadar work throughout India in the annual session of the Congress at Cocanada in 1923. This time Utkal Provincial Khadi Board came into being with Niranjan Patnaik as the President. Berhampur became the headquarters of Khadi Board.

Gandhi was released from jail in early 1924. Soon after he concentrated on constructive programme, particularly Khadar and prescribed spinning franchise for every regular Congressman. The All-India Congress Committee in its meeting at Ahmedabad in June 1924 decided that every member of elective Congress bodies was to send to All-India Khadi Board two thousand yards of self-spun yarn every month. On 11 July 1924, Niranjan Patnaik appealed to the Congressmen of Orissa to implement the above decision of AICC.[87]

Gopabandhu Das, on 19 July 1924 appealed to the people of Orissa through 'Samaj' not only to implement Khadar Programme but also to produce cotton in their fields because he considered it economically unprofitable to spin yarns out of the imported Nagpur cotton. He made certain arrangements for the implementation of Khadar programme like in every district there should be khadar centre. Besides the Khadar centres, in some appropriate places, able and honest workers should be employed for reorganising village life through promotion of spinning, enrolment of Congressmen, raising handfuls of rice for Tilak Swarajya Fund, establishing Primary schools on the model of national education and inculcating the habit of newspaper reading among the villagers.[88]

Despite the leaders' effort, a lot of sincerity and irregularity was noticed. In the Utkal Dipika, dated 16 August 1924, it was pointed out that except a few workers and professional spinners and weavers nobody in Orissa was associated with the Khadar programme. By the mid-August of 1924, only 19 Congressmen and 5 non-Congressmen could send to the All-India Khadi Board two thousands yards of self-spun yarns out of a total number of 412 Congressmen.[89] Later it was found that 5 out of 12 members of AICC, 4 out of 9 members of Provincial Congress Working Committee, 73 out of 100 members of Provincial Congress Committee and 178 out of 235 members of District Congress Committee failed to send the yarns to the Khadi Board.[90] This decline was natural for the khadi was costlier than the machine made cloth. By June 1925, the All-India Khadi Board took up the direct supervision of the Provincial Khadi Board which was then designated as Khadi Bibhag (Khadi Department), Utkal.

On 25 August 1925, Gopabandhu Das went to Akrai to study the appropriate methods of execution of Khadar programme.[91] The Khadar workers tried to popularize Khadar among the people through lecture programmes along with visual demonstration by magic lanterns and spinning competitions. By the end of 1926, the Khadi work in Orissa became systematic and orderly. Being invited by Niranjan Patnaik, Manager, Orissa Spinners' Association, Shankarlal Banker and Laxmidas Purusottam visited Orissa in February 1927 to examine the Khadi work in the province. They were highly satisfied with the Orissa Charkha organisation, but they found that khadi produced in Orissa was dearer,[92] because there was no cotton cultivation here. Jamnalal Bajaj came to Orissa to study the Khadi work of Orissa. From 7 to 18 April 1927, he visited the Khadi centres of Balasore, Bhadrak, Guamal, Jajpur, Chandol, Kendrapara, Cuttack, Berhampur, Aska, Kodala, Jatni and Puri and discussed the question of improving the Khadi production in Orissa with Gopabandhu Das and Atal Bihari Acharya.[93]

But still there was much lacuna in the implementation of Khadar programme. The sale of Khadi remained confined to four centres in four towns- Balasore, Cuttack, Puri and Berhampur. The sale of Khadi, on the whole was lagging behind the production of Khadi. Consequently there was want of capital for increasing the production of Khadar. In 1927, when Gandhi visited Orissa for the third time, there were four Khadar producing agencies in Orissa- (1) The All-India Khadi Board, (2) Daridra Narayan Seba Sadan, started by Gopabandhu Das in 1925 at Kadua, Puri district to give relief to the famine-affected people through spinning, (3) Cuttack Khadi Sangh, a Cooperative Union organised by

Gopabandhu Choudhury, (4) Gobinda Mishra's Champapur Centre. These Khadi producing agencies lacked coordination and cooperation among themselves which led to rivalry and unhealthy competition.[94]

Gandhi's tour to Orissa produced widespread influence on Orissa. Many sincere workers enthusiastically responded to his advice and worked in the villages to popularise Charkha. In course of time a large number of Khadi and several Ashrams sprang up on the province.

Civil Disobedience Movement in Orissa

The announcement of the appointment of the Simon Commission on 8 November 1927, created a great excitement in the political circles of India. On 3 February 1928, the Commission arrived in Bombay. When the Commission was touring the country, the political parties of India set up a Committee under Motilal Nehru to draft a constitution for India. The Nehru Committee's report was adopted by the Calcutta Congress in 1928 which demanded, unless Dominion status was promised by the British within a year the Congress would declare itself for Complete Independence. Young Congressmen under the leadership of Jawaharlal Nehru and Subhas Chandra Bose grew restive and would have nothing less than Complete Independence. Therefore, the Lahore Congress, 1929 under the Presidency of J.L. Nehru announced that the goal of India's struggle for freedom would be 'Purna Swarajya' or Complete Independence. It was decided too to celebrate 26 January as the Independence Day. Thus started a new chapter in India's fight for freedom.

In different parts of Orissa the pledge of Independence was taken on 26 January. The Utkal Pradesh Congress Committee received reports of Independence Day celebration from 54 places.[95] Mass meetings were organised in many places on the occasion in a large gathering at Cuttack, Gopabandhu Choudhury, the Secretary of the Congress Party in Orissa, read the Declaration of Independence and after silently listening the people gave their assent to it by raising hands. At Bhubaneswar the national flag was hoisted at the top of the Temple of Lingaraj. Police took disciplinary action against some leading Congressmen of Puri like Acharya Harihar Das, Lingaraj Mishra, Krupasindhu Hota, Bholanath Sahu and others.[96]

In the meantime four Oriya members of the Legislative Council of Bihar and Orissa, Godavaris Misra, Lingaraj Mishra, Nanda Kishore Das and Narayan Birbar Samant resigned from their seats. Biswanath Das resigned his seat from the Madras Council. Nilakantha Das also gave up his seat in the Central Legislature.[97]

Towards the end of the February 1930 Gandhiji decided to launch Civil Disobedience Movement by breaking the Law at Dandi. "Salt is necessary for life", said Gandhi, "as air or water, given by nature is essentially necessary".[98] He considered the salt tax to be the most iniquitous of all from poor man's stand point. Gandhi's decision to break the salt law on the Gujarat sea-coast was received with much enthusiasm by the Congress leaders in Orissa. "The UPCC resolved on 28 February 1930 to make effective arrangements to start organised Civil Disobedience in some particular area of the AICC".[99] Gopabandhu Choudhury was authorised to make all preliminary arrangements.

The UPCC at its meeting on 16 March 1930 at Balasore decided to launch the movement in Orissa by breaking the salt law and Gopabandhu Choudhury was given the charge to organise it. The District Congress Committees were directed to recruit volunteers to actively participate in the movement and to carry on other common programmes of the Congress at full speed. Inchudi on the sea-coast, 12 miles from Balasore was selected to be the place where the salt-campaign was to begin.

H.K. Mahtab and Sardar Surendra Nath Das, had prepared the ground at Inchudi for the beginning of the struggle in Orissa. Infact, they had so thoroughly drilled nationalistic ideals into the minds of the villagers and had roused their patriotic sentiments that they showed exemplary tenacity and courage throughout the movement in helping the Congress workers and volunteers and in boycotting the Government officials and police forces. They also participated in large numbers in the actual breaking of the salt law and in preparing the contraband salt. It was claimed on the basis of the Government report that the Salt Satyagraha at Inchudi occupied the second place in India, the first being Gujarat where Gandhi himself led the movement.[100]

On 12 March 1930, Gandhi with his 78 associates of the Sabarmati Ashram started his historic Dandi March. Motibas Das, a Khadi student of Orissa was one among them.[101] Gandhi's march infected the whole nation and there were marches every where.[102] The first batch of 21 volunteers led by Gopabandhu Choudhury and Acharya Harihar Das proceeded from Swaraj Ashram at Cuttack to Inchudi with all solemnity in the early morning on 6 April 1930, the day on which Gandhiji broke the salt law at Dandi. Their aim was to start the movement on 13 April and accordingly they planned their journey of about 120 miles in seven days. The struggle was on. On 8 April Gopabandhu Choudhury was arrested at Chandol on the charge of violating the prohibitory order and was imprisoned for seven days. In his absence the party was led by Acharya Harihar and they reached Inchudi on 12 April.

The second batch of Satyagrahis, known as 'Lauhastambha Vahini' led by Madan Mohan Patnaik set out for Balasore on 9 April from Cuttack, followed by the 'Patitapaban Vahini' of Puri led by Satyavadi Nanda, the 'Ganjam Vahini', the 'Sambalpur Vahini' and the 'Orissa Gujarati Vahini'.[103] The local people also joined the Congress volunteers and atleast in six centres near Inchudi the preparation of contraband salt continued vigorously. Sardar Surendra Nath Das and Jiyaramji Kalyanji Kothari were arrested on 12 April, a day before the beginning of the actual struggle for their experiments to manufacture salt from sea-water on the Balasore Coast. However, soon the movement gathered spectacular momentum, and the people from far and near blocked to the seashore of Balasore which to them was like a place of pilgrimage. Even a batch of Satyagrahi from Gujarat reached Balasore towards the end of April.[104] The volunteers were prepared to court arrest without any hesitation and every day a few of them were taken into custody. The police authorities tried to hamper the preparation of salt by all possible means but they could not succeed.

Gopabandhu Choudhury was released on 19 April and soon he proceeded to Balasore the same evening. The Congress Working Committee sat at Balasore and decided to permit the villagers in general to start mass civil disobedience at different places on the Balasore sea-coast.[105] Chaudhury H.K. Mahtab and Dr. Krushna Prasad Mohanty were arrested near the satyagrah camp. With a previous notice to the District Magistrate a new satyagraha centre was opened at Sartha on 20 April,[106] 10 miles northward from Inchudi. Karunakar Panigrahi, Nilambar Das and Mathuri Behera took leadership of the villagers and volunteers. While manufacturing salt, they were arrested with three other villagers.

By the end of April 1930 contraband salt was manufactured in 21 centres along the coastline of the Bay of Bengal in the Balasore district. The following were the centres-Inchudi, Rasalpur, Srijang, Bardhanpur, Sartha, Bhimpur, Tundra, Kuanrpur, Ratai, Parikhi, Kherang, Gudu, Rajbala, Salgan, Kharasahapur (Athilabaj), Boita, Brahmapur, Mandari, Bachhada, Panchpada and Eram. In all these centres the villagers manufactured salt under the direction of one or two "pledged satyagrahis".[107]

The most conspicuous thing was the prominent role the Oriya women played in the salt campaign at Balasore and other places of Orissa. Smt. Rama Devi and Smt. Malati Devi had thrown themselves in the freedom movement of Orissa from the very beginning. In the company of several women of the neighbouring villages, such as Malati, Kokila, Jahnavi, Kiranbala and Kananbala, they went to the first Satyagraha centre, Inchudi. They addressed a meeting of one hundred women in the Balasore town in the evening of 18 April and tried to impress upon them the importance of women's participation in the movement. Ramadevi and Malatidevi called upon the women to implement such items of the Civil Disobedience movement as boycott of foreign cloth, promotion of Khadar and prohibition.[108] They went to the villages of Srijang and Tundra which were located in the vicinity of Inchudi and asked the village women to take part in the Salt Satyagraha. At their call, hundreds of uneducated women (nearly 1500) came forward and violated salt saw by collecting salt earth at Inchudi on 20 April. The police did not interfere with this women's satyagraha. On 22 April the local woman satyagrahis again manufactured contraband salt at Inchudi.[109] In the meantime 10 woman Satyagrahis with 25 male satyagrahis proceeded from Sambalpur to Balasore.[110]

On 21 April, about 700 person of different villages including 30 women of Kuanrpur went out on the second day of mass Civil Disobedience and manufactured mounds of salts openly at different centres, "60 Oriya ladies of the neighbouring villages manufactured salt at Tundra, Boita, Inchudi, Kuanrpur, Koligaon, Rasalpur and Kasha".[111] About 20 mounds of salt were brought to Balasore under regular satyagrahi escort for sale.

In a number of the centres illiterate women came out of their homes to violate the salt law. On 27 April, some women carried contraband salt from sea shore to the Balasore town without any police obstruction.[112] On 29 April, 17 women manufactured salt at Sartha and brought the same to their home.[113] But on another occasion, while the women were manufacturing salt at Sartha, the police broke their earthen pots.[114] On 28 May 1930, at Iram, 500 women took parts in the manufacture of contraband salt.[115] On 8 June, 600 women again manufactured salt in the same centre.[116] Soon the contraband salt was sent to the towns of Balasore and Cuttack where the people readily purchased them.

The Salt Satyagraha was a great success in the district of Balasore. Inchudi was the second Dandi in the history of the freedom movement in India.

When Gandhi decided to break the salt law, there was serious talks in Cuttack regarding the Salt Satyagrah in Orissa. The movement received an impetus from the public meeting of women representing all classes on 22 April at Cuttack held under the Chairmanship of Mrs. Kumudini Dasgupta. Seventeen ladies of 'Purdanasin' (veil) Hindu families enrolled themselves as volunteers to start picketing the liquor shops.[117]

By the middle of May 1930, preparations were being made for the launching of Salt Satyagraha in the Cuttack district. On 8 May Narayan Birabar Samanta, an ex-M.L.C. and scion of the former ruling family of Kujang (which was at that time a zamindary estate of the Maharaja of Burdwan) announced at Cuttack that he would start the salt manufacture on the sea coast of Kujang. The Satyagrah started in the district under the guidance of Malati Devi, Rama Devi and Narayan Birabar Samanta assisted by Narayan Patra, Sharat Chandra Das, Natu Mohanty, Raghunath Satpathy and Maheswar Pradhan. Narayan Samanta was arrested.[118]

Protest meetings were held for the arrest of their leader. Malati Devi and Rama Devi toured the entire area with indomitable zeal creating unbelievable enthusiasm among the workers and the common men. After sometime he was set free. Youthful volunteers (called Vanara Sena or Monkey Brigade) also played an important role in carrying on the satyagraha at Kujang. On 17 May a meeting was held on the Katjuri river-bed to give send off to the first batch of Satyagrahis for the Kujang Satyagraha, where Malati Choudhury felicitated the Satyagrahis with flower and sandal paste. By the end of May not less than four batches of Satyagrahis had violated salt law in Kujang.[119] Inspite of the harassment and repression by the police the Kujang Satyagraha went on. By the first week of June 56 Satyagrahis were manufacturing salt in three places of Kujang.[120] On 6 June the former Rani of Kujang Bhagyabati Pata Mahadei violated the salt law at Kaliapat with 500 satyagrahis which roused great enthusiasm among the villagers, particularly the village women who came out of their houses with baskets to collect salt earth along with the Rani. On 7 June the Rani violated again the salt law with more than 3,000 men and women.[121]

The salt manufacture was carried on in eight centres of the district-Garh-Kujang, Chatua, Kaliapat, Paradip. Ersama, Kankardia, Dardia and Ratua.[122] The major credit for organizing the salt satyagraha in the Cuttack district would go to two women Satyagrahis - Malati Devi and Rama Devi. They not only mobilized the people for the movement but persuaded them to carry on the movement peacefully "inspite of the crudest forms of repression adopted by the authorities".[123]

By the end of April 1930 Pandit Nilakantha Das again resigned from the Central Legislative Assembly to organise the salt satyagraha in Puri district.[124] Regular salt campaign at Astarang, Latra, Singheswari, Khandasahi, Mandanki, Kuhudi and Olanger under the distinguished leadership of Pandit Nilakantha Das began on 22 May 1930. On the opening day, there were brutal lathi charges on the satyagrahis. Many of them including Nilakantha, Jagannath Rath, Krupasindhu Hota and Mohan Das were arrested, but the campaign resumed full swing. Kakatpur was the major centre in the district, Puri.

Ganjam was the second district to launch the campaign for the manufacture of contraband salt. Salt satyagrah in this district began under the leadership of Niranjan Patnaik and Biswanth Das. Sarala Devi and Niranjan Patnaik made intensive tours throughout the district and enrolled men and raised money for the Civil Disobedience. At the instance of Sarala Devi 'Udyog Mandira' was opened in Berhampur for imparting training to the satyagrahis.[125] On 7 May 1930 these satyagrahis led by Niranjan Patnaik broke salt law at Ganjam "before a gathering of 4 to 5 thousand including more than thousand women".[126] Biswanath Das, Sashi Bhusan Rath, Narasimha Sahu and Dibakar Patnaik took active part in the salt-campaign in Ganjam and Huma.

On 8 May, a meeting was addressed at Huma by Biswanath Das and Sarala Devi and both appealed to the people to wear self-spun khadar and join the Civil Disobedience movement.[127] In the district contraband salt was manufactured at six places-Huma, Ganjam, Lakshmipur, Pallibandh, Jayanti-garh and Baruva, but large scale manufacture was carried on at Ganjam and Huma. A contemplated plan of the Ganjam Congressmen for a raid on the salt depot at Huma could not materialise because of want of clearance from the President and Secretary of the UPCC[128] and preventive measures by the police. The salt satyagraha in Ganjam went on upto 20 June.

Three favourite items of Gandhi at this time were Khadar, abstinence from drink and removal of untouchability. A programme for intensive boycott and picketing campaign was prepared by the U.P.C.C. It was sent to all District Committees urging them to organise a widespread, vigorous and aggressive propaganda covering urban and rural areas against the dealers of foreign cloth and liquors.[129] In the Cuttack town the picketing of foreign cloth shops began on 20 June 1930.[130] Earlier in May, a meeting of the Cuttack lawyers under the Chairmanship of Janakinath Bose, a famous lawyer and father of Subhas Chandra Bose was held where they decided not to wear foreign cloth and if possible, wear khadar.[131] By 23 June, twelve satyagrahis who were found picketing the cloth shops had been sentenced to six months' rigorous imprison-ment.[132] Early in July picketing of liquor shops began in Motiganj Bazar and Nua Bazar of Balasore.[133] By the first week of August picketing of excise (liquor and opium) shops began in Cuttack.[134] Some picketers were arrested and jailed.

Yielding to the pressure of picketers the cloth dealers in important towns pledged not to import foreign cloths. Mrs. Malati Choudhury played a leading role in the boycott of foreign cloths. The official report shows that picketing of cloth shops had become "very troublesome" in most districts of Bihar and Orissa province and many dealers were "apparently suspending dealing in foreign cloth, outwardly at any rate".[135]

Children under 16 were enrolled as volunteers[136] to picket the foreign cloth and excise shops. In Orissa, small boys formed 'Vanar Sena'. In Cuttack and Balasore according to Government report, "picketing is carried on mainly by women and boys who stand in rows in front of the liquor shops and be the would-be purchasers to abstain".[137] Oriya women, supposedly conservative and shy, boldly picketed before foreign cloth and never cared for police bludgeons or arrest or imprisonment. At Berhampur, picketing was carried on under the leadership of Mrs. J.V. Narayana.

The children did wonderful work in Orissa as in other provinces. They performed many odd jobs. Besides popularising home-spun cloth, they hawked cyclostyled Congress bulletins, carried letters, cooked food, hoisted flags, pasted posters and circulated leaflets and pamphlets.[138] They largely relieved the work of the ladies. In Cuttack, picketing of liquor shops and foreign cloth shops was successfully done by Rama Devi and Malati Devi with the help of their 'Vanar Sena'.[139] About 50 women worked as volunteers, but only five of them, Sarala Devi, Rama

Devi, Malati Devi, Chandramani Devi and Sunamani Devi courted arrests.[140]

In May 1930, in the Balasore sadar subdivision the Congressmen were thinking of launching a campaign against the payment of Chowkidari tax.[141] After the suspension of salt manufacture with the advent of monsoon, the UPCC authorised the launching of Civil Disobedience by the non-payment of Chowkidari tax in one particular area of Balasore district where intensive constructive work was taken up. The place selected was Inchudi-Srijang area.[142] Thirteen villages contiguous to Inchudi joined the no-tax campaign. Gour Mohan Das, Abhiram Mohanty, Bhagabat Bhuyan, Niranjan Mohanty, Bipra Charan Mohanty, Rama Chandra Pradhan and Sachi Behera started organising the villagers nearly, for the no-tax campaign.

In order to fuse the plan of no-tax campaign, the government sent one Sub-Inspector and some constables to Srijang on 11 July 1930. The Sub-Inspector brought certain charges on some persons as a result on 12 July three satyagrahis and two prominent villagers were accused and arrested. This provoked the people who demanded an impartial enquiry into the case. Getting no response from the police, about 600 to 700 people gathered round the police demanding the release of the arrested persons. It resulted in violence. The police were manhandled. The District Magistrate and the Superintendent of Police arrived at the place with an armed force. The people were brutally assaulted. Three women were raped.[143]

The indiscriminate assault of the police on the unarmed and harmless people attracted the attention of Laxmi Narayan Saha of the 'Servants of India Society' and Bhubanananda Das, M.L.A. who toured the villages and exposed the stories of police suppression outside. As a protest, Bhagabat Prasad Mahapatra resigned from the Bihar and Orissa Legislative Council.[144] Sashi Bhusan Rath the editor of 'Asha' was arrested for publishing the accounts of naked police atrocities at Srijang in his daily, the 'Asha', Gopal Narayan De of Balasore was also prosecuted for publishing cyclostyled pamphlet entitled 'Lawlessness in Balasore'.[145] With a view to collecting the expenses of keeping extra police at Srijang, punitive tax was imposed on the villagers. According to the report of the police, 48 persons in Balasore were convicted under the unlawful instigation Ordinance.[146]

Gandhi had asked the people to cut off all the palm trees in the villages.[147] People were making a country liquor, called toddy from date and palm trees. In Orissa, picketing of excise shops went on side by side with the cutting of date-palm trees in all districts. In the district, Balasore, by 14 June 1930, 1941 date trees had been cut.[148] According to Pranakrushna Padhiary by the end of September 1930 in the whole of Orissa 7,000 date trees had been cut.[149] According to the official report the picketing of excise shops resulted in heavy loss of revenue and a considerable amount of illicit distillation.[150] Picketing of liquor and opium shop was more rigorously suppressed than that of foreign cloth shops and police guards were posted in excise shops.

By the time the Civil Disobedience Movement started, the 'Asha' was the only daily newspaper in Oriya. Because of the splendid enthusiasm roused by the movement, the two weeklies, the 'Samaj' of Cuttack and the 'Prajatantra' of Balasore started daily editions. To curtail the growth of public support and sympathy for the movement through the Press, the Government subjected the Samaj and the Prajatantra to the stringent restrictions of Press ordinance asking them heavy security deposits. Thereupon, the Samaj and the Prajatantra stopped publishing from 16 and 8 May respectively. The 'Utkal Sevak' of Sambalpur also stopped its publication. A warning was given to the Gopinath Press, Bhadrak for publishing a leaflet entitled, 'Luna Mara Gita' (A song on Salt-manufacture) and was banned. Two pamphlets entitled 'Rana Nimantrana' (The War Call) and 'Rastriya Taranga (The National Wave) had also been prescribed.[151]

The Congressmen published two unauthorised cyclostyled bulletins, 'Bidrohi' and 'Biplabi' from Cuttack and Balasore respectively almost daily but were located by the Government and sooner the cyclostyle machines were seized.[152] On 14 May 1930, the Samaj office was searched by the police for tracing out a manuscript, called 'Vidrohi Vina' (The Seditious Violin).[153] In the Cuttack Town a daily news sheet, called 'Sambad' was being brought out 'Sambad' was publishing accounts of Civil Disobedience Movement. Therefore, it became a special target of attack in the pro-government newspaper, 'Satya Samachar' which was started in June 1930 by Braja Sunder Das, M.L.C. and Gopal Chandra Praharaj.

In the Kuhudi centre of Puri district, on 25 May 1930, five satyagrahis were arrested and severely beaten by the police.[154] In Kujang area of Cuttack district the subdivisional magistrate shabbily treated the satyagrahis by uttering abusive language and breaking their earthern pots, used for boiling brine, cooking rice and storing drinking water. The drinking water which the satyagrahis were bringing in buckets from a place, one and a half miles away from the salt manufacturing centre was thrown away by the police.[155]

The Salt Satyagrah inspired the lawyers and students to a large extent in Orissa. Many students left schools and colleges. Surendra Nath Patnaik was expelled from Ravenshaw College School for hoisting the Congress Flag on 12 March in a meeting on the river-bed of Katjuri. Balaram Pati, Bipin Bihari Mohanty, Krupasindhu Khuntia, Bhupendra Nath Bose, Niranjan Ghose, Braja Mohan Singh, Chintamani Misra, Chakradhar Satpathy, Gatikrushna Swain, Sadasiv Sarangi and Akulananda Behera left their schools to join the Satyagrah camp.[156]

The students of Cuttack had expressed their solidarity for the Civil Disobedience Movement by accompanying Rajkrushna Bose to the Collectorate, holding Swaraj flags and raising slogans of victory when he was arrested by the police on 17 April 1930.[157] The same day a meeting was held in Katjuri by the students where they resolved to join the movement and observe 19 April as a day of hartal, protesting against the arrest and imprisonment of Bose.[158] Bose was quite popular among the students. The Government readily arrested and jailed him to prevent the large scale involvement of students in the movement. In the Cuttack district, during the first phase of the Civil Disobedience Movement, 21 students left schools to join the movement and about 75 young men under the age of twenty joined it.[159] Three well-known freedom fighters- Surendra Nath Dwivedy, Surendra Nath Patnaik and Binod Kanungo discontinued their studies in the High School and joined the movement.

At Balasore, Rabindra Mohan Das, Gajendra Nath Sahu, Gaura Chandra Das, Nityananda Mohapatra, Kshetra Mohan Rout, Trilochan Panigrahi and Gouragopal Das left their schools and enrolled themselves as Satyagrahis. They started wearing Khadar cloth, shirt and cap.[160] In Bhadrak subdivision of Balasore district three young graduates- Bhagabat Sahu, Gokulananda Mohanty and Kamalakanta Mahapatra (The son of Chaudhury Bhagabat Prasad Samantray Mohapatra) courted arrest and imprisonment for taking part in the movement. According to Nilamani Pradhan, ten college students participated in the Civil Disobedience movement and courted imprisonment. But as he points out, primary and secondary school students "constituted the greater part of the prisoners".[161]

In the Puri and Khurda towns a student, Nrusingha Charan Samanta Simhar was externed from Puri town as he was organising a hartal in the town.[162] In Khurda, Samanta Simhar alongwith two student satyagrahis named Shyam Sundar Senapati and Balaram Patra was moving from village to village, asking the students to boycott the schools and the villagers to defy government officials and violate laws.[163] Senapati and Samanta Simhar were arrested on the charge of intimidating the village Chowkidars and tearing foreign cloth.[164]

An Oriya student of Benaras Hindu University, named Sharat Chandra Pattanayak, was arrested in Rae Bareli, U.P. and sentenced to six months' rigorous imprisonment for participation in Civil Disobedience Movement.[165] Chintamani Mishra, a law student of Ravenshaw College was imprisoned for his activities as a satyagrahi. On 17 October 1930, the Congress volunteer boys, about 20 in number, staged a black flag demonstration before the Maharaja of Parlakhemindi (who had already been nominated to the Round Table Conference) in Shriramchandra Bhavan and shouted, "Shame ! Shame ! do not go to the Round Table Conference. Go back".[166]

During the first phase of Civil Disobedience movement the total strength of enrolled volunteers was almost 1700.[167] There were many teenagers among the volunteers. But because of Gandhi's instruction and U.P.C.C's decision, young men below the age of sixteen were not enrolled as volunteers. Later on they were enrolled. The teenager volunteers, popularly known, Banar Sena, showed exemplary courage and undauntable fortitude in the movement.

Participation of urban as well as rural women in the Civil Disobedience Movement in Orissa was a spectacular feature. In the Non-cooperation movement of 1920-21, Saraladevi, the wife of Bhagirathi Mahapatra, the Secretary of U.P.C.C was the only woman participant. But, in 1930, a considerable number of women joined the Civil Disobedience Movement. The wives of some Congress leaders made up their minds to take part in the nationalist movement. Ramadevi (wife of Gopabandhu Choudhury), Malatidevi (wife of Nabakrushna Choudhury), Saraladevi, (wife of Bhagirathi Mahapatra), Janhavidevi (wife of Mukunda Prasad Das) Prafulla (wife of Biswanath Hota, a Balasore Congress Worker), Laxmi (wife of Puri Congress worker, Satyavadi Nanda), Shobha (wife of Ganjam Congress worker Antaryami Panda), Gunamanjari (wife of Puri Congress worker, Lal Bihari), and Sarojini

Choudhury (wife of Late Munsif Gagan Bihari Choudhury) and others took active participation in it.[168]

In 1928 Miss Shailabala Das had organised a women's conference in Ravenshaw girls' school in order to establish a branch of All India Women's Conference in Orissa.[169] The Calcutta Congress of 1928 was attended by a number of ladies from Orissa, such as, Ramadevi, Saraladevi, Sarojini Choudhury, Jahnavidevi and Kokiladevi.[170] By 1930 there were women workers in the Congress Ashrams at Kadua (Sakshigopal) and Alaka. Ramadevi was trying to enrol female members for the Congress. In the meeting held in Katjuri river bed on 13 April 1930 to bid farewell to the fourth batch of satyagrahis, Ramadevi, Malatidevi, Prafulla, Laxmi and Sarojini Choudhury were present. Mrs. Sarojini Choudhury appealed to men as well as women to join the peaceful Civil Disobedience movement and thereby prove themselves worthy men and women.[171] In this meeting, in response to Malatidevi's appeal and request, 200 foreign cloths were surrendered by the people for the sake of bonfire.[172]

Ramadevi, Malatidevi, and Kiranbala Sengupta decided to organize a women's campaign for participation in the salt satyagraha at Inchudi. On 19 April 1930, they mobilised the women of Srijang, the neighbouring village of Inchudi for the salt campaign. On 20 April, hundreds of rural women under the leadership of Ramadevi and Malatidevi manufactured contraband salt at Inchudi.[173]

On 22 April 1930 a meeting of women was held in Gopabandhu Choudhury's residence in Cuttack to plan the participation of women in Civil Disobedience Movement. "The significance of this meeting", as the Deshakatha observed, "lies in the fact that it marks the beginning of organised participation of women workers in the nationalist movement".[174] By the middle of May 1930, Ramadevi, Malatidevi and Prafulla Kumari Hota were busy mobilizing men and women for the salt campaign in Kujang. The Rani of Kujang, Bhagyabati Pata Mahadei took active participation and at her call hundreds of housewives came out with baskets and manufactured contraband salt at Kaliapat.[175]

By the time the salt campaign was suspended because of the break of monsoon in 1930, most of the Congress leaders were in jail. But mainly the two housewives of Choudhury family-Ramadevi and Malatidevi tried to keep up the organizational work as well as the movement of the Congress. When Atal Bihari Acharya was arrested in August 1930, he nominated Ramadevi as the President of Cuttack District Congress Committee.[176] From 26 September 1930 till her arrest in the first week of November 1930 she acted as the President of UPCC.

Ramadevi, Malatidevi and other lady Congress workers (almost 50 in number) worked enthusiastically; they worked "more strenuously and bore greater hardships than many of the men leaders could have done".[177] Sunamanidevi was arrested at Puri and imprisoned in July 1930 for delivering speech in violation of police law (1) on her return from Sabarmati Ashram.[178] From Patna camp jail the Congress leaders such as H.K. Mahtab and Pranakrushna Padhiary, were trying to issue secret instructions to Ramadevi, Malatidevi and Saraladevi to carry on the salt campaign. When Pranakrushna Choudhury was released from Patna camp jail, he carried three letters from Pranakrushna Padhiary, intended for Ramadevi, Latikadevi and Saraladevi. But the police seized those letters from Choudhury at the Balasore railway station.[179]

The women in the villages discarded their purdah and greeted the satyagrahis as the latter marched through the villages. In the villages of Balasore seashore such as Inchudi, Iram, Sartha, Tarei, Chhanua, Parikhi, Kherang and Rupakhanda and in Kujang villages (particularly Kaliapat) hundreds of village women took part in the manufacture of contraband salt. On 21 July 1930, when 700 women were coming back from Iram with salt earth, the police charged them with lathis. But they remained firm.[180] On 6 June 1930, a meeting of 300 women was held in Shyamsundar Temple of Balasore to take decisions about women's role in the ensuing Civil Disobedience movement.[181] On 8 June 600 women took part in the manufacture of salt at Iram. But this time police did not obstruct them.[182]

The women who came out of their houses in the face of opposition from family members identified the women's urge for emancipation and self-respect with the country's struggle for freedom. Ramadevi and her daughter Annapurna Maharana had recorded the extraordinary courage, shown by a village widow named Sushila, belonging to Ramapur village of Binjharpur thana of Cuttack district, in joining the Congress movement.[183]

The Civil Disobedience Movement of 1930 prepared the ground for large scale involvement of women in the organizational work of the Congress as well as the Civil Disobedience movement of 1932. Fourteen women delegates from Orissa (5 from Balasore, 2 from Sambalpur, 6 from Cuttack and 1 from Puri) attended the Karachi Congress of March 1931 held after the withdrawal of Civil Disobedience Movement.[184] Many women came forward to act as volunteers in the annual session of the Congress, proposed to be held in Puri in 1931, from the remote villages like Bari, Kalyanpur, Purusottampur and Ahiyas in the Jajpur sub-division. They also went to jail by participating in the Civil Disobedience Movement of 1932.[185]

After the arrest of Gopabandhu Choudhury at Balasore on 26 April 1930, the Presidents of Orissa Congress one after another were convicted. Before she was convicted, Ramadevi who was the President of the U.P.C.C. at that time nominated Golak Nath De as 'dictator' (sole organizer of the Congress party) to manage the party affairs as normal functioning of committees was impossible in those circumstances.[186] Golak Nath De, towards the end of November 1930 issued a statement that as the repressive measures of the Government had failed to coerce the movement, new satyagrahis should work with greater zeal and enthusiasm, and resume the manufacture of salt from December when the climatic conditions would permit such operations.[187] But soon Government ordinance declared all Congress Committees, Satyagraha Committees and such other associations or institutions for Civil Disobedience as unlawful organisation. Empowered by such an ordinance, the police took possession of the Congress offices, 'ashrams' and other such institutions in December. Many volunteers were also arrested.[188]

In January 1931 the salt satyagraha was resumed in many places in coastal Orissa. At Balasore the Congress office had been shifted to a French enclave known as Pharasidinga within the town over which the British authorities had no control. From that place Sardar Surendra organized the movement at Inchudi again and many volunteers including women began the work in right earnest.[189] Such operations also continued at Krushnapur, Kakatpur, Latra and other places. The success of the movement in Orissa was highly commended by Gandhiji and Jawaharlal wrote : " My greetings to the people of Utkal. I have heard of their sacrifice and sufferings in the national struggle for freedom. I congratulate them and trust they will carry on the good fight till our motherland is free".[190] The political atmosphere in the country was however changed with the signing of the Gandhi-Irwin Pact on 5 March 1931. Till the end of the year there was comparative lull, but once again the storm broke out with full fury soon after the return of Gandhiji from the second Round Table Conference without achieving any success.

With the resumption of Civil Disobedience from January 1932 the people of Orissa whole- heartedly plunged into the movement. Prominent Congress leaders who had come out of the jails and a large number of volunteers were once again arrested.[191] Most of them were sent to the Patna camp jail. The Congress was declared unlawful.[192] The press was kept under strict censorship. The Samaj and the Prajatantra suspended their publication for sometime, Orissa, therefore, could not host the Indian National Congress.[193] The Reception office and the volunteer camps were immediately closed. All Congress offices and ashrams at Cuttack, Puri, Kadua, Jagatsinghpur, Bargarh and Balasore were also closed. It was rather tragic for the people of Orissa, who were preparing in a big way for the first time to host the 46th annual session of the Indian National Congress at Puri, to find all of a sudden the cancellation of the session due to the decision of the Government in declaring the Congress and its associate organisation as unlawful bodies.

Gandhi's arrest led to a good deal of activities, such as demonstrations and "meetings in the river-bed of Katjuri after dark".[194] Interestingly, the powerful police failed to arrest Surendra Nath Das who concealed himself in 'French-Balasore' and issued inflammatory leaflets such as 'Rana Veri' and circulated them with the help of his closest associates in Balasore.[195] In the Athgarh area, there were intensive underground Congress activities under the leadership of Binod Kanungo, Surendra Patnaik and Bhramarbar Routray. After 12 months, Surendranath Das was arrested and convicted in February 1933.[196]

In August 1932, efforts started by the Congressmen all over the province to recover the Congress offices which had been locked by the Government Swaraj Ashram at Cuttack was recovered after strenuous efforts. Balasore Congress office and the Balasore Nari Ashram were also reoccupied at this time.[197]

In May 1933, Gandhi suspended the satyagrah unconditionally. The Congress leaders of Orissa, therefore, interested themselves in constructive work.[198] In Balasore, Harekrushna Mahtab formed a 'Krishak Sangh' with the intention of starting a no-tax campaign. He was able to rekindle the feeble flame of enthusiasm by organising Khadar and spinning centres at different places.[199] Gandhian constructive work continued in full swing in Orissa till Gandhi started the Harijan Movement. Despite the stern repressive measures of the Government, the movements did not completely stop until it was called off by the Congress in 1934.

Constitutionally, in 1934-35, India stood at the threshold of a new era because of the certain provisions envisaged in the forthcoming constitutional reforms. As per the provision of provincial autonomy a separate province was promised to the Oriyas. In 1935, while Congress party was celebrating its golden jubilee, the Oriyas were looking forward to form a separate entity of their own. However, in 1936, Orissa got her provincehood enjoying full autonomy and in 1937 elections were also held for the Orissa Legislative Assembly. The Congress party won the election and formed the ministry.

Meanwhile, the Second World War set in in 1939 and the British Government promised India many things after war provided the Indians helped the Government heart and soul. By October 1939 the Congress party decided to quit office since the Government refused bringing any substantial change of the old imperialistic policy. All Congress Ministries in several provinces resigned by November 1939. The war situation in Europe gradually deteriorated and by the middle of 1940 Hitler had overrun the whole of Western Europe. The Viceroy issued the "August Offer" on 8 August 1940 in response to the Congress demands which neither satisfied the Congress nor the Muslim League. The Congress Working Committee decided to launch the Individual Satyagraha Campaign.

The Utkal Provincial Congress Committee at its general meeting on 15 April 1940 got itself changed into Satyagraha Committee. The anti-war agitation continued in Orissa by the Congress, the Socialists as well as the student community. The Individual Satyagraha movement was inaugurated on 1 December 1940 by H.K. Mahtab who delivered anti-war speech near Balasore. He with other nine M.L.A.'s were arrested. This movement continued for a long time and many Congress leaders went to jail in turn. The war situation in the meantime deteriorated day by day. Mahatma Gandhi could realise the aggressive imperialism of Japan and its subsequent attack on India. Realising the war situation Gandhi threatened the British to quit India soon, otherwise he would launch a "Quit India" movement.

Quit India Movement in Orissa

The war impact in Orissa took a serious turn in the month of March 1942. After the fall of Singapore on 15 February 1942, the evacuees from Burma began to pour into Orissa. The loss of Rangoon (modern Yangoon) on 8 March 1942 made the situation more implicated. A close connection existed between Orissa and Burma and a large number of Oriyas were working there. Evacuees from Burma contributed in some measure to spread alarm in Orissa. Sri W.H. Lewis, the Governor of the Province, brought the matter to the notice of the Governor-General in New Delhi, but the latter could not give any assurance to protect Orissa. He did not propose to squander troops in erecting a more facade which would crumble if the Japanese landed.[200]

In that criss-cross phase of time, the situation in Orissa took a turn towards the worse. The danger of Japanese invasion loomed large in the Orissan sea coast when as a result of enemy action, some British ships were wrecked in April 1942 which led to drastic Government measures for the security of the province. The people were asked to remove all kinds of vehicles, boats, cycles and cars from the coastal region to atleast twenty miles inland. Strict restrictions were also imposed on the use of light in the coastal villages for evading the Japanese air-raid. The Government records were removed for safety to far-off Sambalpur which was called the base headquarters.[201]

Pandit Nilakantha Das who was the Provincial Organiser of the National War Front in Orissa toured different districts and tried to convince the people to support the war measures. But the greatest efforts to maintain public morale were made by the Congress volunteers and leaders who kept constant touch with the people. They formed voluntary defence organizations throughout the province without cooperation of the people to instil fearlessness in their minds and to counteract false propaganda.[202] Anticipating the Japanese invasion Gandhiji sent his disciple, Mira Ben to work in the province in order to create confidence in the minds of the people and also to prepare the atmosphere of 'Swaraj' to face the enemy. She stayed for some time in the 'Swaraj Ashram' in Cuttack and worked with other Congress leaders.[203]

Thus, the people of Orissa were being prepared to meet the enemy if they ever invaded the province. However, the Government did not hesitate to take strong action against the leading Congressmen if their action endangered war efforts in any way. Biswanath Das, the Congress ex-Premier and Leader of the Opposition in the Orissa Assembly, was arrested at his residence in Berhampur on 30 June 1942 under the Defence of India Rules in connection with his speech at Aska.[204]

Gandhiji, in the meantime, was thinking to launch a new movement in India to ventilate the grievances of the people against the British Raj. The Congress Working Committee in their meeting at Wardha passed a long resolution on the matter, popularly known as the 'Quit India Resolution' which initiated a new phase of the freedom struggle in the country. The Congress demanded the withdrawal of the British from India which would enable the people to shape their own destiny. However, the working committee thought it necessary to refer the matter to the All India Congress Committee for final decision. The meeting of the AICC was fixed on 7 August 1942 at Bombay.[205]

The historic resolution with its call for open rebellion against the British authorities alarmed the Government who made elaborate plans to nip it in the bud. The Provincial Governments were immediately consulted in this matter. In Orissa, the Governor despatched a secret report to the Viceroy conjecturing several reasons for Congress campaign. The location of Orissa in a potential war zone, absence of communal problems and the existence of a Coalition Ministry were some of the important reasons for which Orissa was to be selected as an important place for the Congress campaign. Thus, despite a Ministry functioning in the province, the British authorities took the upperhand in suppressing the movement which broke out in Orissa a week later.

The resolution was adopted in the night of 8 August 1942 and the Government swiftly moved its machinery of repression throughout the country against the Congress leaders and their organisations from the early morning of 9 August 1942. Most of the Congress leaders including Gandhiji were arrested at 4 A.M. of 9 August. Prominent leaders of various states were interned one after another and soon after 'Do or Die' movement started. People in groups in the entire country carried on wide efforts to collapse the prevalent administrative machinery of the Government. The students, youth, labourers and cultivators in large number joined this people's movement.[206]

In Orissa, as in other parts of the country, early in the morning of 9 August 1942 all important Congress leaders including the ex-ministers and legislators were rounded up by the police. Some of them were 'underground' workers. Mainly, Surendra Nath Dwivedy was managing the whole movement in Orissa as a secret worker. The revolutionary movement got much of its momentum because of the inspiration from Ram Nandan Mishra, a Congress Socialist leader of Bihar who was there in Orissa that time.[207] It picked up its speed in the second week of August. People were fired protesting against the arrest of popular Congress leaders. Terrible violence started at places. Everywhere started the boycott of schools and colleges and defiance of government laws and officers. The violent mob burnt down government offices at many places and the jailed Congress leaders openly disobeyed the jail laws.

In the first week of September 1942, the Government Communique reviewed the political situation in Orissa and revealed that the mob violence had been witnessed in the districts of Cuttack, Balasore and Koraput.[208]

In the district of Cuttack the movement began from the town itself and the students of Ravenshaw College, the premier institution in the province, launched a strike which was followed by other educational institutions in the town. On 14 August some students of the Ravenshaw College set fire to the office room of the college which damaged records and furnitures. Student leaders like, Banamali Patnaik, Ashok Das, Biren Mitra, Suraj Malla Saha, Bibhudhendra Mishra, and Mayadhar Mohanty, the Private Secretary of H.K. Mahtab were arrested followed by the imprisonment of many college as well as school students including Amitabh Mohapatra, Debendra Nath Mohanty and Trailokya Nath Mohanty and others.[209] Particularly in Jajpur and Kendrapara subdivisions, violent activities took place in several places. People attacked post offices, Canal Revenue offices and P.W.D. Bungalows and some of them were burnt. Telegraph and telephone wires were cut in several places and Chowkidars' uniforms were snatched away and put to flames.

The Congress Ashram at Bari in the Cuttack district was seized by the police soon. The Ashram was reoccupied by the villagers and the property seized by the police was destroyed. The Government took drastic steps against the people of Bari area by imposing a heavy amount of collective fine which was fully realised.[210]

Another incident took place in Kaipada, a village near Bari where the people had destroyed a post office. Subsequently a small police party was attacked which led to police firing and five persons were killed and several others were injured. In Jajpur town several thousand people marched in a mammoth procession towards the police station and S.D.O.'s office. As it was a huge gathering the police did not take any immediate action. An aeroplane came to the rescue of the police and it dropped dynamites to disperse the gathering. The people withdrew and on the way they burnt a post office. Disturbances also took place at Ersama, Tirtol and Jagannathpur area where the people succeeded in burning police stations, post-offices and such other Government institutions.[211] On 26 August, Biswambhar Parida and Jayaram Panda from Jagatsinghpur, Surendra Nath Patnaik and Maulana Atahar from Salepur, Raghunath Mohanty, Sachidananda Mohanty, Dukhi Bandhava Mishra and others from Kendrapara, Jagannath Das, Dwarika Nath Das, and Annapurna Maharana and others from Jajpur were arrested.[212]

Surendra Nath Dwivedy, Lokanath Mishra, Padmanabha Ray, Krushna Chandra Rout and others were famous as the underground Congress workers who distributed revolutionary leaflets secretly among the Congress workers and the police failed to detect them. However, the district collector and the police carried on their efforts to imprison these workers. Even cash award was declared by the administration to bring them into limelight. Finally on 11 October, Sri S.N. Dwivedy was arrested from a house in the Alishabazar of Cuttack town and many secret papers were seized. The medical students of Cuttack were lathicharged and some of the student doctors like, Dr. Motilal Tripathy, Dr. Rabindra Ghosh and Dr. Birakishore Mohanty were put behind the bar. The daily 'Samaj' published from Cuttack stopped its publication protesting against this heinous oppression.[213]

The August Revolution took a violent turn in the district of Balasore in which maximum persons lost their lives. The news of the arrest of H.K. Mahtab on the morning of 9 August in Bombay electrified the people's resentment in the state. Before an outlet was thought, leaders like Sardar Surendra Mohan Das, Nilambar Das, Karunakar Panigrahi, etc. were interned. Goura Charan Das, Secretary, District Congress Committee and Pyari Mohan Das, a member carried this people's war clandestinely. The students and the public not only disobeyed the laws of the Government, organised 'hartals' and carried on picketings in front of Government offices and courts but also set fire to dak bungalows, post offices and police stations, cut telegraph lines and in some cases also stopped the payment of taxes and rents. On 17 August 1942, a huge crowd (around five thousand) of villagers attacked the police station of Bhandari Pokhari and set fire to it. They also burnt the post office of the locality and demolished a road-bridge to prevent the police force from reaching the place. The government took strong action against the people of the locality and a punitive fine of six thousand rupees was imposed.[214]

The villagers in several remote places in the district of Balasore agitated against the British Raj. Several incidents occurred in the district and the police had to open fire in many places killing a number of persons at Khaira,Turi Gadia, Dhamnagar, Eram and other places. The atrocity of the police was manifested at Eram in Basudevpur Police station on 28 September where they fired on the unarmed villagers and killed 35 people on the spot and perhaps nowhere in India so many people were killed in a single police action during the movement.[215]

The Eram incident took so sordid a way that it was called "the Jalianwallah Bagh tragedy of Orissa". On that fateful day a few thousand villages of the locality had assembled in an open space which was surrounded on three sides by thorny bushes, muddy fields and ponds. They had gathered there on hearing the usual sound of conch-shells to listen to their leaders on the possible course of action against the police and Government supporters of the locality. A strong police contingent headed by a D.S.P arrived on the scene and asked the people to disperse. The police had already decided to take strong action against them because of their snatching the 'dak' from a post-peon and some belongings of the police party from a chowkidar. When the people could not be dispersed, the police opened fire and several rounds of bullets were fired on a thick crowd which led to serious repercussions.[216] For this heinous and brutal event caused, the Government was vehemently criticised and was ultimately forced to institute an official enquiry into the matter.

Virtually, Eram was a geographically isolated village which did not allow government officials to enter into it. If any official was seen the villagers blew conch-shells and gathered around. This symbolised the unity exhibited among the local people against any police or government official taking recourse to the concerned village. The Eram incident was not a great conspiracy. Also there was no grand design. Some of the Congress workers wanted the villagers to boycott the police and other officials in order to establish a 'Swadhin Chakada' (parallel administration) of their own. The incident involved remarkable enthusiasm and spontaneity. The atrocity manifested was no doubt great.

The August Revolution also took a serious form in the district, Koraput which was chiefly noted for its tribal population and its literacy was the lowest in the province. However, the people of the district were not unaware of the message of Gandhiji. In August 1942 when the news spread that Gandhiji had given a call for open rebellion, the people started no-rent campaigns with the belief that the British rule had come to an end. Violence, rioting, sabotage albeit cropped up in the district. Minor disturbances occurred at Nandupur, Potangi, Jeypore and other places.[217] The most violent incident happened at Matili. Lakshman Naik, the prominent Congress leader of the area, assisted by a large number of tribal people and armed with cudgels and lathis and carrying Congress flags, moved through dense forest areas where he destroyed liquor shops and agitated the people for destroying the British authority in the district. Finally they attacked the Matili police station on 21 August 1942. One forest guard was killed and some Government servants were injured in the scuffle. The police opened the fire which caused the death of five persons and seventeen agitators were injured including their leader Lakshman Naik[218] who was arrested, tried and subsequently hanged on 29 August 1943 in the Central Jail of Berhampur.[219] The memory of a martyr of his statute inspired the people of the Province to fight for the cause of their motherland.

Protesting against the incident on 21 August 1942 at Matili while an agitated mob was proceeding on 24 August 1942 to burn down a police station, the police opened fire at them which led to the killing of eleven persons and injuring of fourteen according to the press communique issued by the Government.[220] Large number of suspected participants in the disturbances were arrested. The Government also ordered the seizure of gun-powder and caps from licensed shops and thus the movement in the district was brought under control to a great extent.

In the district Puri, the Congress leaders like Nilamani Routray, Sriharsha Mishra and Baishnab Patnaik and others were arrested.[221] On 16 September 1942 the people in the villages round Nimapara decided in a meeting not to pay rent, etc. to Government and Zamindars. On the same way, they proceeded to the police station in order to persuade them to give up their jobs. The people also tried to hoist the Congress flag in the compound of the police station. When the police prevented them from doing so, the trouble began and the agitated mob pelted stones at them. Fire was opened from the police side which resulted in the death of one and injury to 16 others on the spot. The people became more violent too.

In Ganjam district, the agitation took the usual form of burning a number of Government buildings (thatched sheds) in the agency area and of destroying telegraph lines. The Government controlled the situation without much trouble. There was no report of any firing in the district.

In Sambalpur, the students went on strike and organised demonstrations at several places. Objectionable pamp'ılets were found to have been circulated in the district. All leading Congress men and workers suspected of unlawful activities, were arrested.[222]

However, some prominent Congress leaders went underground and tried to lead the mass movement through secret instructions. Jayprakash Narayan, Aruna Asaf Ali, Ram Manohar Lohia and others took over leadership of the underground organisations in the country in those critical days. In Orissa such an underground organisation was secretly established by Surendra Nath Dwivedy, a member of AICC from Orissa. He averted arrest soon after his return from the crucial meeting of the AICC at Bombay and remained in Cuttack town itself by deceiving the Government authorities and supplying secretly cyclostyled bulletins to the Congress leaders of the province for their guidance and necessary action. For about two months he ran his underground organisations. But finally he was arrested on 12 October 1942. He and fifteen others were involved in "Orissa Conspiracy Case" and were tried in the Court of J.E. Maher, Special Judge of Cuttack in early 1943 and fourteen of them were sentenced to various terms of imprisonment.[223]

No doubt remained that the exciting revolutionary bulletins considerably roused public sentiments in many parts of the province. Surendra Nath Dwivedy even tried to encourage his comrades from inside the jail by some dare-devil means. When that was detected the Government transferred Sri Dwivedy from Cuttack to Koraput jail and he was kept under very strict vigilance.[224]

The British authorities took sweeping actions against the prominent Congress leaders in the state soon after the Quit India Resolution was adopted by the AICC. Within two days they were all arrested and put behind the prison bars. So, they could not provide any leadership to the movement. Basically, the local leaders in different parts of the province carried on the revolutionary activities and agitations according to their own ideas. It was of "Do or Die" struggle throughout India and the people in many cases voluntarily and spontaneously jumped into the fire. Finally, the British Government emphasised upon the Defence of India Rules according to which fifteen members of the Orissa Assembly were under detention. Nand Kishore Das, Deputy Speaker of the Orissa Assembly had also been arrested under the same rule.[225] The institutions of local self-government both in Cuttack and Balasore districts had been superseded by the Government for proper maintenance of vital services in the event of hostile attacks.[226] Thus by the end of October 1942 the Government succeeded in curbing out the movement by strong repressive measures under the Defence of India Rules.

The Government of India Act, 1935 brought significant changes in the administration of the provinces. In 1937 part of it was enacted since elections were held for the Legislative Assemblies of the few provinces excluding the federal government at the centre. Of course, all were the fostered ministries since they collapsed due to the breaking of the Second World War. In Orissa, the Congress was voted to power inspite of the fact that the rajas and maharajas of the princely states were arrayed on the other side who had played an important role in formation of a separate province for Orissa. But the election results reflected the dichotomy in Orissa.

By the end of December 1941 some of the Congress M.L.A's who were in jail had been released. Biswanath Das, ex-Chief Minister of Orissa came out of the Cuttack jail on the expiry of his full term of imprisonment on 4 December 1941.[227] H.K. Mahtab was released from the Berhampur jail on 1 December 1941. The Congress leaders including Sri Das now decided to remain prepare to attend the Assembly session in order to defeat the Co-alition ministry under the Premiership of Maharaja of Parlakhemindi.[228]

In the second half of 1942 the situation in Orissa took a turn towards the worse. The danger of Japanese invasion loomed large in the Orissan sea coast where as a result of enemy action, some British ships were wrecked in April 1942. Thus, the people in Orissa were being prepared to meet the enemy if they ever invaded the province. Even the Governor admitted : "In public Congress speakers have been keeping more or less to a moderate line and are occasionally helpful..."[229] However, the Government did not hesitate to take strong action against the leading Congress men if their action endangered war efforts in any way. Biwanath Das, the leader of the Opposition in the Orissa Assembly, was arrested at his residence in Berhampur on 30 June 1942 under the Defence of India Rules in connection with his speech at Aska.[230]

In one of the sessions of the Orissa Legislative Assembly Bichitrananda Das, Deputy Leader of the Congress wanted to move an adjournment motion regarding lathi charge on political prisoners and inhuman treatment meted out to them in Berhampur jail on 26 January 1944 in connection with the hoisting of the National Flag.[231] The Speaker did not allow the matter to be discussed on that day. However, it was taken on the next day, 2 March 1944.

The Deputy Leader of the Congress Party vividly narrated the incident in the house. It occurred on 26 January 1944 between 2 P.M. and 4 P.M. and the lathi charges were made twice on the freedom-fighters. Biswanath Das, Nityananda Kanungo, Uma Charan Patnaik and others sustained grievous injuries on that day. The Government had not yet come to their hospitality and the Premier tried to refute the allegations regarding the injury sustained by Sri Das. He said : "when a lathi charge was made, Mr. Das was caught by the crowd and most probably he was pushed over and fell down and no injury was done to his body as a result of lathi charge. He might have fallen down and sustained the injury. I have personally gathered the information and the Officer-in-charge solemnly declared that nothing of that sort happened".[232] However, that unfortunate incident created suspicion in the minds of Congressmen about the bad intention of the Government. Throughout the budget session, the Congress members repeatedly raised this matter in the House in order to open up the mask of popular so called ministry in the public eye.

Meanwhile, the Congress leaders in Orissa had been released from detention. As the province was being administered under Section 93 of the Government of India Act,1935, the question of the formation of a ministry was raised by once again. In that connection, Biswanath Das in an interview on 9 May 1945 said that there was no intention on the part of the Congress to form a ministry so long as the Indian political dead-lock continued.[233]

The Indian political situation took a crucial turn after the General Election in Britain in 1945. The Labour Party succeeded in defeating the Conservatives and won a clear majority for forming the Government. In the Cabinet headed by Attlee, Lord Pathick Lawrence became the new Secretary of State for India. The Labour Party had considerable sympathy for the freedom struggle in India and under the changed circumstances after the war, it was certain that they would grant self-government to the Indians fulfilling their long cherished desire. Soon after its assumption of power, it was announced that the election to the various Indian Legislatures would be held in early 1946. The Governor of Orissa dissolved the Orissa Legislative Assembly by a notification in September 1945. Thus ended the existence of the First Legislative Assembly of Orissa elected under the Act of 1935 after more than eight years during which three Ministers had functioned, a global war and a great national upheaval had taken place.

The preparation for election to the Second Assembly in Orissa began towards November 1945. In the meantime, Biswanath Das, the former Premier of Orissa had been disqualified to become a member of the Orissa Legislative Assembly for a period of 6 years from 28 August 1943 for his alleged malpractice in the election of Uma Charan Patnaik from Baliguda constituency in the Ganjam district. The case was disposed of when he was in jail and he had hardly any opportunity to defend himself. Attempts were made to remove this injunction order so that he could take charge of the election affairs in the province and also could stand as a Congress candidate to the Assembly. After legal scrutiny it was not found possible to remove the ban on him and, therefore, he was not able to stand as a candidate in the election. However, the Central Parliamentary Board gave joint responsibility to him and H.K. Mahtab to manage the election affairs in the province.[234]

Sardar Patel asked them to recommend the names of the candidates whom they considered to be loyal and faithful to the Congress. He wrote to Sri Das : "I donot know exactly when the period of your disqualification is to expire but there must be some candidate selected for the provincial Assembly who would be willing to make way by vacating his seat for you whenever he is asked to do so. We would have escaped much of these difficulties if your disqualification had not come in the way and your services had been available to us for legislative work. I know that you will do your best even from outside, but your position as the leader of the Assembly Party would have spared us all this trouble".[235]

Under the able guidance and leadership of H.K. Mahtab and Biswanath Das, the Congress did fairly well in the election of 1946. It could secure as many as 36 seats uncontested in the House of 60. It was almost equal to the strength of the Congress Party in 1937. The final party position out of 56 elective seats were as follows : Congress 47,

Muslim League 4, Communist 1 and Independents 4.[236] On 20 April 1946, the Orissa Assembly Congress Party met at Cuttack to elect its new leader. Forty-six out of 47 members attended the meeting, presided over by Sri Das and Mahtab was unanimously elected as the leader of the Assembly Party and was authorised to select his colleagues. Four members were nominated by the Governor out of which three were taken according to the suggestion of H.K. Mahtab.[237] Thus the Congress Party in Orissa entered the legislature in 1946 with tremendous confidence and hoped not only to adopt a comprehensive programme for amelioration of the masses, but also to see the fulfillment of the long cherished goal, the achievement of freedom.

The Ministry took the office on 23 April 1946 and H.K. Mahtab the new Premier spoke with much confidence : "Independence is not now a distant object to be gazed at like star of one's choice in the distant horizon. It is now on the point of being realised and all of us believe that we will have it before the year is out. Independence is a must urgent matter for, without it, poverty and squalor of the country can not be effectively dealt with. To me independence has no political charm, if through it I can not tackle the problems of the masses i.e., their abject poverty, disease and ignorance".[238]

The First task of the Congress ministry after their assumption of power was the release of all political prisoners in Orissa irrespective of undergoing transportation for life for revolutionary activities during the Quit India Movement. Within a week the release of prisoners was complete. Another bold step which the Ministry wanted to take was the appointment of the former I.N.A. Medical Service. The public at the same time urged that Oriya I.N.A. men who were gradually returning home from various camps from Burma, might also be usefully employed under the popular administration.[239]

In the first week of May 1946, the Premier also announced in a press conference that collective fines realised during the Quit India Movement would be refunded to the villagers. Accordingly, orders were sent to Collectors of different districts to refund the fines to the respective persons. With regard to the damage caused to the buildings and properties of various institutions, which were taken possession of by the then Government in 1942, the new Government considered the question of awarding compensation for the damages. There was a popular demand for the enquiry into the excesses committed by the police and other

Governmental and semi-Governmental authorities during the Quit India Movement. The Premier averted any vindictive action because of so many urgent problems the country faced that time. However he said, "We are prepared to make sifting inquiry into specific cases of gross illegalities and corruptions wherever they may have been committed and to take suitable action against any officers proved guilty of the charges".[240]

The Second Session of the Assembly was summoned on 17th July 1946 for transacting special business, the election of members from Orissa to the Constitutional Assembly.[241] Nine members were elected to the Constituent Assembly from Orissa and they were : Harekrushna Mahtab, Santanu Kumar Das, Malati Choudhury, Rajkrushna Bose, Bhubanananda Das, Bodhram Dube, Nanda Kishore Das, Biswanath Das and Lakshmi Narayan Sahu.

Communal problem became very much acute with the decision of the Muslim League to observe "Direct Action Day" on 16 August 1946. It led to the worst holocaust in Calcutta where thousands of men and women were butchered and many more rendered homeless. The Congress Ministry of the province had to think of prompt measures not only to pacify the people of the province, but also to give necessary help to the Oriya population in greater Calcutta area in order to rehabilitate them.

It was decided to enquire into the matter and the Government entrusted the problem to Sri Das, the Ex-Premier of Orissa who volunteered to go to Calcutta in order to see for himself the condition of the Oriya population. The Government wanted him to have a semi-official inquiry to ascertain the correct position. He reached Calcutta on 5 September 1946 and submitted a report to the Government, on 15 September 1946. He visited the affected areas, gathered information from all sources and finally concluded that 750 Oriyas lost their lives and 1500 received injuries during the communal riot in Calcutta and the loss of property of the Oriyas was estimated at almost 25 lakhs.[242] Sri Das recommended to the problems created by riots and also wanted that they should call upon the Government of Bengal to provide compensation to the families victimised.

The Government took prompt action to mitigate the distress of the people. Provisions were made for the maintenance of the Riot Distressed Oriya Enquiry Office at Calcutta. Applications were sent to the Government of Bengal for the rehabilitation grants. The Provincial Government also called for applications from the relatives of the victims of the Calcutta riots who were residing in the province.[243] Such steps by the Government restored confidence in the minds of the Oriya Community working and residing in Calcutta. Much praises were offered to Sri Das in this respect for his accurate and articulate report on the said riot.

'Noakhali Day' was observed as a mark of protest against the communal disturbances in different parts of India and this protest led to further communal troubles in some parts of the country. People in Orissa observed the 'Noakhali Day' on 31 October 1946. In Cuttack, the capital of the province, it was decided to observe complete hartal and to take out a procession in the town on that day. Two days before it, H.K. Mahtab, the Premier of the province, got a secret report that some Hindus in the town had prepared themselves to murder the Muslims. But the Premier in a public meeting explained the indispensable necessity of maintaining communal harmony in the country for larger interest. He did not like that there should be any retaliation in any place in India against the Muslims as a protest of the incidents at Noakhali. His speech satisfied both Hindus and Muslims and specially the fear of the Muslims was dispelled to a great extent and communal harmony was not disturbed in Orissa for a long time.[244]

The post-war development schemes assured much importance during the days of the Congress Ministry in 1946-47. Of course, tentative proposals and the first draft of the plan of reconstruction and development in Orissa had been outlined as early as January 1945. But the plan could not make any headway that year. Much importance was, therefore, attached to these projects when the popular Congress Ministry took over the administration of the province in 1946. In the budget estimates for the year 1946-47, H.K. Mahtab gave a detailed account of various projects to be undertaken by the Government for post-war reconstruction of the province. Though Orissa was a poor province and its budgetary position was rather gloomy, yet the Premier desired to take bold steps for amelioration of the condition of the masses.[245]

With the achievement of freedom, India entered a new phase of her history. The Provincial Legislatures began to play a different role as the representative institutions of a self-governing people. The special session of the Orissa Legislative Assembly, which met on 27 August 1947, might be regarded as a filling epilogue of the legislative struggles and achievements of the preceding two generations. The Orissa Assembly passed one memorable resolution on that very day. H.K. Mahtab, the Premier, himself brought the resolution in the House as follows :

"This Assembly expresses its heartful joy at the advent of Independence and ushering in of the real Provincial Autonomy on the 15th of August 1947 and records its deep gratitude to the great national leaders, Mahatma Gandhi and Pandit Gopabandhu Das (who was the father of nationalism in Orissa) and to all these workers who have perished in the struggle for freedom in the course of the last quarter of a century. This Assembly hopes that the people and the Government of the Province will take necessary steps to commemorate the 15th of August by raising monuments in memory of the leaders and martyrs in suitable places in Orissa".[246]

Even though the early years of British conquest of Orissa in the first half of the nineteenth century was marked with several resistance movement, yet, the Congress-led nationalist movement had made rather a slow beginning in Orissa. The late-nineteenth and early twentieth centuries were dominated by the movement for a separate province of Orissa. Thus, Orissa did not lack inactivity or awakening, rather, for justifiable known reasons the freedom struggle in Orissa picked up vigour in the post First World War era. Mahatma Gandhi was the greatest influence on the Congress leadership in Orissa. The Non-Cooperation movement in Orissa brought the waves of changes. Congress emerged as an important organisation under Gopabandhu Das. The Civil Disobedience movement was vigorous in Orissa bringing out the youth and women in large number to the forefront. The Quit India movement had a larger mass base involving the tribals, peasants and others. A detailed discussion on the nature and contradiction of the movement shall be taken up later.

References

1. *Young India* (YI), 10 Mar 1920
2. P. Sitaramayya, *History of Indian National Congress*, Vol.I : 199
3. UD, 11 Sept 1920
4. Ibid, 18 Sept 1920
5. H.K. Mahtab, *Sadhanar Pathe* : 28
6. Ibid : 24-25, Also *Utkal Prasanga* (UP), August 1972 : 25
7. Sadhanar Pathe : 31
8. Samaj (SJ), 19 Mar 1921
9. P.Kar, *Congress and Orissa* : 104

10. Gandhi to C.F. Andrews, Jubbalpur, 21 Mar 1921. From a photostat : G.N. 961, Gandhi National Museum and Library (GNML)
11. Annual Administrative Report (AAR), Bihar and Orissa, 1920-21 : 150
12. P.Kar, op.cit. : 105
13. Ramadevi Choudhury, Jiban Pathe : 52-53
14. H.K. Mahtab, Gandhi O Odisha : 13
15. SJ, 28 Mar 1921
16. Ibid, 28 Mar/2 Apr 1921
17. The Collected Works of Gandhi : 550
18. SJ, 28 Mar 1921
19. H.K. Mahtab, *Dasha Varshara Odisha* : 29
20. AAR, Bihar and Orissa, 1920-21 : 150
21. Gopabandhu Choudhury, *Gandhi and Utkal* : 16-17
22. *Ibid* : 26
23. *Ibid* : 17
24. *Ibid* : 4
25. *Orissa District Gazetteer*, Sambalpur : 79
26. Mahtab, Dasha Varshara : 24
27. SJ, 4 Sept 1920
28. UP, August 1972 : 34
29. S.N. Patnaik, Odishare Swadhinata Andolana : 39
30. Nilakantha Das, Nilakantha Granthavali : 27 and 127
31. UP, op.cit. : 42
32. Mahtab, Dasha Varshara : 29
33. YI, 2 Mar 1921, Also UP, op.cit. : 26
34. S.N. Patnaik, *op.cit.* : 39
35. SJ, 21 May 1921
36. Nilakantha Das, *op.cit.* : 87 and 127, Also S.N. Patnaik, *op.cit.* : 39
37. *Sadhanar Pathe* : 42-44
38. P.K. Nayak, *Biswanath Das* : 59-60
39. P.Kar, *op.cit.* : 97-98
40. YI, 2 Mar 1921
41. P. Sitaramayya, *op.cit.* : 212
42. SJ, 16 July 1921
43. Mahtab, *Dasha Varshara* : 33

44. A.C. Pradhan, *The Nationalist Movement* : 49
45. SJ, 17 Sept 1921
46. AAR, *op.cit.* : 153
47. Mahtab, *Dasha Varsha* : 35
48. Ibid.
49. Chittaranjan Mishra, *Freedom Movement in Sambalpur* : 199
50. Gopabandhu Choudhury, op.cit. : 28
51. Chittaranjan Mishra : 205
52. AAR, *op.cit.* : 153
53. Sadhanar Pathe : 55
54. *The Bombay Chronicle,* 14 Jan 1922
55. YI, 2 Mar 1921
56. Nilakantha Das, op.cit. : 87-89, Also SJ, 22 Jan 1921
57. P. Kar, op.cit. : 103
58. *Orissa District Gazetteer,* Sambalpur : 79
59. *Ibid* : 79-80, Also Nilakantha Das : 87-89
60. *SJ*, 5 Mar 1921
61. *Ibid,* 12 Mar 1921
62. Chittaranjan Mishra, *op.cit.* : 196
63. A.C. Pradhan, *op.cit.* : 53
64. SJ, 26 Nov 1921
65. *Dasha Varshara Odisha* : 44
66. A.C. Pradhan : 54
67. SJ, 3 Dec 1921
68. Proceedings of the Legislative Council of Bihar and Orissa, 1921 : 721
69. *Ibid* : 730-32
70. *Ibid*, 1923 : 405-6
71. SJ, 27 May 1922
72. *Ibid*, 13 Aug 1921
73. *Home Political Proceedings,* No. 18, April 1922
74. P. Kar, *op.cit.* : 115-16
75. *Sadhanar Pathe* : 67
76. *Proceedings of the Legislative Council of Bihar and Orissa,* 1922 : 1006
77. *Ibid* : 1047
78. Dasha Varshara Odisha : 33

79. Bipan Chandra, India's Struggle for Independence : 285
80. Dasha Varshara Odisha : 61-62
81. N.K. Das, Mo Jibana O Janjala Kahani : 40
82. Home Political Proceedings, F. No. 25, Sept 1924
83. Ibid, F.N. 122, March 1925
84. SJ, 10 June 1922
85. UD, 5 May 1923
86. SJ, 19 July 1924
87. UD, 26 July 1924
88. SJ, 19 July 1924
89. UD, 30 Aug 1924
90. Ibid, 27 Sept 1924
91. Ibid, 5 Sept 1925
92. YI, 12 May 1927
93. Ibid, 5 May 1927
94. Mahtab, *Gandhi O Odisha* : 54-55
95. Home Pol. Progs., F.No 5/62/1932
96. SJ, 29 Jan 1930
97. Ibid, 5 Feb 1930
98. L. Fischer, *Life of Mahatma Gandhi* : 17
99. Home Pol. Progs, F. No. 5/62/1932
100. *Sadhanar Pathe* : 129
101. YI, 12 Mar 1930
102. P. Sitaramayya, *op.cit.* : 403
103. UP, op.cit. : 46, *Also Dasha Varshara Odisha* : 85
104. *UD,* 26 Apr 1930
105. *YI,* 1 May 1930
106. Ibid, 1 and 8 May 1930, And SJ, 23 Apr 1930
107. Pranakrushna Padhiary's Report, AICC, Files (NMML)
108. UD, 26 Apr 1930
109. *Ibid.*
110. *Ibid.*
111. *YI,* 8 May 1930
112. UD, 3 May 1930
113. Ibid.

114. Ibid, 10 May 1930
115. Ibid, 7 June 1930
116. Ibid, 21 June 1930
117. YI, 8 May 1930
118. UD, 24 May 1930
119. Ibid, 31 May 1930
120. Ibid, 14 June 1930
121. Nilamani Pradhan's Report, AICC, Files (NMML)
122. Ibid.
123. A.C. Pradhan, op.cit. : 128
124. Home Pol. Progs., 18/6/1930 (NAI)
125. UD, 10 May 1930
126. UP, August 1988, Dandapani Behera "Ganjam Jillare Ain Amanya Andolana"
127. Nilamani Pradhan's report
128. Dandapani Behera, op.cit.
129. Home Pol. Progs, F. No 5/62/1932
130. UD, 10 May 1930
131. *Ibid,* 28 June 1930
132. *Ibid,* 12 July 1930
133. *Ibid.*
134. *Ibid,* 9 Aug 1930
135. *Ibid,* 25 May 1930
136. B. Kanungo, *Jatiya Kabi Birakishore* : 62
137. Home Pol. Progs, F. No. 18/Jan 1931 and 18/IV Apr 1931
138. Ibid, F.No. 18/Jan 1931
139. S.N. Patnaik, *op.cit.* : 82
140. P. Kar, *op.cit.* : 176
141. UP, August 1986
142. Dasha Varshara Odisha : 88
143. P. Kar, op.cit. : 172-73
144. UD, 31 July 1930
145. *Ibid,* 6 Sept 1930
146. *Dasha Varshara Odisha* : 89
147. P. Sitaramayya, *op.cit.* : 390

148. Padhiary's Report
149. L.S.S.O' Malley, Bihar and Orissa District Gazetteers: 2
150. Padhiary's Report
151. Home Pol. Progs., F.No. 18/VIII July 1930
152. Ibid, F.No. 5/62/1932
153. Satya Samachar, 6 Aug 1930
154. UD, 31 May 1930
155. Padhiary's Report, Appendix-C.
156. S.N. Patnaik, op.cit. : 74
157. UD, 19 Apr 1930
158. Deshakatha, 18 Apr 1930
159. Nilamani Pradhan's Report
160. UD, 10 May 1930
161. Purusottam Singh, Swadhinata Sangramare Banar Sena
162. Satya Samachar, 30 July 1930
163. Ibid.
164. Ibid, 22 Oct 1930
165. Ibid, 5 July 1930
166. A.C. Pradhan, op.cit. : 156
167. Ibid : 157
168. Ibid : 161-63
169. Ramadevi Choudhury, Jivan Pathe : 86
170. Dasha Varshara Odisha : 80
171. UD, 19 Apr 1930
172. Ibid, 26 Apr 1930
173. Ibid
174. Ramadevi Choudhury, op.cit. : 89-91
175. UD, 16 Aug 1930
176. Ibid, 21 June 1930
177. Padhiary's Report
178. Acc. No 27. W.W.C.C., 1930 (Orissa State Archives)
179. Padhiary's Report
180. UD, 21 June 1930
181. Ibid.
182. Ramadevi Choudhury, op.cit. : 94

183. A.C Pradhan, op.cit. : 167
184. Ramadevi Choudhury : 94
185. A.C. Pradhan : 168
186. SJ, 19 Nov 1930
187. Ibid, 3 Dec 1930
188. Ibid, 17 Dec 1930
189. Ibid, 21 Jan 1931
190. Ibid, 4 Mar 1931
191. Ibid, 16 Jan 1932
192. Home Pol. Progs, F.No. 18/I, Jan 1932
193. Nilakantha Granthavali : 101-103
194. Home Pol. Progs., F. No. 18/I Jan 1932
195. Ibid, F.No. 18/II Feb 1933
196. Ibid, F. Nos. 18/I Jan 1933 and 18/II Feb 1933
197. Sadhanar Pathe : 151
198. Home Pol. Progs., F.Nos, 18/4 May 1933 and 18/6 May 1933
199. Ibid, F.Nos. 18/9 Aug 1933 and 18/12 Nov 1933
200. N. Mansergh (ed), *Transfer of Power,* Vol. I, 1970: 298-99
201. *Sadhanar Pathe* : 223-24
202. K.M. Patra, *Orissa State Legislature* : 186
203. B. Parida, Mukti Sangram O Odisha : 46
204. Amrit Bazar Patrika (ABP), 2 July 1942
205. P. Sitaramayya, *op.cit.* : 340-42
206. B. Parida, op.cit. : 48
207. *Ibid.*
208. A B P, 7 Sept 1942
209. B. Parida : 53-54
210. K.M. Patra, op.cit. : 190
211. A B P, 13 Sept 1942
212. B. Parida : 56-57
213. Ibid : 64-65
214. ABP, 7 Sept 1942
215. B. Parida : 71
216. H.K. Mahtab, *History of Freedom Movement in Orissa,* Vol.IV : 81-85
217. K.M Patra, *op.cit.* : 193

218. B. Parida : 51
219. Mahtab, *op.cit.* : 91
220. *ABP,* 7 Sept 1942
221. B. Parida : 75
222. Mahtab, *op.cit.,* Vol.V : 83-89
223. K.M. Patra, *op.cit.* : 195
224. S.N. Dwivedy, *August Revolution* : 210
225. ABP, 16 Oct 1942
226. *Ibid,* 26 Sept and 27 Oct 1942
227. *Ibid,* 5 Dec 1941
228. *Ibid,* 1 Jan 1942
229. N. Mansergh (ed), *Transfer of Power,* Vol. II, 1971 : 121
230. ABP, 2 July 1942
231. *Orissa Legislative Assembly Proceedings* (OLAP) Vol. X, 1944 : 15
232. *Ibid* : 69
233. *Indian Annual Register* (IAR) 1945, Vol. I : 64
234. K. M Patra, op.cit. : 224
235. Durga Das(ed), *Sardar Patel's Correspondences,* Vol II : 159-60
236. ABP, 18 Apr 1946
237. *Sadhanar Pathe* : 255
238. ABP, 24 Apr 1946
239. Ibid, 29 Apr 1946
240. K.M. Patra : 228-29
241. *OLAP*, Vol I, 1946 : 226
242. K. M. Patra; 243
243. OLAP, Vol. III, 1947 : 935-42
244. *Sadhanar Pathe* : 276-78
245. K. M. Patra : 237
246. *OLAP,* Vol. V, 1947 : 7

4

THE POPULAR MOVEMENTS IN THE PRINCELY STATES

Conquest of Orissa by the British during the Second Maratha War in 1803 brought about significant changes into the body politics of the then Orissa. Miracle was exhibited because the 'garjats' or the Tributary Mahals or the Feudatory States or the Princely States of Orissa came into administrative relation with the Mogulbandi areas (the level and cultivated portion of Orissa from which the Mogul Emperors derived their revenues; coastal districts of Orissa, Balasore, Cuttack and Puri) which were under direct control of the British authorities. Though the British regulations were not introduced into the Tributary Mahals and the avowed policy of the government was non-interference in their internal administration, yet at times the government took decisive action to preserve peace and tranquility in those territories. By 1837, there were 18 Tributary Mahals of Orissa under the control of the Superintendent the office of which was established in 1814 by the then Governor- General, Lord Moira. The Superintendent was however, authorized to exercise a discretionary power of interference in any 'heinous crime' brought to his notice, where such interference might appear to him indispensably necessary to secure the 'end of justice'. The British authorities, while tenaciously upholding the policy of non-interference in relation with the Tributary Mahals or Princely States, empowered the Superintendent to take suitable action in extreme cases.

The number of the 'Garjats' or the Princely States was reduced to 16 from 18 in 1848 when Banki and Angul were confiscated in 1840 and 1848 respectively. Later on by the division of one Princely State into two distinct units, the number was raised to 17. There was no further change throughout the 19th century.

In 1862 sanads were granted to all the chiefs guaranteeing them the right of adoption. Another significant administrative change took place in 1888 by a judicial decision of the Calcutta High Court which ruled out those 17 Princely States as the party to British India. As a result, new sanads were given to all the Chiefs, defining their status, powers and positions.[1] Lord Elgin issued such sanads from Shimla on 27 October 1894. In 1908, in consequence of memorial submitted by several chiefs to the Viceroy, revised sanads were issued by Lord Minto. Definite limitation of criminal powers laid down in the sanads of 1894 was replaced by a liberal clause. It required the Chief of a Princely State to conform "in all matters concerning the preservation of law and order, and the administration of justice generally, within the limits of your state, to the instructions issued from time to time for your guidance by His Honour, the Lieutenant- Governor of Bengal".[2] The Feudatory Chiefs were also directed to administer justice 'fairly and impartially' to all alike.[3]

The Feudatory Chiefs of Orissa were supposed to conform to the advice of the Commissioner on all important matters at all times. But doubt remains if there was any real improvement in the administration of those territories as the British laws and regulations were not directly introduced and the government took action against the rulers in extreme cases only. Due to dismemberment of Orissa under the three presidencies, the Feudatory States were grouped under the three categories, namely, Central Provinces States, Chhotnagpur States and Cuttack States. The States of Bamra, Kalahandi, Patna, Rairakhol and Sonepur were known as Central Provinces States; Bonai and Gangpur as Chhotnagpur States and nineteen others, namely, Angul, Athgarh, Athmalick, Banki, Baramba, Baud, Daspalla, Dhenkanal, Hindol, Keonjhar, Khandpara, Mayurbhanj, Narasinghpur, Nayagarh, Nilgiri, Pal-lahara, Ranpur, Talcher and Tigiria were called the Cuttack States.[4] Kalahandi was then a dependency of Nagpur Zamindary but later came under the Central Provinces.

The Nizam of Hyderabad had ceded Northern Circar to the British under which the princely states of Ganjam, Koraput and Vizagpatam tracts were included. Several estates under these districts, namely, Jeypore, Parla, Bobili, Tekkali, Manjusa, Madgul, Khallikote, Dharakote and Ghumsur etc. remained under the British Agent at Vizagpatam. They were popularly known as agency area. However legally though the princes continued to control the internal administration they were Zamindaries only. In 1906, a Political Agent was appointed under the control of the

Commissioner for the 24 States of Orissa. In 1916, Saraikella and Kharswan were also added to the charge of the political Agent. Finally in 1922, the Political Agent was designated as the Political Agent and Commissioner of Orissa Feudatory States, 26 in number. At the same time, an Assistant Political Agent was also appointed to help him in the better management and administration of the States.[5]

In 1933, the Eastern States Agency comprising 26 Feudatory States of Orissa and 14 States from the Central Provinces, was brought into existence for greater control and better management of those states directly under the Government of India. The headquarters of the Agency, which was first situated at Ranchi, was shifted to Calcutta and the Agency was administered by a Resident controlled by the Political Department of the Government of India. Such an arrangement continued till the end of the British rule in the country.

Growth of Political Consciousness

Political activities in British Orissa very much influenced the neighbouring princely states. The people of the States resuscitated their own spirit to know about the movement. The Feudatory Chiefs patronized and participated the political organisations of British Orissa. A slow but steady impact fell upon the body-politic of the Feudatory States. Political organisations were gradually established in those areas to arouse consciousness among the people.

Printing press, journals and newspapers played a dominant role in rousing political consciousness among the people. Till 1866 there was no such press or periodicals which made any contribution towards the growth of political consciousness among the people of Orissa, although the Christian Missionaries brought out some religious publications for their own purposes.[6] Towards the later part of the sixties and in the rest of the 19th century Orissa evinced keen interest in journalism. 'Utkal Dipika' was the pioneer periodical under the editorship of Gourishankar Ray. The first periodical of the garjats of Orissa named 'Sambalpur Hitaisini' was published in Bamra in 1885 under the patronage of the Raja of Bamra.[7]

The newspapers and periodicals of the period highlighted the political, social, religious and cultural aspects of the life of the people and added flavour to the intumescent consciousness among them ventilating their buzzing hopes and sizzling aspirations. Albeit, exchange of ideas took the room between the people of British Orissa and the garjats. Early in 20th century a few more periodicals were published in the garjats. From Talcher was brought out 'The Gadajata Basini' and from Patna, 'The Sanatan Dharma'.[8] These periodicals made the people conscious about their socio- economic condition as compared to their counterparts in the British Orissa, who were in better condition.

Political activities first grew in the garjats of Orissa. But due to lack of support, modern facilities and education, political organisations or institutions could not be brought into limelight. The greatest lacuna that remained with the leaders and workers of British Orissa in the early decades of 20th century was that they hardly pressed upon including in their demands the garjats the most vital portion of the natural Orissa. Impact of the West and contact with the West touched the princely states as much as the coastal Orissa under the British. At the beginning the rajas and zamindars took the leadership in the movement for a separate province of Orissa and naturally they were partly responsible for arousing consciousness in their respective states. This consciousness did not limit itself to the question of linguistic province only. It was certainly directed against the feudatory elements taking recourse to the subjugation of the people.

The Utkal Sammilani (Utkal Union Conference) which was established in December 1903 in British Orissa was attended by some feudatory chiefs, zamindars and the common people of the princely states. Forty-four (44) branches of the Sammilani were established in the princely States of Mayurbhanj, Talcher, Kharswan[9] and others. Talcher was the first state where one branch and four sub-branches of Utkal Sammilani were established and the second being the feudatory state of Mayurbhanj,[10] Ananta Mishra was entrusted with the propaganda work in the princely states for launching democratic movement. He toured in the states of Ranpur, Nayagarh, Athgarh and Tigiria and preached among the people about the aims and objectives of Utkal Sammilani. He was well received by the feudatory Chiefs and was assured of better administration in their respective states.[11]

By the time the World War I broke out in 1914, the feudatory Chiefs of Orissa contributed a sum of Rs. 54,000 at the initiation of the Maharaja of Sonepur for the purchase of two aeroplanes as gift to the British army for use in the War. Mayurbhanj too donated another aeroplane for the War.[12] During the War political activities and organisational works were slow in British Orissa. But a few anarchical activities were seen both in British Orissa and the princely states.

Right from the beginning of the First World War, a group of 'Babajis' under the leadership of Shreemat Goswami Aguya Maharaj alias Divyasingha Dev, the exiled Gajapati of Puri, started anti-British activities moving from place to place. He started a Math at Jagulipatna in Khurda.[13] In 1915 he went to the princely states of Baramba and Narasinghapur and preached that the British would be defeated and driven from India and that he would be made the Emperor. Since the group was operating from Khurda and was under surveillance, the Government of British India thought to be vigilant on the group so that it did not disturb the people of the princely states.[14] Immediate steps were taken to arrest the involved characters. Their movements were prohibited in the garjat states as well as in the British India provinces.

Militant nationalism grew in Bengal. The anarchical activities had a tremendous impact upon the garjats, the first being Nilgiri.[15] Taking into account the severity of the activities every possible steps were taken to prevent the feudatory states 'being used as hiding place or rendezvous for these anarchists'.[16] Strict precautions were observed against suspicious strangers and characters. Police and Chowkidars were organised 'to track them down and arrest them and also to detain any suspicious person passing through or any stranger in disguise'.[17] A constant watch was kept over any such persons and of any matter affecting the 'internal political situation'.[18]

With the emergence of M.K. Gandhi in the national struggle, a change took over in the political activities all over the country. Satyagraha started every where and Gandhiji's clarion call flared the atmosphere. The princely states stood no exception to it. The satyagrahis started hawking proscribed literature and circulating unregistered papers in the states of Orissa.[19] Gandhiji's urge for non-co-operation movement in 1921 awakened everybody in the country. His visit to Orissa had a great impetus on the people of both British Orissa and the feudatory states. There was immediate response in the state of Sonepur.[20] Gradually it spread to other areas, such as Keonjhar and Kharswan.

The administration of the rulers of the princely states of Orissa had evoked deep reaction from the people at different times. During the first three decades of the 20th century there were several small risings in those states primarily aimed at the removal of maladministration and other economic grievances and in most of the cases the rulers suppressed those risings with strong hands.

The impact of the mass movements of the freedom struggle in 1921 and in 1930-32 slowly penetrated into the inaccessible land and the people realised the importance of basic civil and political rights.

The political history of 1930-31 is a tale of constant agitation.[21] The Utkal Congress organisation opened a branch named 'Garjat Praja Sammilani' (Orissa States' People's Conference) in May 1931 in order to organise the people of the princely states.[22] The Congress workers poured into the garjats for propaganda. Some of them went to Nayagarh and persuaded the people to use 'Charakha' and hand-spun cloths.[23] The Congress workers of Sambalpur instigated the people of Bamra not to pay high rents and thus, a no-rent campaign began there.[24] The Congress, too, openly condemned the autocratic rule of the feudatory chiefs. The Congress workers advised also the rulers to introduce election system and to hand over the responsibility of administering the state to those elected persons. A democratic form of government was proposed in every princely state. At the same time, the Congress demanded that people should be given liberty of speech, liberty of holding meetings and for changing the old fashioned laws. The Congress proposed a free press in every state and emphasised giving independence to the people in the garjats. But the ruling chiefs did not pay any heed to it as they themselves stood anti-Congress and anti-nationalist.[25] Still, organisational work in the garjats continued.

A meeting of the 'Garjat Praja Sammilani' was convened on 19-20 June 1931 at Cuttack[26] under the guidance of Radhanath Rath, Balunkeshwar Acharya, Madhusudan Patnaik and Govinda Chandra Mishra and Braja Sundar Das which was presided over by Bhubanananda Das, Member of Indian Legislative Council. Many people from the princely states of Talcher, Hindol, Pal-lahara, Dhenkanal, Athgarh, Tigiria, Narasinghpur, Nayagarh, Daspalla, Ranpur, Nilgiri and Keonjhar attended the meeting.[27] The objectives of the meeting were to keep good relationship between the rajas and the subjects, to improve the standard of living of the people, improve education, health, agriculture, trade and commerce and industry of the garjats and to establish night school and to distribute books and to do all other general village development works of the garjats and etc. But the organisation soon 'sank into a state of inactivity'.[28]

Representatives from different princely states of Orissa went to attend the All India Native States' People's Conference so that they would be able to discuss about the socio-economic and political situation of the states. About three to four representatives went to participate the meeting of the conference held at Bombay in June 1931, in orde · to ventilate their grievances and to seek the co-operation of the national leaders.[29] The Indian States People's Conference issued a leaflet from Bombay regarding the celebration of the 'State People's Week'. The week fixed for the Orissa states was the third week of August 1931. And during that week, efforts were launched by the volunteers to approach people of the states in order to obtain their signatures to a mass memorial and to enrol them as members of the conference.[30] Bidyadhar Singh Deo, a representative from Orissa was elected member of a committee of the conference who made a tour in the princely states of Mayurbhanj and Dhenkanal in order to mobilise the people's movement. He persuaded the people to join the movement in large numbers.[31]

In the meanwhile, an Enquiry Committee had been formed to know in detail about the oppressive acts of the ruling chiefs and the socio-economic condition of the people. Such an attempt was most welcome to all the native states of the country. In March 1930 public opinion was raised to form such a committee in Orissa.[32] But the people of the garjats of Orissa could not appreciate it as it had no impact upon them. They could not also join the All India Movement. On the other hand, exploited and tortured by the ruling chiefs, many people left their homes and took shelter in the neighbouring areas of British Orissa[33] where the nationalist movement was at its height. British Orissa became the training ground for those immigrants, who afterwards, led the democratic movement in the princely states of Orissa.

Within a couple of years political situation in Orissa changed to a great extent. On 1 April 1936 Orissa became a separate province comprising six British administered districts of Balasore, Puri, Cuttack, Angul, Sambalpur and Ganjam. The Princely States were not included and hence a different feeling spread in these areas. The Orissa States People's Conference (Garjat Praja Sammilani) became very active in its organisation and upheld the same tempo to lead the movement in the princely states.

In 1936-37 fresh attempts were made to revitalise the organisation by Sarangdhar Das and others and the second session of Orissa States' People's Conference was held at Cuttack on 23 June 1937 under the presidency of the Congress leader Pattabhi Sitaramayya. He emphasised the need for awakening the people of the Feudatory States of Orissa and claimed that their immense potentialities must be unfolded before their vision.[34] He also appealed to the people of the states to come in line with their fellow country men in British India for the national cause.

The conference adopted several resolutions and also its constitution. The object of the conference was declared to be the attainment of responsible government by the people of the states and all bonafide residents of the Orissa states above the age of 18 who subscribed to the object of the conference were eligible for membership. Provision was also made for starting State People's Association in each of the Orissa States. The conference also strongly urged upon the rulers of the Orissa State for immediate conferring upon their subjects rights of occupancy on their holdings and fundamental rights of citizenship.[35]

The attention of the rulers was also drawn to the widespread distress among their subjects caused by the illegal exactions like 'Rasad', 'Magan', 'Bethi', etc. and the conference strongly urged upon them for total abolition of such evil practices. In order to investigate and report on such illegalities in the states, the conference appointed a committee consisting of Satish Chandra Bose, Balabanta Rai Mehta and Braja Sundar Das as members and Sarangdhar Das as the Convenor.[36] The Orissa States People's Conference in 1937 paved the ground for the formation of political associations in the states to awaken its people and also tried to focus the attention of all concerned in removing their grievances. The situation took a favourable turn by the installation of a popular Congress ministry in Orissa in July 1937 which inspired the people in the princely states and kindled new hopes in them. Some Congress leaders also were now interested in the problem and devoted their time and energy to rouse the people against their oppressive rulers.

The second meeting of the working committee of the Orissa States People's Conference was held at Janakinath Swaraj Bhavan of Oriya Bazar Cuttack on Sunday, 3 July 1938[37] under the chairmanship of Kabiraj Balunkeswar Acharya. Radhanath Rath, Govind Chandra Mishra, Madhusudan Patnaik, Gadadhar Mishra, Harmohan Patnaik and Sarangdhar Das were present in the meeting along with the invitee-members, Balabanta Rai Mehta, Lalmohan Patnaik, Harekrushna Mahtab, Narayan Charan Samanta Simhar, Srikant Rout and Banchhanidhi Senapati.[38] Among others, the most important resolution passed, was that the members of the Conference would be deputed to procure documentary evidence of the existing grievances in the states. The Working Committee too accepted the creed of the Conference and desired to work under its general guidance and supervision. The Working Committee of the All India States' People's Conference was requested to grant affiliation to the Orissa People's Conference as soon as possible.[39]

'Prajamandal' Movement

Under such political situations, some Congress leaders- Nabakrushna Choudhury, Malati Devi, Harekrushna Mahtab, Bhagabati Charan Panigrahi, Surendranath Dwivedi and Ananta Patnaik among others became interested in the problem and exerted to organise "Prajamandals" or People's Associations in the States. They were organised to secure better administration and legitimate rights and privileges for the subjects. The rulers were not prepared either to redress wrongs or grant rights and privileges to subjects. Consequently the problem became complex and serious and widespread unrest prevailed in several states.[40] A brief account of the movement is given here to understand the unrest.

The period of movement has suitably been divided into three phases- first phase, 1938-39, from the post 1936 to the outbreak of 2nd World War, second phase, 1940-44, the War period and the last phase, 1946-1947, the post war period to Independence of India. Towards the end of the last phase of the movement a new political trend was seen, which resulted in the take-over of the feudatory state of Nilgiri and subsequently, merger of rest of the princely states.

With Nilgiri in the beginning, the Prajamandal movements in the princely states of Orissa reached a degree with much vigour and dynamism. The leaders demanded the formation of democratic institution through elected representatives of the people in the States. To spread up the movement different political parties such as the Congress, the Socialists and the Communists came forward. The Congress and the Socialist leaders realised that the federation of India according to the provision of the Government of India Act, 1935 had strengthened the position of the feudatory chiefs who were thus emboldened to persist in their repressive policies. The leaders of the movement strongly condemned the inhuman practices prevalent in the states and so started a campaign to expose the conditions that were the direct cause of the sufferings of the people. The Communists too supported the movement because of the growing economic condition of the people.

In the first phase, the princely states of Nilgiri, Talcher, Dhenkanal, Nayagarh, Khandpara, Ranpur and Athgarh took prominent role. Comparatively less degree of role was played by Hindol, Athmalik, Bamra, Sonepur and Boudh. Nilgiri was the first state in Orissa where the movement manifested itself in a vigorous form.[41]

After the formation of Prajamandal in June 1938 in **Nilgiri**, the people started their movement to secure legitimate rights such as recognition of the elementary rights of citizenship and removal of restrictions on the civil liberties of the people.[42] They sent memorials both to the Raja of Nilgiri, Kishore Chandra Mardaraj Harichandan and to the Political Department of India. Since this ended in fiasco, the people took resort to non-violent agitation against which the Raja promulgated strict rules and orders. But people defied the orders. The Congress and the Socialists patronised the movement. Congress workers from Balasore poured into Nilgiri to activise it. Consequently, 116 persons were arrested.[43] But they went on a hunger strike. In support of them and against the repressive act of the Raja of Nilgiri a meeting was held on 9 June 1938 in Cuttack Town Hall organised by Kabiraj Balunkeshwar Acharya, Sarangdhar Das, Harekrushna Mahtab and Radhanath Rath.[44] The meeting made several allegations against the Raja of Nilgiri.

The Congress ministry in Orissa under the premiership of Sri Biswanath Das openly condemned the autocratic rule of the feudatory chiefs. The leaders at Cuttack planned to spread the Prajamandal Movement to other princely states later.[45] The Congress leaders of Nilgiri under their chief, Kailash Chandra Mohanty took active initiation in driving the movement intensively. Similarly, the Communists under Banamali Das championed the cause of the poor peasant of Nilgiri.[46] Thus, political movement rapidly grew under the leadership of three politicai organisations : the Prajamandal, the Congress and the Communists.

As situation became serious, a settlement was thought to be an immediate need. Negotiation for amicable settlement started between the Political Agent and the ruling chief on one side, and the President and the Secretary of Nilgiri, on the other. But no fruitful result came out. Agitational activities continued and the arrest of Banamali Das added much dimension to them. The state authorities reacted sharply and applied wanton force on the agitators. On 10th August 1938 the State Police resorted to firing on the agitators and injured many. The ruthless measures continued for three days.[47]

At that critical juncture, H.K. Mahtab, a prominent Congress leader of Orissa and Chairman of the State People's Enquiry Committee, began negotiation with the ruler of the state and the Political Agent for some settlement of the issue. Finally, the Raja agreed to concede all the demands of the Prajamandal except those that referred to the formation of the State Assembly and control of the State Budget. Peace was restored for the time being.[48]

People's agitation in the states of **Talcher** and Dhenkanal, in the border of the district of Cuttack, took a serious turn by September 1938. Talcher Prajamandal was formed on 6 September 1938 at a meeting held at Kosala in Angul presided over by Pabitramohan Pradhan. Other prominent leaders of the movement were Dasharathi Pani, Maguni Chandra Pradhan, Gaurisankar Pradhan and Krutibash Rath. On 16 September another mammoth gathering of several thousand persons was held at the same venue where the people openly accepted the call of the Prajamandal and declared their intention to fight till the last for fulfillment of their demands.[49]

Soon after the Prajamandal submitted its charter of demands to the ruler of Talcher, severe suppressive measures followed from the state authority to break the backbone of the movement. Inspite of arrests, firings, loot and arson the people did not give up their fight.

Being restive of the repressive measures of the ruler, the people of Talcher by November 1938 decided to adopt a novel course of action. They started pouring down from their own villages to the neighbouring area of Angul in British Orissa. The Prajamandal leaders claimed that influx to be about 60 thousand. By a modest estimate atleast 30 thousand people had actually come away from the state.[50] Such an unprecedented exodus drew the attention of many Congress leaders and philanthropists in the country including Gandhiji. It was no doubt, a novel method in the movement for liberty in the states. The camp works were supervised by leaders like Girijabhushan Dutta, representative of Angul, Laxmidhar Rai Choudhury and Saibani Dei.[51] Immediately, there was an urgent meeting among all the feudatory chiefs of Orissa on the issue of 'hizrat' in Talcher. As a result, extradition warrants were issued by the feudatory chiefs against the agitators who left their states. Simultaneous oppressive measures were intensified to quell the movement in Talcher. The people, however, remained undaunted and fought for freedom with resolute earnestness.

In January 1939, A.V. Thakkar Bapa, Prof. N.G. Ranga, M.L.A of Madras, Rajendra Prasad, a veteran Congress leader, Miss Agatha Harrison, Lady Member of British Parliament, and C.F. Andrews, a philanthropist visited the camps of the people who had migrated from Talcher narrated harrowing details of the sufferings of those people. Gandhiji was very much moved to hear the details of the episode and appealed to the philanthropic institutions and relief societies to rush succour to the people. The Congress Ministry in Orissa also did their best to mitigate the distress of the people. Prof. Ranga advised the Congress leaders to start a 'State Refugees Relief Fund', at the same time, issued a statement to the press regarding the inhuman cruelty meted out to the innumerable persons of Talcher. Similarly, Miss Agatha Harrison took keen interest in the problems of the refugees. She assured them of redressing their grievances. Captain Woods of the Salvation Army interviewed Kishore Chandra Birabar Harichandan, Raja of Talcher, the leaders of the camps and other important persons in an attempt to effect a solution to the refugee problems. However, his attempts proved failure since the raja refused to cancel the extradition warrants, or to allow the tenants to participate in the state administration.[52] C.F.Andrews who had himself seen the miserable condition of the people in the camps, brought it to the notice of the British authorities in New Delhi and also gave it publicity outside India. The unprecedented migration of the people from Talcher created a lot of sensation in different circles.[53]

In the meantime, attempts were made to bring about a reconciliation between the ruler and his subjects. By the force of the ruler finally agreed to give some important concessions to the people and an agreement on the matter was signed on 21 March 1939 between Major Hannessey, Assistant Political Agent of Orissa States and H.K. Mahtab, the former representing the ruler and the latter the aggrieved people of Talcher.[54] This was popularly known as the Hannessey- Mahtab Pact. But even after the agreement was signed, the ruler tried to play mischief and he did not make an open declaration to that effect. Naturally, the people refused to return to their villages without a positive assurance. Gandhiji took up the issue with Lord Linlithgow[55] and finally the ruler of Talcher yielded to the political pressure from above and a declaration granting important concessions to the people was made on 23 June 1939.[56] The people returned to their villages by the end of June, and peace was restored. At last extradition warrants were withdrawn from 42 persons in August 1939.

The World War II broke out on 1 September 1939. And the Talcher Prajamandal movement took altogether a different course.

Political agitation started in **Dhenkanal** in the first quarter of 1938. The Socialists first raised their voice in April 1938 against the oppressive ruler, Shankar Pratap Singh Deo Mahindra Bahadur, Raja of Dhenkanal.[57] Gradually the Congress leaders too supported the Socialists. Prajamandal was formed in Dhenkanal in the first week of September 1938. The Prajamandal workers demanded for grant of constitutional rights. Haramohan Patnaik, a student leader and Brundaban Dhal, an ex-Assistant Commissioner of Police, took keen interest in mobilising the people against the unnecessary taxation of the ruler.[58] The Prajamandal advanced their 39 demands repeatedly in meetings, through papers and their representative body.[59] The agitators of Dhenkanal and of the neighbouring areas armed with weapons, assembled in large number and started demonstration. The situation became so tense that the state authorities resorted to open firing on the Prajamandal workers. Still, agitation continued. A futile compromise reached between H.K. Mahtab, Sarangdhar Das and Malati Choudhury from the side of the Prajamandal, and the Political Agent and the Raja of Dhenkanal from the Government side.[60]

Radhanath Rath, Sarangdhar Das and other organised meeting in the Town Hall of Cuttack in support of the agitators of Dhenkanal.[61] The Congress ministry in Orissa refused to provide police force to the ruling chiefs of the garjats and thus only supported the cause of the garjat people.[62] Laxmi Narayan Sahoo, Nabakrushna Choudhury and Malati Choudhury held several meetings at Sukinda and Jenapur in the district of Cuttack to gain their support in shape of money and men.[63] These leaders also persuaded the people of Dhenkanal to leave the state in order to be saved from oppression. Consequently, a large number of people fled to Mogulbandi areas.

Inspite of this exodus of people, the Prajamandal Movement in Dhenkanal never died down. A historical episode took place on 11 October 1938 in Dhenkanal. The State Police fired upon the people at Nilakanthapur near the river-bank of Brahmani.[64] The Prajamandal worker, it is said, resisted the State Police to cross the river. As the Police rowed over the boat, the agitating people, it is alleged, stoned them and the Police began firing on the mob to disperse them. Consequently, six persons, Laxmana Malik, Nata Malik, Raghu Naik, Guri Naik, Hurushi Padhan and a twelve-year old boy, named Baji Rout, were shot dead.[65] Such heinous treatment meted out to the agitators was strongly resented by the public of Orissa. The dead bodies were then carried to Cuttack where post-mortem was done and then taken to the burial ground of Khannagar on a large procession on the bank of river Katjuri, for cremation.[66] But it was mentioned that the dead-bodies were cremated in the burial ground of Kaliaboda of Cuttack.[67]

All over Orissa people of all sections condemned such an act and sympathised with the people of Dhenkanal. Sarangdhar Das suggested that henceforward the Prajamandal workers, instead of taking shelter in Mogulbandi areas, should start non-violent agitation in garjats. Prof. N. Ranga and Gandhiji desired to know details of the incident.[68]

Prajamandal movement continued unabated. The people pledged to 'Do or Die' and shouted in the name of Mahatma Gandhi hoisting the Congress flag. But there was mass arrest in Dhenkanal. The Government of India sent the Resident of the Orissa Feudatory States to Dhenkanal to study the situation. The Raja of Dhenkanal, finally promised to redress their grievances. He released some prisoners, reduced the cess-tax by two pices, allowed to cut down wood from the reserve-forests, to kill the wild animals who destroyed the crops and lifted license on contract over betel leaves. But the people were dissatisfied since the Raja warned the people of the withdrawal of these concessions if the agitators did not refrain from agitation.[69] Hence the agitation continued.

The Congress and the Socialist leaders of Orissa fully supported the Prajamandal movement in the states and denounced the oppression of the rulers on their subjects. It was Pandit Godavaris Misra who advocated the cause of the ruling chiefs of Orissa in his paper, entitled 'Lokamata'. His resignation from Orissa Assembly was demanded by the Socialists.[70] Throughout December 1938 the political affairs in Dhenkanal engaged the attention of the leading politicians of Orissa. People fought with unstinted vigour. The Raja of Dhenkanal had no option but to allow the representatives of the Prajamandal to associate themselves in the administration of the state. Though the gesture was conciliatory to some extent, it could not fulfil the aspirations of the people as their demands fell nothing short of the establishment of a full responsible government and guarantee of civil liberties.[71]

Prajamandal movement in Dhenkanal was steered more towards constitutional way during the first quarter of 1939. In May 1939 the movement entered a quieter phase with the hope of getting legitimate grievances redressed by the authorities. On 26 June 1939, the Raja of Dhenkanal, Shankar Pratap Singh Deo Mahindra Bahadur announced in his 'darbar' a number of measures regarding reforms for improvement of administration in the state. Since no fixed date was earmarked as to when the proposed reforms would be implemented, it brought considerable doubt in the minds of the agitators as to integrity of the ruler's purpose. Thus, the situation in Dhenkanal did not apparently improve and the movement continued till the demands were achieved.[72]

Prajamandal was formed in **Ranpur** followed by Nilgiri in June 1938. To know the political developments elsewhere, people subscribed to different local and national newspapers and periodicals. Birabar Krushna Chandra Singh Deo Bajradhar Narendra Mohapatra, Raja of Ranpur prohibited the people from reading those newspapers but himself subscribed to English newspapers.[73] As a result, people reacted to such an action of the Raja. The Prajamandal of Ranpur vehemently criticised the state activities. It also condemned the Raja who had not made land settlements since sixty years. The Prajamandal leaders planned to give a new direction to the movement-first, educating the workers about the democratic organisation, its aims and objectives ; second, proper discipline and co-ordination among the workers.[74] While the democratic organisation was mobilising, atleast, 14,000 people out of total population of 47,711 of Ranpur, within a short period, a violent incident occurred in the first week of January 1939, which shocked and alarmed the whole country.

The Prajamandal was declared unlawful and some of the leaders were imprisoned. The situation was tense and on 5 January 1939 a large number of people gathered near the palace and demanded the immediate release of their leaders. The ruler informed the matter to Major R.L. Bazalgette, the Political Agent, who was present in Nayagarh, a neighbouring state, and soon the latter arrived on the scene. He wanted to disperse the crowd, but they refused to listen to him. As violence broke out Major Bazalgette fired two shots from his revolver with provocation from the people on the spot and two persons died instantaneously. It further incited the mob and they attacked the Major with their bamboo sticks and snatched away his revolver. He succumbed to the violence of the people in no time. H.K. Mahtab gives a graphic account of the scene in his autobiography 'Sadhanar Pathe'. By a strange coincidence he reached the spot a few hours after the death of Bazalgette in that evening and promptly cautioned the people about possible repercussions of the incident.[75]

The killing of the Political Agent was condemned by the Congress leaders in the country. Gandhiji, Subhas Bose, Jawaharlal Nehru, President of All India States People's Conference, Biswanath Das, Premier of Orissa and many others issued strong statements regarding the matter. The Congress Working Committee passed the following resolution :

"The Working Committee record their deep regret at the killing of Major Bazalgette by a crowd at Ranpur in Orissa and are of opinion that such acts of violence do great injury to the course of freedom in the States. The Committee have welcomed the awakening among the people of the states and look forward to their deliverance, but they are convinced that resort to mob violence will delay that deliverance. The Committee, therefore, earnestly trust that the people of the states as well as those in other parts of India strictly adhere to peaceful methods in the struggle for freedom".[76]

The aftermath of murder of Bazalgette was very serious. Most of the people of Ranpur and its adjoining villages left their homes and took shelter in the jungles in Mogulbandi and in the Khasmahals like Khurda, Sunakhala, Bolgarh, Siko, Tangi, Olasingh and Banpur.[77] The Government of Orissa sent police force from Cuttack and Puri to Ranpur. Ranpur turned into a desert, having no men, women, children, cattle etc. Every house was searched by the Police Force and looted. Order to 'shoot at sight' was issued. Further, 200 British soldiers were sent to Ranpur to maintain peace and orders.[78] Preliminary enquiry into the murder of the Major was entrusted to the Deputy Magistrate of Puri, the Inspector of Police and to the C.I.D. Six persons involved in the murder case were arrested by 15 January and thirty-one by 4 February 1939.[79]

Later on, Raghunath Mohanty, Dibakar Parida and Chintamani Naik were sentenced to death. Hata Naik, Bhagabat Behera, Krushna Rout, Antar Kailash, Banka Swain, Bhagaban Sahoo, Maji Naik and Narasingha Sahoo were transported for life. Six persons were acquitted and sentenced to transportation for life, were sent to Keonjhar jail.[80] The Raja of Ranpur was deprived of his ruling power in July 1940 and consequently, the state was taken under direct administration of the British Government.[81]

Before the Prajamandal could be effective in **Nayagarh** the people exasperated by the most pitiable socio-economic condition had been striving with discontent. From the thirties of the 20th century, injustice, corruption, extortion and maladministration reigned supreme in Nayagarh. All the time Krushna Chandra Singh, Raja of Nayagarh, lived in foreign countries and the entire state administration was entrusted to the diwans who were mostly recruited from outside the state.[82] Early in 1938 situation suddenly began to deteriorate in Nayagarh.

The state officials were very much oppressive. More than half of the state income went to the pockets of these officials. Illegal taxes on road, opium, betel, ganja etc. were imposed on the people. No native people were given appointment even in the low salaried employments of the state Darbar.[83] The little welfare works were done even on 'bethi'. The Public Works Department of the state was running on loss. There was acute shortage of water and people had to trek long distance for the collection of the same in summer. In the rainy season the torrential rivers overflowed and inundated their paddy lands and houses. Many did not even get straw to thatch their houses. They had to live in open air under the scorching sun.[84] When people went to appeal to the Raja of Nayagarh, the State Officials did not allow them to do so.

The most devastating condition of the people was in regard to the imposition of monopoly of betel and 'tamakhu'. It was famous as 'betel agitation' in Nayagarh. Betel was sold at high rate. People started boycotting consuming betels. About 500 agitators made appeal to the higher authorities, stating the fact that this newly introduced betel monopoly was made due to extra expense incurred in the frequent tours of the Raja to Puri and Calcutta.[85] The agitators like Narayan Nanda and Bharat Sahoo, Biswanath Mishra, Ganapati Ram, Banchhanidhi Panda and Akrusa Mohanty were dragged to the Police Station and were severely beaten by the Police.

General condition of people was very much miserable as there was no rain in the months of June, July and August 1938 for cultivation of their lands, and no food for them to survive. Persons owning acres of land had to go for cooli work on the streets.[86] There were cries for help everywhere in the state. At such a cross-road of socio-economic crisis the Prajamandal was formed following Nilgiri. Guided by the Congress, the Nayagarh Prajamandal first started Swadeshi movement in the state.[87] People used 'charakha' and wore hand-spun khadar. The movement continued for months together. As Nayagarh was famous for agrarian revolution in the past, a Kisan Movement started in December 1938. When the movement went out of control, an ordinance was issued by the ruler prohibiting meetings and processions within the limits of his state. But the ordinance went in vain. A large section of the people assembled before the palace of the raja and demanded the release of their leaders. The raja, out of fear, released them and the Prajamandal workers on 9 January 1939.[88] With the outbreak of the Second World War in September, the movement entered into a quieter period.

The princely state of **Khandpara** underwent socio-economic and political deterioration during the first three decades of the 20th Century. In the thirties, things went pitiful. Extra illegal taxes were imposed on betel, beedi, salt and sugarcane. 'Bethi' and 'Begari' were in vogue. No communication facility existed in the state. On the other hand, Harihar Singh Mardaraj Bhramarbar Ray, Raja of Khandpara, enjoyed flying by purchasing aeroplane and motor cars. Hundreds of educated people rose against the oppression and misrule of the Raja in August 1935. When rigorous repressive measures followed, large number of persons fled, out of fear, to the neighbouring British administered territories.[89]

Prajamandal was formed in Khandpara towards September 1938. People through the Prajamandal demanded civil liberty and self-government.[90] In July 1939 the Prajamandal further demanded recognition of the Association of the elected representatives of tenants. The agitation assumed its much velocity. So, the Raja applied all methods of repression including severe assault, rigorous imprisonment and social boycott.[91] Even the family members of the leaders who lived in British territories, were tortured and forcibly driven back to the state homes. Despite the opposition, the Prajamandal movement carried on its struggle for independence in the latter half of 1939.

Sparkles of political events were clearly visible in the feudatory state of **Athgarh** right from the third decade of the 20th century. Srikaran Radhanath Bebarta Patnaik, Raja of Athgarh spent 10% of the total income of the state in purchasing motor cars and aeroplane.[92] He also prohibited export of goods from his state to Cuttack which caused a great harm to the trading circles of Athgarh.[93] In 1935 the Raja by stamp abolished 'bethi' from his state, but the people continued paying bethi and other illegal taxes.[94]

After the historic episode of October 1938 in Dhenkanal, Prajamandal was formed in Athgarh. With its birth political situation underwent a metamorphosis. Repressive acts were started by the Raja. The state authorities resorted to firing on the Prajamandal workers causing the death of one person. Besides, many were arrested on various charges as well as they attended the political meetings at Cuttack.[95] Leaders like Ananta Mohapatra, Achyutananda Das and Radhanath Rath, Raghab Gajendra, Raghunath Dalsinghara and Dhaneswar Dhal led the movement in Athgarh. A procession of 400 people marched to the Raj palace through Darshanpur and Birakishorepur and shouted slogans like 'Inqulab Zindabad', 'Mahatma Gandhi ki Jai' etc. The police charged the mob with lathis and arrested many of them.[96] Nevertheless, the movement continued under the guidance of Radhanath Rath and Chakradhar Patnaik who had been conducting it from a village called Malabiharpur.[97] The state officials were kept vigilant to maintain peace and order in the state. About 12 armed police and a few volunteers were posted at Athgarh from 26 October to 31 October 1938 to safeguard the town and the Raj Palace. People, out of fear fled to the nearby areas of Banki and Gholapur. The Prajamandal leaders persuaded the people to leave the state for Mogulbandi areas. Such a political situation in Athgarh drew the serious attention of all concerned. The Raja of Athgarh, finally, held a darbar on 12 November 1938 in which he issued a proclamation giving certain concessions to the people's demands like monopoly-licence on betel, beedi, tamakhu and kerosene etc. was lifted temporarily, interest on arrear Taccavi loans was exempted and the Panchayat System in vogue was replaced by another specially meant for the welfare of the people, etc.[98] These concessions, somehow, pacified the movement and throughout the Second World War, Athgarh passed through a dormant period.

Sambalpur Group of States

The tyrannical monopoly of the feudatory chiefs of Orissa evoked among the people of Sambalpur a strong feeling of resentment against the rulers, and aroused their sympathy for the oppressed mass of the states. Meetings on 13, 24 and 25 June 1938 were held at Sambalpur under the leadership of H.K. Mahtab, Balabanta Rai Mehta and Sarangadhar Das in which the Congress leaders vehemently criticised the evils prevailing in the feudatory states.

'Nilgiri Day' was observed in Sambalpur in a meeting held on 27 July 1938. On 1 September 1938 'Kisan Day' was observed in various places of Sambalpur. Congress people who organised this meeting, discussed about the Kisans who dealt on various ills and injustices, and untold sufferings both in the state and British India. An All India crisis was felt impending. Therefore, a meeting was held on 12 February 1939 at Balibandan of Sambalpur town where resolutions were passed 'expressing grave concern of the people over the situation arising out of the warpath adopted by Rajkot and other states authorities, and calling upon the people of Sambalpur to be ready for the movement, apprehended by Pandit Jawaharlal Nehru against the repressive policies of the state rulers'.[99] The political unrest in different princely states and crisis in the Congress circle were discussed in the meeting and the people were exhorted to unite in combined strength against the British Government.

Prajamandal in Sonepur was formed towards the last quarter of 1938. By 1939 about two thousand people were enrolled as members of Prajamandal. Mohan Mishra and Lakshman Satapathi, on behalf of the Prajamandal, presented a demand sheet to the ruler of Sonepur on 15 March 1939, but were arrested. Soon, Bhimsen Bhoi and his friends offered Satyagraha on 23 March. Thus, started an agitation against Sudhanshu Sekhar Singh Deo, Raja of Sonepur, early in 1939. The state authorities arrested some of the leaders. Nevertheless, the movement continued, the village Gond Turum being the centre of their activities.[100]

Intermittent campaign and vigorous agitation since 1937 were already directed against the neighbouring states of Orissa. Burma was one of the feudatory states where Congress activities were dynamic and strong. Dibakar Mishra, an active Congress Worker of Bamra, since 1937, joined the Bamra Prajamandal movement, and hence was banished from the state by the ruler. Managovind Das, an active Congressite of Bamra suffered imprisonment at the hands of the state authorities because of his participation in the Non-cooperation movement of 1921.[101]

Prajamandal activities albeit spread to Boudh, Hindol, Athmalik, Rairakhol etc. Consequent upon the formation of Prajamandals in Hindol and Athmalik, the state authorities adopted suppressive measures quickly. The agitators were implicated in false cases. In December 1939 the Prajamandal leaders and the refugees of the camps in Hindol were greatly agitated at such actions of the ruler. 'Bethi' continued in the state. A booklet named 'Hindol Rahashya' deprecating the repressive acts of the ruler was widely circulated.[102] In Athmalik too, oppressive measures were adopted by the ruler to quell the agitation. But the leaders did all they could to strengthen their organisation.[103]

The agitation in the princely states was thus transformed into a part of the wider movement carried on in British India for the achievement of independence and the establishment of a popular democratic government in the whole country. The agitation in the state was intensely associated with support to the All India Policy of the parent national organisation.[104]

The outbreak of World War II brought about predominant changes in the politico-economic parlance of India including the states. The Government of India launched war time measures and issued instructions to the ruling chiefs to put down any squabble in the states under the Defence India Rules. Mahatma Gandhi urged the people to suspend Satyagraha for the time being. But people throughout the country grew violent against the British Government in August 1942. The princely states of Orissa had upheld the banner of the agitation even from 1940.[105] Constitutional and administrative reforms were introduced since 1939 in the states of Baramba, Narasinghpur, Tigiria, Dhenkanal, Athmalik, Nayagarh, Ranpur, Bonai, Gangpur, Boudh, Rairakhol and Saraikella by the authorities in order to divert the agitators' attention from further agitational course. Still the movement continued.

'Bethi' and 'Begari' were long standing customs in the states. The abolition of such systems was introduced in 1923. But the abuses were not completely annihilated. During the agitation of 1938 and 1939 many concessions including the abolition of 'bethi' and 'begari' were granted to the people of the states. People were hardly satisfied and therefore the movement was kept alive.

In early 1940 the Prajamandal of Khandpara discharged a bulletin (No.2) entitled 'Juddha Nian' (war fire) and distributed copies of it in Cuttack. The two persons who were in charge of distribution, were captured at Cuttack by the Police. The bulletin severely condemned the prevailing administration in the feudatory states, and the support of the British in repressing the agitating people.[106] Towards the middle of 1940 situation in the states changed. The refugees posed a great problem both for the states and the British Government. H.K. Mahtab intervened in the affair and gradually Khandpara entered into a normal phase.

Besides, democratic movements started early in 1940 in the states of Talcher, Nilgiri and Dhenkanal. Pabitramohan Pradhan, President of Talcher Prajamandal complained against the oppressive acts of the state officials. He accused the British Government of helping the rulers of the feudatory states in oppressing their subjects. In May 1940 he began enrolling satyagrahis from among the leaders and workers of Talcher Prajamandal. Moreover, he organised and convened several meetings of the Prajamandal for which he was arrested on 15 December 1940. Still meetings were held criticising the maladministration, absence of justice in the State Court, lack of constructive works such as arrangements for irrigation, education etc. But the real object was to condemn the action of the state Darbar and the Political Department in arresting the prominent members of Talcher Prajamandal.[107]

Prajamandal was started afresh in January 1941 with Kalandi Charan Pradhan as its President. Cyclostyled leaflets narrating the repressive acts of the state authorities were distributed on 7 January in Angul. A memorandum was given to the Political Agent describing the excessively high rents and demanding the remission of the same.[108] In May 1941 the Talcher Prajamandal strongly objected to the establishment of 'Byabastha Parishad' by the ruler, and criticised the state Darbar for having failed to the promises and declarations made by the Raja in 1938 regarding the constitution of the 'Byabastha Parishad'. In addition to usual criticism against the activities of the Darbars, anti-war speeches were also made in the meetings held in the British territory by the Prajamandal leaders.

The Prajamandal of Nilgiri remained very much active. In January 1940 its leaders formed a Defence Committee to render financial assistance to the victims and the socio-politically harassed people of the state. Kailash Chandra Mohanty, President of Nilgiri Prajamandal, delivered an anti-war speech at Amoodia hat (Market) in Balasore. He was arrested, tried and convicted to six months rigorous imprisonment. Banamali Das was expelled from the state as he was preaching Communism. Despite these, volunteers were recruited and selected to enrol satyagrahis in different places of the district including Nilgiri.[109]

While the people of Nilgiri strove hard to achieve the democratic form of government in the states, the state authorities persisted in quelling the movement ruthlessly. H.K. Mahtab rushed to Nilgiri to tackle the situation.[110] Mahatma Gandhi deputed Sarangadhar Das to move to the district of Sambalpur and addressed several meetings in the first week of

1941, explaining the Congress attitude towards the war and the Imperial Government.[111] He was arrested in February.

There was no political movement of any significance in any other states of Orissa during the period. The next step of agitation was taken up during the Quit India Movement of August 1942. People of both the British territories and the states joined the movements.

Impact of the Quit India Movement

Gandhi's clarion call once again was vibrated in the veins of India in August 1942. Not only the British provinces responded it with full zeal and zest but also the princely states including those of Orissa. The most immaculate movement set in motion in Dhenkanal, Talcher and Nayagarh.

The political movement in **Dhenkanal** started simultaneously with the August revolution of 1942 in the British Provinces. But the character of the movement charged with the appearance of Baishnab Charan Patnaik, a veteran leader of Dhenkanal who had been imprisoned in Sadar Jail under Section 29(1)(b) of the Defence of India Rules after the outbreak of the second World War. He was released in April 1942 under certain terms and conditions. As per the August Resolution of the Congress Working Committee at Bombay, leaders of the Congress all over India was arrested. In such a situation, Baishnab Charan Patnaik entered into Dhenkanal secretly and organised the villagers of the interior areas of the states to fight against the authorities. Shri Patnaik launched his political movement unabated.

On 25-26 August 1942, at night, he with his followers attacked and burnt the police station and the sub-divisional offices at Murhi. The party then moved towards Malpura where they were joined by about 500 people of more than 12 villages. The agitators looted the *debottar* granary of the place and distributed them among the poor people of the villages. From the above two places they looted a sum of Rs. 20,000 and some arms and ammunitions.[112] The party further moved towards Bhuban and to the state headquarters via Gandia with slogans the main content of which was that when Mahatma Gandhi was dying in prison, it was shame on the part of the state employees to serve the autocrats.

Such a grave situation compelled the Raja of Dhenkanal to seek help from the Political Agent, Orissa Feudatory states. The Raja telegraphically requisitioned a police contingent of 30 men with 15 armed men and two platoons of Joint Police Force to move to Bhuban, Murhi and Parja respectively. Further precautionary measures were taken against the agitators. The Political Agent, Orissa States, instructed the rulers of Pal-lahara, Keonjhar, Hindol, Talcher, and the Dewan of Athgarh and Tigiria to strengthen their police force on the common borders of Dhenkanal, and to cooperate with the state Darbar in providing information about the movement of Baishnab Charan Patnaik and his party, and if possible, to arrest them. To round up Baishnab Charan Patnaik and his party the raja was advised to organise immediately a mobile force of 50 constables on bicycles. Extensive and rapid patrolling started from 31 August 1942 in the northern part of Dhenkanal. At the same time, the Political Agent advised the Raja 'to cease of barking and take the reins in his own hands',[113] and tackle the situation with the help of the government force.

Despite every measure of the authorities, Baishnab Charan Patnaik ceaselessly went ahead in his political movement. His followers were very much active in Parjang and Palasuni and the enraged insurgents burnt the police station and the school at Chandpur on 4 September 1942. The attack on police station was, infact, a victory for Baishnab. Further plans were to attack the Motanga police station near the Meramundali Railway Station, then Bhapur and at last, the Dhenkanal town.

Such an alarming news made the Raja more vigilant and careful. Immediately, he sent his spies all over the state to dissuade the people from joining the agitation. More than 600 licensed guns were seized from the people. In addition to these, the Raja recruited Muslims from the districts of Cuttack and Puri for police work in the state.[114] Agitation continued, an exchange of fire took place at Jahnapara school in which one person from Baishnab's party was severely wounded and then imprisoned. In the encounter with the state police Baishnab got wounded by his forearm and head. His comrades sprang up from Angul, Talcher, Dhenkanal, Sukinda and Jajpur. Hiding themselves in the jungles of Sukinda and Palasuni Bisos, they used to get help from the nearby villages. The important leaders of the agitators moved to different places in the guise of girls, milkmaids, Kendera jogis and bearded sadhus.[115]

Meanwhile, the Congress and the Socialist leaders of British Orissa got themselves involved in the garjat movement. Nabakrushna Choudhury, Nityananda Kanungo, Rajkrushna Bose, Nilamani Panda etc. took active interest in the affairs of Dhenkanal and Talcher, but they were arrested and sent to Angul as security prisoners. Undaunted

Rajkrushna Bose instigated the school boys to cut down the telegraph and telephone lines, remove railway lines, and leave the schools to join Baishnab Charan Patnaik. Nabakrushna Choudhury took a bold step in propagating the Congress creed. He invited the Raja of Dhenkanal to join the Congress Party and be renowned among the Princes of India. He expressed his feelings that Indians of all ranks-officials and non-officials were internally inclined towards the great and only cause-independence of the country. It so happened, he went on saying, that the policeman did not actually carry out the order of the S.P. of Cuttack, but only made a show of force.[116]

In the meantime, Baishnab Charan Patnaik's head carried a reward of Rs. 3,000, but he was not traced out. One of the main supporters of him was Jayakrushna Mishra, District and Sessions Judge of Dhenkanal. He was in 'hand and gloves'[117] with Baishnab and his party and was responsible for injecting fear in the minds of the officers and others through a net-work of secret propaganda in the last agitation. Till the end of January 1943 the agitation continued. Some Mahajans (landlords) including the Marwaris played a great rule in helping the agitators with money and other necessary things.[118]

Since the situation did not improve by the end of 1942 and Baishnab Charan Patnaik could not be captured, the Political Agent, Orissa Princely states, suggested to form a 'Special Task Force' to ceaselessly pursue the agitators till they were captured. The Raja of Dhenkanal convened police cooperation meetings of all the neighbouring feudatory states in order to capture the agitators. Police officers from Keonjhar, Pallahara, Talcher, Hindol, Angul, Sukinda and Tangi attended the meetings. The Raja also convened a meeting of the people at Murhi on 2 January 1943 and advised them to refrain from agitational activities.[119] The spies employed for the purpose, proved useless.

Towards the end of 1942 Baishnab came back to Orissa after getting his medical check up at Jamshedpur and made his sojourn in Dhabaleswar and Paschimeswar of Athgarh. He also stayed at Puri, Sakhigopal, Olansingh, Khurda and Charchika. In January 1943 he went to Berhampur to seek help from Gorachand Patnaik, Biswanath Das, the reputed congress leaders, and then went to 'Madhusudan Gramyodota Sangha' to seek the advice of H.K. Mahtab.[120]

Meanwhile, the Task Force Operation started in January 1943 under the charge of Deputy Superintendent of Police of Dhenkanal. It worked out successful in curbing out the agitation in the state. Twelve out of twenty-four followers of Baishnab Charan Patnaik were arrested by March 1943. The state authorities tried to capture him from the train during his movement, but they failed. Finally, he took shelter in Sukinda under the protection of Narendra Pradhan, leader of the Bhumijas of Natum.[121] Then peace prevailed in Dhenkanal.

The Quit India Movement also had its dynamic echo in the princely state of **Talcher.** Pabitramohan Pradhan, leader of the Talcher Prajamandal joined the movement led by Baishnab Charan Patnaik. Shri Pradhan formed a parallel government in Talcher derecognising the administration of the Raja.[122] On 7 September 1942 the Talcher Prajamandal started railway strike. As per the plans, the people removed railway line, cut off telegraph lines, ransacked the post office and murdered a man in the north Talcher.[123]

The Murhi incident of 26-27 August 1942 in Dhenkanal added faggots to the fire of Talcher. The agitators detracted rail engines and displaced twenty yards of the rail on 6 September. The next day they destroyed police outposts and looted the post office at Sipur. On 9 September bridges and telegraph lines were damaged. The state authorities resorted to 12 rounds of firing killing one and wounding two other.

The Prajamandals of Dhenkanal and Talcher combinedly programmed to attack the places of the Raja of the latter state. About 8,000 agitators moved towards the place. With limited resources the Raja faced the mob with guns, spears, axes and bows. But in the encounter the Raja won the victory. When necessity arose, machine guns were used to disperse the mob.[124] In the attack 217 persons were arrested, 5 were killed and many turned injured.

Repressive measures started from the side of the state authorities. A reward of Rs. 1,800 was declared for the capture of Pabitramohan Pradhan. Later on, the amount was raised to Rs. 10,000. As a result, he had to leave Orissa and joined the 'Azad Hind Fauz' of Subhas Chandra Bose.[125] Collective fines were imposed on 35 affected villages out of a total number of 438 in the state. Criminal cases were filed against 367 persons, 211 were arrested for joining the unlawful mob. On the other hand, those from the depressed classes like Panas, Hadis (Mehentars), Doms, and aborigines like Kandhs and Savaras who did not take part in the movement, were amply rewarded by the British Government. The

Raja of Talcher was also awarded the title 'Raj Bahadur' as a personal distinction in recognition of his good and meritorious service during the August movement of 1942.[126]

The spirit of agitation in Talcher gradually died down. But the Prajamandal workers devoted themselves in constitutional works and forming the democratic organisations for the smooth running of the state administration.

In **Nayagarh** mounting tension was further aggravated due to failure of the Raja to meet the demands of the Prajamandal. To the precipitation of the situation the Raja arrested the leaders like Sridhar Das, Banchhanidhi Senapati, Laxmana Maharana, Sukru Behera, Udaynath Prusti and Bidyadhar Mantri, on 19 July 1942.[127] People started Satyagraha in the state. About 400 weavers assembled at Bolgarh on 28 September 1942 demanding the release of the Khadi centre of Dighi which had been in the possession of the police.[128] The people were determined to secure their demands through peaceful Satyagraha. But the Raja adopted repressive measures. As a result, a clash arose between the armed police and the peaceful procession of the people on 10 October 1942. On the spot Kasti Dakua was shot dead and a number of persons were wounded.[129] Oppression continued inside the jail. It was alleged that, Kanduri Parida and Budhi Parida were beaten to death inside the jail.[130] But the movement continued unabated.

Nilgiri too reacted significantly during the 1942 movement. At the outset, the elected members of the Praja Sabha of Nilgiri refused to attend the meetings convened by the Raja.[131] Two platoons of force were sent soon to the troubled spot. In the encounter, Raghu Naik and Ganga Mallik were shot dead and many persons were wounded. Ultimately, the people won and the Raja was deprived of the ruling power and sent to Ranchi in November 1942.

After the disturbances were subdued temporarily, the people settled down peacefully and the administration got good co-operation from them. A meeting of the state Praja Sabha called by the Diwan and the Assistant Diwan, and all the elected members had a discussion. A slight change in the constitution of the Praja Sabha was thought desirable. The elected members offered to cooperate in the revival of the Praja Sabha.[132]

A peaceful and constitutional movement ran amok in the feudatory state of **Majurbhanj** during the period of the World War II. Prajamandal came up in 1939 under the leadership of Sarat Chandra Das.[133] Village economic funds were created demanding legitimate civil and political rights. Elements of political agitation were slowly introduced into the state. To counteract such a strong move, the ruling chief of Mayurbhanj made a declaration to establish a Praja Sabha early in 1940. But it could not attract the people nor could it mislead the Prajamandals. In the Manitri Conference of the state Prajamandal process started for the establishment of democratic administration in the state. There was an another Conference at Ambajoda on 18 December 1940.[134] The Raja's Darbar met at the sametime to create disturbances in the state Prajamandal activities. However, the plan ended in fiasco. Albeit, the achievement of the Prajamandal drew the attention of the Congress leaders.

The first annual session of Prajamandal of Mayurbhanj was held at Kumdhia on 9-11 May 1940 under the Presidentship of Sarangdhar Das. In 1941 Prajamandal activities spread to Panchapidha, and constructive works were stressed upon. The police declared the Prajamandal illegal.Sarat Chandra Das attended the All India State People's Conference held at Bombay in 1942. But he was arrested later on. Several meetings of the Prajamandal were organised during the Quit India Movement uninterrupted by the state darbar.The third session of the Prajamandal was held in 1944 at Madhunanda of Manitri Pargana. After the collapse of the Parished another state-sponsored organisation called Prajamandal was established to counter the activities of the Prajamandal.Finally,both the counter organisations worked in the state to win over the people.But within a couple of years the Prajamandal died a natural death.[135]

Final Phase (1946-1947)

No doubt, the cataclysmic Second World War ended in May 1945, but it brought in its train tremendous political changes not only to the British provinces but also to the princely states of India. The Prajamandals became once again active. Fresh attempts were launched to instil the sense of patriotism into the minds of the people of the states under the same umbrella of the Prajamandals. The press, the students and the political parties played viable roles in materialising their goals into reality. Towards the close of the war in 1945, everybody assumed that India would get her self-government in not very distant future. The rulers of the princely states of India rightly realised that the time had come to reorganise the administration of the states lest there would be 'unfavourable criticism of states'.[136] The Government of India, at a later time, advised the rulers, especially of the states of Orissa thus : "You are entrusted with the destiny of the state, the welfare and contentment of its people. You have had time to see and gauge for yourself the trend of affairs both within and without the state".[137]

Soon after the war the Central Government decided that 'the ban on the All India Congress Committee and any existing bans on Provincial, District or lower Congress Committees or on the All India Spinners Association or branches there of should be removed'.[138] The Provincial Governments were asked to take necessary action. The Provincial Government of Orissa which was formed in April 1946[139] gave sufficient impetus to the democratic movements in the feudatory states.

Under the cloak of reforms in the states, oppression, despotism and tyranny were attempted to be hidden from the eyes of the people. But it could not remain so. As dissatisfaction continued to prevail among them, agitation went on in the states, immediately after the Second World War. The Prajamandals demanded for representing the Constitutional Assembly to be free from the exploitation by the tyrant rulers. People's struggle for freedom aroused strong sympathy in the hearts of the local public, the students community and different political parties as well as local and national press. Students were exhorted to start agitating the maladministration of the feudatory chiefs, and to organise the people of the states towards achieving the goal. The States Students' Conference was held at Cuttack on 10 February 1946, where the speakers criticised the administrative system prevailing in the states and demanded release of all the political prisoners, restoration of civil liberties and amalgamation of smaller states with the British India.[140]

Different political parties came forward with their resolutions to support the cause of the people of the states. The District Congress Committee of Sambalpur convened a meeting in October 1945 and resolutions were passed to fight against the alleged measures of reprisals adopted against the Congress by the feudatory chiefs. On 1 March 1946 'Sahid Day' was observed in various places of Sambalpur and on that occasion there was complete hartal in the district. The Communists held a mass rally on 29 May 1944 at Cuttack in order to bring about cooperation among all the political parties in achieving the common goals.[141] Congressites like N.K. Choudhury, S.N. Dwivedy and others advised the students who held a meeting of the Cuttack District Students' Congress at Cuttack on 3-4 August 1946, to be more organised to free the people from the British yoke and pressed for withdrawal of warrants of arrest and cases against the political absconders of the states.[142]

The press, both local and national, came forward in rousing the enthusiasm of the people of the states for freedom. The newspaper named 'Gadajata Tara' made a general attack on the administration of the states and drew attention to the complaints against the police and other departments of the states government.[143] 'The New Orissa' described administration of the ruling chief of Dhenkanal as 'a veritable hell on earth', since the most terrible atrocities were committed there. The paper also described the Orissa states as the creation and manifestation of British imperialism. It, therefore, urged the British to 'pension off the Ruling Chiefs and thus close a dark chapter in Indian history'.[144] 'The New Orissa' in a strong rejoinder demanded afresh the 'liquidation of the states' as soon as possible.[145] 'The Samaj' and the 'Dainik Asha' highlighted all the proceedings of the States' Workers' Conferences. H.K. Mahtab, at a meeting of the Garjat Students' Conference, remarked, "There is no legal, moral or historic justification for the retention of the Orissa states as separate entities".[146] The press immediately commended the move of H.K. Mahtab in assuring the amalgamation of the administration of the Orissa States and the Orissa Province.[147] The highlights in the press created vigorous enthusiasm among the people of states. The movement gradually took a definite course to achieve its goal.

Merger of the Princely States

The wave of nationalism helped to a great extent the integration of the princely states with the rest of India. The merger of the smaller states began in Orissa and then it spread to different parts of the country culminating in the complete elimination of the yellow patches from the map of India.

In Orissa H.K. Mahtab formed the Congress Ministry in April 1946 and then he made serious attempts for bringing about a complete change in the position of the states which ultimately ended with their merger with the province.[148]

Mahtab met the Cabinet Mission on 6 April 1946 and while discussing the political settlement of India, he raised the problem of the princely states of Orissa and pleaded for amalgamation of those states with the Provinces. He also placed a memorandum before the Mission on this matter.[149] The rulers opposed the plan of amalgamation. But Mahtab not only pleaded the case before the Cabinet Mission but also tried to convince the rulers about its urgent necessity. On 26 April he wrote to Sir Stafford Cripps complying his interest in the amalgamation of 26 Orissa states with the province of Orissa.[150]

But the Cabinet Mission was busy finalising other important matters and could not look into this specific issue. Mahtab sent two circular letters to all chiefs of the princely states of Orissa during May-June 1946. Nothing tangible came out of such endeavours–which aimed at bringing about a solution of the problems.

As soon as the proposals of the Cabinet Mission were announced, some of the rulers of Orissa and Chhatisgarh states decided to form a federal union. These rulers met at the Rajkumar College at Raipur on 21-22 December 1946 and subsequently formed the Eastern States Union which started functioning from 1 August 1947. It had an elaborate constitution and was financed by contributions from the constituent states.[151]

An attempt was made to escape harsh realities of time before the lapse of British paramountcy over those states. In fact, with the dawn of independence things began to develop so rapidly that the fond hopes of the feudatory chiefs to maintain their statusquo were completely shattered. The states ministry under Sardar Patel was compelled by the force of circumstances to take necessary steps to arrest the process of 'balkanisation' of India.

The process of integration of the Indian States began in Orissa with the assumption of administration of the Nilgiri State by the Dominion Government. Nilgiri, much discussed in this chapter, was the first state to start the popular Prajamandal movement against its autocratic ruler. It had spread like wild fire to other Orissa states. Though there were temporary settlements with the rulers, the root cause of the grievances was not removed. So the trouble started once again with the revival of the Prajamandals whose leaders aimed to capture power from the rulers in order to establish responsible governments. The rulers did not hesitate to resort to all kinds of repressive measures, lathi charges, arrests and detention without trial, etc. In Nilgiri the Prajamandal decided to form a parallel government and to occupy government offices and property. In a desperate effort to maintain his position, it was alleged, the ruler recruited some Pathans in his military force and finally instigated some 'adibasi' people to plunder the villages. It led to complete anarchy in that state.[152]

Situation in Nilgiri deteriorated fast. The aboriginals grew in vehemence in the state politics. Their unrest came to a head. Towards the end of October 1947 it became clear that the small contingent of the Eastern States Union Armed Police Force which was posted at Nilgiri, proved incapable of affording protection to the ruler. The ruler was mostly responsible for instigating his aboriginal subjects to indulge in an organised orgy of loot, murder and arson. There was practically no administration worth the same in the state from the beginning of November 1947. The aboriginal rising in Nilgiri and its probability of spreading to the neighbouring districts of Orissa made the situation very critical both for the Government of Orissa and the Indian Dominion.[153]

The agitation for responsible government in Nilgiri led to a serious trouble. As no solution could be made between the ruler and the Prajamandal, ultimately, the latter decided to go ahead. Its ideas were to form a parallel government, to occupy the villages, and to take over government offices and property. In fact, a free provincial government of the Nilgiri state entitled, 'Azad Nilgiri Government' was formed at Balasore early in first week of November 1947 with Kailash Chandra Mohanty as President and Sarangdhar Das as Adviser.[154] On the other hand, the ruler, in order to maintain his position, formed a loyalist party, recruited a force of Gurkhas and obtained assistance from the Raja of Dhenkanal. Besides, his aboriginal subjects occupied the cultivated fields of the peasants and harvested the grain. They affixed blue flags to the property they seized, attacked villagers and looted their property. The ruler was alleged to have set them deliberately against the Prajamandal, as a result of which the state police did not check those depredations.However, the situation in Nilgiri became further gnawing when the Communists were involved in the affairs.[155]

Such a grave situation compelled the Government of Orissa to seek advice from the Government of India which thought it wise to put check on the rising aboriginal unrest. All the press expressed bitter resentment at the conduct of the ruler and urged immediate intervention of the Dominion Government. 'The Prajatantra', a local newspaper, also urged the ruler of Nilgiri to seriously consider for the merger of his state with the province of Orissa. It was also an unanimous opinion of all the press that 'merger was the only solution of baffling problem and the natural goal of the states peoples democratic aspiration'.[156] Despite this, the ruler took his own decision to form a ministry on the basis of election. However, realising the complete break down of administration and an outbreak of lawlessness in the state, the Government of India authorised the Government of Orissa to send the Collector of Balasore to Nilgiri to take over the administration of the state.[157]

The operation started in the morning of 14 November 1947. Military Force, Air Force and the Provincial Police Force rushed towards Nilgiri. Kishore Chandra Mardaraj Harichandan, Raja of Nilgiri, atleast, proclaimed his unwillingness to provide his state a modern administration.[158] The take-over of Nilgiri administration was made feasible. The Government of Orissa appointed B.B. Patnaik as the administrator of Nilgiri in place of Mohinimohan Mukherjee, Dewan of the Raja. 'Nilgiri ... was then administered as an occupied territory by the Orissa Government till the 1st Jan 1948 when the occupation was legalised as merger'.[159] On two occasions the aboriginal mobs armed with primitive weapons, were fired upon. In such circumstances, it took sometime in re-establishing the rule of law and to completely withdraw all the armed forces from the state.

The press and the public praised the decision of taking over of the administration of Nilgiri. There was wide expression of hope and sizzling aspiration that the incident would serve as an object-lesson to the rulers of other states and would convince them of the futility of any attempt to follow a policy of 'divide and rule' with a view to retaining all power with themselves.[160] The bold action of the Government of Orissa in taking over the administration of Nilgiri gave a fresh impetus to the agitation of the Prajamandals in other states. The Prajamandals then reaffirmed their stand for the establishment of responsible government in the states and accelerated their movement in order to attain that end. The Working Committee of the Regional Council of the Orissa and Chhatisgarh States, in its meeting held on 15-16 November 1947 at Balasore, recorded its appreciation of the steps taken by the Dominion Government and the Government of Orissa, in respect of Nilgiri.[161]

The Prajamandal insisted upon the rulers with ultimatum to introduce popular administration in their respective states. The Prajamandals of Patna and Dhenkanal declared their intention to take over the administration of those states into their own hands, if their demands were not fulfilled by December 1947. Similarly, the rulers of Bamra, Kalahandi, Narasinghpur and Keonjhar were given ultimatum to grant full responsible government to their subjects latest by April 1948.[162] The high handedness of the Darbar of Saraikella was also severely condemned. The Prajamandal workers of Athmalik resolved to form village defence committees and voluntary corps for protection against any attack by the aboriginal. The Prajamandal members, as a protest against the atrocious activities of the ruler of Bamra, successfully induced the people of the state to resign from the state-sponsored Prajamandal.

As a result of the vigorous agitation of the Prajamandals, some of the rulers yielded to the people's demands and declared their intention of transferring the states administration of the people where as rulers of other states decided to form an Interim Government based on adult franchise. The ruler of Athgarh was the first among all the rulers of Orissa, who issued an appeal to all the rulers of the Eastern States Union to dissolve the Union which proved an administrative failure.

Simultaneously, the rulers of Bonai, Sonepur, Baramba, Athgarh, Mayurbhanj and Rairakhol surrendered all powers unconditionally to the Prajamandal by the end of November 1947. Because of the unwillingness of the ruler of Khandpara to it, the Prajamandals declared a policy to start parallel governments in such states in order to combat their administration. Of course, the ruler of Khandpara, afterwards, conceded all powers to the Interim Ministry formed in the state.[163] Thus as a post precedence of the take-over of the feudatory state of Nilgiri, most of the rulers in Orissa seriously pondered over their failure. Those who could imagine every running-spell of time, yielded to the people's demands, and those who could not were engaged in nefarious and subversive activities. The attention of the public was focussed on those states and the developments were closely observed till a final decision was reached on 14 December 1947 with their merger into the Government of Indian Dominion.

The take-over of the administration of Nilgiri by the Government of Orissa offered a new direction to the Prajamandal movement in the states. The subsequent formation of the interim ministries in some princely states also brought new hopes and beliefs for the Prajamandal leaders who assumed offices in the ministries. After November 1947 democratic movements in the princely states came to an abrupt halt. In substitution was launched the effort for the merger of the states with a view to uniting the natural Orissa under one politico-administrative set-up.

With the problem of Nilgiri solved, the States Ministry decided to retain initiative on the problem of the princely states of Orissa. At a high level meeting of the Ministry on 20 November 1947 in which Mahtab was also present, it was decided not to recognize the Eastern States Union and to explore possibilities of associating the states with the provincial administration in mutual interest. It was further decided to meet the rulers at a conference at Cuttack in December in order to resolve the problem. Accordingly Sardar Patel with V.P. Menon and other officials of the States Ministry arrived at Cuttack on 13 December. On that evening serious consultations were held with the Government of Orissa. Mahtab narrates the situation as follows :

"After some discussions he (Sardar Patel) scrapped straightaway the conclusions which were arrived at in Delhi on 20th November 1947. He made up his mind and gave his decision that these states should be amalgamated with the province. He asked me if our memorandum was ready. I said it would be circulated early next morning. The memorandum which was prepared at the instance of the states ministry was scrapped and a new memorandum was quickly prepared... The whole night, Sardar again discussed with me all the future possibilities. He repeatedly told me that responsibility in the case of Nilgiri was entirely mine but in the present case it is shared by him as well. I assured him that in case the Rulers did not agree to his proposal, there was bound to be serious lawlessness in the states and Orissa Government would not allow such a situation to develop. If necessary, all the States would be taken over on the same day".[164]

The historic conference began in Raj Bhavan at Cuttack in the morning of 14 December, The first meeting was with the rulers of 'B' and 'C' Class States. Out of fifteen such states, twelve rulers were present and Sardar Patel inaugurated the proceedings with almost persuasive speech. He explained that the states possessed no resources to maintain any stable government. Therefore, it was desirable for them and for the people to merge in the province so that Orissa could thrive on progress as a compact whole in the new federal setup. It was not difficult to persuade them and in the evening twelve rulers who were present agreed to sign the document for merger with the Indian Dominion. It was decided that the rulers of the remaining three States of that category, who were unable to be present, would be asked to sign the agreement later.

The rulers of 'A' Class States were more difficult to be tackled. At the meeting in the afternoon, Sardar Patel tried to convince them. At the outset, the ruler of Mayurbhanj pointed out that he had already transferred power to the hands of the representatives of the people and he was unable to make any commitment without consulting the ministry. Therefore, Mayurbhanj was excluded from the discussion and it alone remained outside the periphery of the agreement. Other rulers agreed ultimately after a good deal of pressure and persuasion to accept the plan of merger and the documents were signed by the morning of 15 December 1947.[165]

On 23 December 1947, in exercise of the powers conferred by the Extra Provincial Jurisdiction Act, 1947, the Government of India delegated to the Orissa Government the power to administer the Feudatory States 'in the same manner as the districts in that province'.[166] It became effective from 1 January 1948. Mayurbhanj signed the Instrument of Merger on 17 October 1948 and the State was taken over by the Government of India on 9 November and was administered by a Chief Commissioner for some time. Then it was handed over to Orissa on 1 Jan 1949. Meanwhile, trouble had begun in the two States of Saraikella and Kharswan and soon it became a bone of contention between the two neighbouring provinces of Orissa and Bihar. Finally, by the arbitration of the States Ministry, those two States were handed over to Bihar on 18 May 1948.[167]

Finally, twenty-four Princely States were merged with Orissa and were subsequently integrated with the province. Such an event of historic significance had its echoes in its sixth session of Orissa Legislative Assembly on 7 January 1948. With a sense of profound understanding of the importance of the merger, Dr. Kailash Nath Katju, Governor of Orissa, addressed the members of the Assembly and observed : "I consider it an act of far-sighted statesmanship on the part of the Rulers of these states that they bowed to the inevitable and in the end they willingly and voluntarily agreed to part with their power whatever it was, and to hand over administration to the Indian Union with a view to the merger of the States with the Province. The 15th of August 1947 will for all time be a landmark in our national history, and in Utkal the 14th December 1947 would also be treasured as a day of historic significance".[168]

On the same day, a resolution was moved in the House on the merger issue. With a profound sense of relief and satisfaction, the Premier,

Harekrushna Mahtab, himself moved the resolution. The long resolution, which expressed the all-pervasive feelings of the people of that event of historic significance, was as follows :

"In placing on record its sense of deep appreciation of the decision of the Dominion Government to make over the administration of the Orissa States to the Government of Orissa, this Assembly expresses the hope that this historic and momentous decision will be followed by the complete merger of the States in the province of Orissa when the new constitution is framed and the provincial boundaries are finally settled by the Constituent Assembly ; it records its great admiration for the high patriotism of the Ruling Chiefs which has made this decision possible, and the farsighted political wisdom displayed by them in divesting themselves of all administrative powers and political responsibilities; it sincerely congratulates the people of the States and shares their rejoicing on their successful achievement of political freedom and looks forward to welcoming their representatives in this Assembly before long;...."[169]

Thus, ended the movement of the Prajamandals that sprang up as a protest against the recalcitrant, exploitative and oppressive rulers of the Princely States of Orissa who reigned undaunted and unhindered paying ever possible least attention to developing the all-round socio-economic standard of their subjects. People tolerated the mischievous nature, its bubonic drought and plaguey distress since they were helpless and handicapped before the catastrophe of the nature. But they hardly tolerated the mischief of a creation of the same nature, its manifestation in ruling chiefs and their cliques. Time went on and the subjects did not lethargically die down in the cocoon of their self complaisance. They resuscitated their own strength and vigour, merged themselves in the mainstream of nationalist struggle, challenged the sanguinary authority launching various movements against autocratic handling of situation in the states and streamlined their movements into a coherent whole (Prajamandal) putting sincere efforts and perseverance. Finally the situation gained momentum and gathered public support in favour of the people. The Congress involved itself in the dispute, mediated properly and prepared the grounds for its amicable solution. In due time, with a historic decision on 14 December 1947 a 'New Orissa' was born when all the Princely States of Orissa agreed unanimously for their merger with Orissa. And they were subsequently integrated in the Province.

References

1. C.U. Aitchison (ed), A Collection of Treaties, Engagements and Sunnuds relating to India and neighbouring countries, Vol.II (Calcutta, 931):323
2. Ibid : 418, Clause III
3. Ibid : 419, Clause V
4. Jagannath Patnaik, Feudatory States of Orissa, 1803-1857:25
5. C.U. Aitchison, op.cit., Clause V:321
6. Orissa Records, Board's Proceedings, Acc.No.120, Commissioner of Cuttack to Govt. of Bengal, No. 389, 22 December, 1855
7. Sambad Bahika (SB), 12 March 1885
8. UD, 4 February and 3 June 1905
9. UD, 21 January 1905, Two Bachelors of Arts : 329.
10. Sambalpur Hitaisini (SH), 17 and 24 December 1904.
11. UD, 7 April 1917.
12. Ibid, 30 June 1917.
13. Orissa Records, Kalahandi Papers, Acc. No. 5 Kal., Political Agent, Orissa States to Superintendent, Kalahandi Feudatory State, No.T/17 Con, 1 March 1916
14. Ibid, Political Agent, Orissa States to Raja of Kalahandi, No. T/Con/141, 21 September 1919
15. Ibid, Political Agent to Superintendent of Kalahandi, No. 180 Con., 14 September 1915
16. Ibid, No. 212 Con., 18 September 1915
17. Ibid
18. Ibid, Political Agent, Orissa States to Raja of Kalahandi, D.O. No. TC/38, 23 February 1919
19. Ibid, Raja of Kalahandi to Political Agent, Orissa States, No. 4 Con., 11 July 1919
20. UD, 31 March 1923
21. P.T. Mansfield, Bihar and Orissa in 1930-31:1
22. Satya Samachar, 13 May 1931
23. Ibid, 14 January 1931
24. Ibid, 28 March 1931

25. Ibid, 21 November 1934
26. UD, 27 June 1931
27. S. Pati, Democratic Movements in India : 82-83
28. L.M. Patnaik, Resurrected Orissa : 329
29. Deshakatha (D'katha), 1 June 1931
30. S. Pati, op.cit. : 85.
31. Vaitarani, Vol.IV, No. VI : 212
32. D'katha, 7 March 1930
33. Ibid, 9 December 1930
34. Indian Annual Register (IAR), Vol.I, 1937:356
35. Ibid : 357
36. Ibid : 358
37. Orissa Records, Kalahandi Papers, Acc. No. 4 Kal, Resident, Chhatisgarh States Agency to Maharaja of Kalahandi, D.O. No. G-64-CR/37, 16 August 1938
38. Ibid
39. Ibid, Chhatisgarh Agency to Maharaja of Kalahandi, Proceedings of the Orissa States People's Conference, 3-4 July, 1938
40. L.M. Patnaik, op.cit. : 330
41. Orissa States Enquiry Committee Reports (Cuttack, 1939):99
42. S.C. De (ed), Diary of Political Events in Orissa : 18
43. S. Pati : 94
44. D'katha, 10 June 1938
45. Ibid, 26 July 1938
46. Samaj, 19 January 1943
47. Orissa Records, W.W.C.C. Acc. No. 38 : 28
48. H.K. Mahtab, Sadhanar Pathe : 185-86
49. History of Talcher Praja Mandal (ed) : 17
50. K.M. Patra, Orissa State Legislature and Freedom Struggle : 273
51. History of Talcher Praja Mandal : 23
52. Orissa Records, WWCC, Acc. No.38 : 40

53. History of Talcher Praja Mandal : 27-28
54. Ibid : 33
55. Sadhanar Pathe : 193-94
56. History of Talcher Praja Mandal : 37-38
57. D'katha, 21 April 1938
58. Ibid, 23 August 1938
59. Orissa Records, Dhenkanal Papers, Acc. No.1026 S, Baishnab Charan Patnaik to Chief Minister of Dhenkanal, 21 June 1946
60. WWCC, Acc. No.-38:29-30
61. D' katha, 18 September 1938
62. Ibid, 24 September 1938
63. Ibid, 25 September 1938
64. B.K.Dhal, Bhulibu Nahin : 17-18

    S.N. Patnaik, Odisare Swadhinata Andolana :145

    B.C. Patnaik, A Pamphlet in Oriya, 9 August 1980
65. B.K. Dhal : 18
66. Sahakara, 1939-40 : 245-46 (Preface to a poem on Baji Rout by Ananta Charan Patnaik)
67. S.N.Patnaik, op.cit. : 145
68. S. Pati, op.cit. : 105
69. D'katha, 5 November 1938
70. WWCC, Acc.No.38:34-35
71. Ibid : 33-34
72. Ibid : 60
73. D'katha : 17 July 1938
74. Ibid, 4 December 1938
75. Sadhanar Pathe : 194-200
76. IAR, Vol.I, 1939 : 308-9
77. D'katha, 6 January 1939
78. Ibid, 7 January 1939
79. Ibid, 4 February 1939

80. Ibid, 5 May 1940
81. Orissa Records, Sambalpur Papers, Acc. No. 9695, A Note on Ranpur
82. D'katha, 22 February 1938
83. Ibid, 21 March 1938
84. Ibid, 24 April 1938
85. Ibid, 31 May 1938
86. Ibid, 21 August 1938
87. S.C. De (ed), op.cit. : 18
88. Orissa Records, WWCC, Acc. No. 34 : 35

    S.N. Patnaik, op.cit. : 147-48
89. S. Pati, op.cit. : 117
90. D'katha, 24 January 1939
91. WWCC, Acc. No. 38:56
92. D'katha, 23 March 1931 and 25 April 1938
93. Ibid, 31 October 1933
94. Ibid, 15 January 1935, 15 November 1937, 21 August 1938
95. Ibid, 31 October 1938
96. Ibid, 29 October 1938
97. Ibid, 26 August 1939
98. Ibid, 13 November 1938
99. Orissa Records, WWCC, Acc.No.13 : 224
100. Utkal Prasanga, August 1972 : 81-82
101. Ibid : 91
102. WWCC, Acc.No. 30:1-2
103. Ibid : 5
104. Ibid : 61
105. Ibid : 65
106. Ibid, Acc. No. 32 : 1
107. Ibid, Acc. No. 30 : 33
108. Ibid, : 35

109. Ibid, Acc. No. 60:4

110. Ibid : 12

111. Ibid, Acc. No. 30:34

112. Orissa Records, Dhenkanal Papers, Acc. No. 1026 S, Raja of Dhenkanal to Political Agent, Orissa State, D.O.No. 404-P/42, 29 August 1942

113. Ibid, A.N. Mitchell to Resident, Eastern States, Calcutta, No. 466 T, 31 August 1942

114. Ibid, Acc.No.1026S, Situation Report of the Dhenkanal State, No. 428-P/42, 4 September 1942

115. S. Pati : 140

116. Ibid : 142

117. Orissa Records, Dhenkanal Papers, Acc.No. 1026S, Raja of Dhenkanal to Commissioner of Police, No. 457/P/42, 9 September 1942

118. Ibid, Raja of Dhenkanal to S.P., 28 January 1943

119. Ibid, Raja's Speech in Oriya, 2 January 1943

120. Ibid, Situation Report, 5 February 1943

121. Ibid, M.G. Patnaik to Captain D.H. Biscoe, D.O.No. 99-CM/43, 9 February 1943

122. Utkal Prasanga, August 1972 : 55 and 57

123. Orissa records, Dhenkanal Papers, Acc. No. 1026 S, Raja of Dhenkanal to A.N. Mitchell, D.O. No. 460-P/42, 9 September 1942

124. Utkal Prasanga, August 1972 : 55, 57 and 58

125. Ibid : 56

126. Orissa Records, Dhenkanal Papers, Acc. No. 1026 S, Raja of Dhenkanal to A.N. Mitchell, No. 445, 15 October 1942

127. Utkal Prasanga, August 1972 : 42

S.N. Patnaik, op.cit. : 179

128. WWCC, Acc. No. 30 : 98

129. Utkal Prasanga : 78

130. S.N. Patnaik : 179

131. Nilgiri Administration Report, 1943-44:35

132. Ibid : 35-36

133. Utkal Prasanga : 58
134. Orissa Records, WWCC, Mayurbhanj : 4

     Utkal Prasanga : 60
135. Orissa Records, WWCC, Mayurbhanj : 5-6
136. Ibid, Sambalpur Papers, Acc. No. 928 S, Notes of M. Worth, Political Agent, Orissa States, 15 February 1945
137. Ibid, Acc. No. 1164 S, Talcher Speech by Resident, Eastern States Agency, Calcutta
138. Ibid, Sundargarh Papers, Acc. No. 2731, Pol. Orissa to All Darbars, No. P, 1-53, 28 September 1945
139. WWCC, Acc. No. 35 : 54
140. Ibid, Acc. No. 50 : 68-70, Acc. No. 10:82-83
141. Ibid, Acc. No. 28 : 16
142. Ibid : 127
143. Ibid, Acc. No. 47 : 5
144. Ibid : 12
145. Ibid : 22
146. Ibid : 12
147. Ibid : 29
148. H.K. Mahtab, Beginning of the End : 17
149. Ibid.
150. Ibid, Appendix VI : 101
151. V.P. Menon, The Story of the Integration of the Indian States : 145-46
152. Prajatantra : 5 November 1947
153. WWCC, Acc. No. 47 : 100
154. Ibid, No.28 : 27
155. V.P. Menon, op.cit. : 147
156. WWCC, Acc. No. 46 : 37
157. V.P. Menon : 147
158. Ibid.
159. Mahtab, Beginning of the End : 27

160. WWCC, Acc.No. 47 : 104-05
161. Ibid, No. 35 : 35
162. Ibid, No. 28 : 27
163. Ibid : 28
164. Mahtab, Beginning of the End : 29,
     Also Durga Das, India from Curzon to Nehru and After : 281-82
165. V.P. Menon, op.cit. : 156-60
166. K.M.Patra, Orissa Legislature and Freedom Struggle : 286
167. Ibid.
168. Orissa Legislative Assembly Proceedings, Vol.VI, 1947-48: 82
169. Ibid : 86

5

THE NATURE, THE INTER-RELATIONS AND THE CONTRADICTIONS

The present work is an attempt to study at the regional level the complexities of various political movements in the era of India's freedom struggle. Orissa in particular presents not only an interesting scenario but also a more challenging and complicated picture. Three movements namely ; movement for the formation of a separate province, the Congress-led movements and the Prajamandal movements in the princely states, dominated the period of the present study. In this chapter attempts have been made to formulate opinions on the issue raised in the introduction. The foremost questions include the nomenclature to be adopted for the various movements and in particular to analyse the nationalistic, democratic and popular contents in them. The inter-relation, the contradiction and the complimentary natures are equally important. The nature of the movements and leadership also deserve equal emphasis. It is felt that such an analysis must be preceded by a very brief summary of the forerun discussion and a review of various works devoted to the study of these movements. This will provide a proper perspective for drawing the conclusion.

Summary

The first chapter of the present work has been devoted to the two questions, a theoretical aspect and the other on the genesis of political movement in Orissa in late nineteenth and first half of twentieth century. The broad theoretical framework may be restated here.

Nationalism is a feeling of a people as having common descent, language, history etc., an emotional and psychological issue involving a feeling of oneness;

a will for self-rule, common political aspiration, memoirs and traditions;

inspired from within or from outside, demanding exclusion of foreigners;

associated in modern times with democracy, equality and liberty, fostered by economic interests, common subjugation, colonialism etc. and it admits allegiance to other groups also.

Broadly the nationalistic movement in India was inspired by the western concepts of nationalism, liberalism and democracy, it was nurtured and fostered by the spread of education, growth of press and other modern elements. The rediscovery of India's past glory and heritage boosted the self-confidence and the desire to be governed by themselves. Various resistance movements spread over more than a century culminating in an unorganised revolt in 1857. This was followed by a constitutional moderate agitation by the early Congress leaders demanding if not freedom, atleast greater participation in the government and a more humane administration. Gradually the demand for agitation became the base for the right of self-governance and self-determination. Besides the Gandhian agitation carried through the Congress, individual extremists, heroes, secret societies, socialists, individual patriots and others furthered the cause of India's freedom movement.

The famine of 1866 in Orissa exposed the devastating economic impact of the British rule, the unsympathetic attitude of the Bengal Government; it taught the people of Orissa the first lesson in forming associations and running organisations. The famine may not be a turning point in British policy in Orissa as held by many scholars, yet it acted as a catalyst for fermenting political consciousness in Orissa. It is one of the earliest events generating the need for formation of Orissa as a separate administrative unit under the Raj. The spread of education had dual role in Orissa. As in the rest of the country it exposed the people, however small a section may be, to the ideals of nationalism, democracy, liberty, equality etc., inculcated a sense of nationalistic pride with the rediscovery of India's past greatness. Unlike in the Bombay Presidency's debate on the use of English versus vernacular medium of instruction, in Orissa it raised the debate of Bengali versus Oriya medium of instruction. This debate became the foundation for arousing a sense of identity among the Oriyas leading to the linguistic movement and making the issue of formation of a separate province of Orissa more important than the question of India's freedom. Interestingly enough, the Bengali intelligentsia was divided in Orissa and thus the microscopic Oriya educated class had brothers in arms amongst the Bengali intelligentsia also. Numerous works on Orissa's history, literature and art remainings appeared in the fag end of the nineteenth century, strengthening and reaffirming the capabilities of the people of Orissa.

Like education growth of press created the necessary consciousness for the development of political movements. Unlike in Bengal and Madras the earliest associations of Orissa were not those of landholders. Early associations were predominantly linguistic and literary in character. The famine had also necessitated relief organisations. The introduction of local self-government also created an awareness for participation in the process of governance. An important section of Orissa elite including M.S. Das attended the 1885 national conference held under the leadership of S.N. Banerjea which merged with Congress the following year. The Utkal Sabha and UUC were established to cater to the regional needs of Orissa. They were not exactly opposed to the Congress nor were prompted solely by the refusal of the Congress to espouse the cause of regional aspiration of Orissa. In simple terms, regional aspiration demanded formation of a regional body and it was common intelligence that Congress was not the appropriate platform for realising the demand of separate province of Orissa. At a later time, this position was vindicated when the UUC adopted the Congress goals in its proceedings in 1920 in addition to its own objectives.

As early as 1876 non-official proposal for a separate province of Orissa was floated by Sri Baikuntha Nath De and Bichitrananda Patnaik. The abolition of Oriya as a court language in Sambalpur region provided the first reason for the demand of a separate province. The subsequent agitation leading to the restoration of Oriya language and its transfer to Orissa in 1905 strengthened the aspiration of the people. Radhanath Ray, Fakir Mohan Senapati, Gangadhar Meher, Madhusudan Rao, Nandkishore Bal, Gopal Chandra Praharaj and Bhima Bhoi, all created a new age in Oriya literature contributing richly to various forms of literature. At a later time, 'Panchasakha' - Gopabandhu and his associates enriched the Oriya literature. The feudal elements consisting mostly of ruling princes and zamindars took a leading role in formation of the Utkal

Sabha and the UUC. The small group of Oriya educated elite class joined hands with the ruling chiefs for demanding formation of a separate province. In the 20's of the 20th century a larger section of educated youth was available to join the ranks of those demanding a separate province. In other words, the nature of leadership gradually underwent a change accepting larger number of educated youth comparatively from humble families. There was near economic stagnation in the later part of 19th century in spite of little improvement in transport and communication. As a whole, the spread of education, growth of transport and communication, awareness of the economic impact of British rule, spread of ideas of democracy and liberty, formation and strengthening of political associations, growth of press, the new era in Oriya literature, continuance of obnoxious medieval feudal practices princely states and above all, the lack of a proper understanding of the aspiration of the Oriya sentiment on the part of the rulers, all combined together to form the backdrop of the genesis of the dominant political movements in Orissa.

The English administration had placed Orissa under three different presidencies, this was not a conscious policy of the Raj. In the 70's of the 19th century the people of Ganjam demanded inclusion of Oriya as a subject of study under the Madras Presidency. Similarly the people of Sambalpur in the 90's of 19th century demanded the restoration of Oriya as the official language. The UUC was established in 1903 with objectives like promotion of unity amongst Oriya-speaking people, development of Orissa's industrial potentialities and natural resources and social reforms through spread of education. H.H. Risley's proposal of transferring Oriya-speaking tracts from the Central Provinces and Madras to Bengal was encouraging. Some officials had sympathy for amalgamation of Oriya-speaking tracts into a single administrative unit even though it could not be established that they fostered the UUC as a part of their imperialistic design of 'divide and rule' or as a part of Bengali bashing in view of their active participation in the freedom struggle.

The formation of UUC and demand for formation of a separate province was intertwined with the Congress in a way. However, M.S. Das held that the UUC did not have a step-motherly attitude towards the Congress. Unlike the Congress there was no streak of demand for self-governance in UUC. As noted earlier it reflected only the aspiration for amalgamation for Oriya-speaking tracts under single administrative unit. It was not solely anti-Bengal for initially it demanded the transfer of Oriya speaking tracts from other presidencies to Bengal Presidency. The agitation for unification was intensified gradually. Various leaders extensively toured the Oriya-speaking tracts. As many as 381 branches of the UUC were opened throughout Orissa. An affiliated association, the Young Utkal Association consisting mostly of students was formed. The UUC advocated Swadeshi; M.S. Das, the father of Swadeshi in Orissa never advocated the Gandhian spinning. He aspired for industrialisation of Orissa on modern terms. The Satyavadi school was opened by Gopabandhu Das in 1909, long before the formation of Santiniketan, Sevagram or the Sabarmati Ashram, which became the training ground for the younger generation. The accession of Krushna Chandra Gajapati, the Maharaja of Parlakhemindi in 1913 and his joining the UUC brought new vigour to the organisation. Anant Misra worked as a roving missionary. Harihar Panda highlighted the need for establishment of Oriya speaking schools in outer tracts. The UUC demanded the introduction of Oriya teaching in Patna University and establishment of Engineering school in Orissa, opening up of M.A. and B.L. classes in Ravenshaw college and a Sanskrit college at Puri.

On the official side the Risley's proposal of 1903 was the first step in this direction. In 1905 Sambalpur was transferred to Orissa. In 1912 the Bengal partition was undone and a separate province of Bihar and Orissa was formed. This was as unnatural as the earlier division was. However, this was still considered to be a step in the right direction by most of the Oriya populace. In 1917 Mr. Curtis suggested the formation of smaller Indian provinces which did not find favour with Montague-Chelmsford.

By 1918 a new class of Ravenshawvians and those educated in Calcutta and Patna emerged in Orissa. Coupled with this was the appearance of Gandhi on the national scene. This new section was led by Gopabandhu Das for whom the national goal of self-governance was as important as the regional aspiration for the formation of a separate province. Finally in its Chakradharpur session of 1920 the UUC adopted the objectives of Indian National Congress in addition to its earlier ones. Simultaneously a separate Provincial Congress Committee for Orissa named UPCC was formed in 1921. Gradually M.S. Das. retired from the agitation and the leadership passed into the hands of Gopabandhu Das and other Congress leaders. However, this did not dampen the spirit of men outside the Congress fold to continue to work for the formation of a separate province. The most notable amongst them was K.C. Gajapati. Of course, the feudal elements continued to work mostly at official level.

The Phillip-Duff Committee advocated the transfer of Ganjam and Vizag estates to Orissa. The Nehru Committee was conspicuously silent on the formation of a separate province excepting for Subhas Bose's note of dissent on the issue. A section of the Oriya leadership welcomed the Simon Commission and represented to it. K.C. Gajapati attended the first Round Table Conference and pleaded forcefully for the formation of a separate province of Orissa. Ultimately on the recommendation of the Round Table Conferences Orissa was formed as a separate province along with Sindh on 1st April 1936.

Orissa also contributed to various resistance movements including the culmination in 1857. In the last two decades of the 19th and first two decades of the 20th centuries though the Congress-led freedom movement had reached Orissa, the dominating note was that of demand for a separate province. Gopabandhu Das can easily be credited as the real founder of Congress movement in Orissa. Mahatma Gandhi visited Orissa for the first time in 1921. The Non-Cooperation movement marked the unique participation of Orissa in India's freedom struggle. Large number of students withdrew from government schools, quite a number of people resigned from government jobs, the message of charkha and spinning reached larger number of people. Orissa fulfilled the quota fixed for it under the Tilak Swaraj Fund. The 'Samaj' and the 'Utkal Dipika' etc. became the mouthpiece of Gandhi. Even people of depressed classes participated in the freedom struggle for the first time. The arrest of the Orissan leaders started. In Kanika a strong agitation followed against the local zamindar. Social reform activities in the wake of Non-Cooperation movement in Orissa were taken up by the Congress leaders. Gandhi revisited Orissa after his 1921 tour. Gopabandhu Das passed away in 1928.

However, by 1930 Congress had a host of important leaders like H.K. Mahtab, Gopabandhu Choudhury, Nabakrushna Choudhury, Bhagirathi Mahapatra, Nilakantha Das, Godavaris Misra, Krupasindhu Mishra, Niranjan Patnaik, Atal Bihari Acharya, Jadumani Mangaraj, Bhagabat Prasad Samantaray Mahapatra, Ramadevi, Malatidevi etc. By that time Congress reached out to the common man and semi-educated people in both smaller towns and villages. Gandhiji's Civil Disobedience movement was more vigorous in Orissa than the earlier agitations and most other parts of the country. The Salt Satyagraha drew women in larger number in Orissa cutting across their social status. It included the queens of the princely states, educated elite and even common villagers.

At Inchudi the Salt Satyagraha was a great success, almost comparable with Dandi. In the whole coastline of Orissa this Satyagraha was a success. The fight against liquor and untouchability continued. Fresh ordinances stifled the press. For the first time students like S.N. Dwivedy, S.N. Patnaik and Binod Kanungo were inspired by both the ideals of the left and the Congress. Large number of volunteers courted arrest. Gandhi commended the response in Orissa time and again.

Of all the phases of freedom struggle the Quit India movement was the most effective one in Orissa. It was not only popular but spontaneous. It survived the repression even without leaders. Mob violence occurred at various places including Cuttack, Balasore and Koraput. The tribals immensely contributed to the success of the movement. Important newspapers were shut down. The arrest of Lakshman Naik at Matili and his subsequent hanging and the firing at Eram are the two most memorable incidents of the saga. Student strikes became common everywhere. However, the movement could not be sustained as in rest of the country due to suppression.

The princely states had retained substantial internal autonomy and princes including some leading zamindars continued to enjoy vast medieval feudal authority over their subjects under the tutelage, protection and even support of the British Raj in India. Many of the princes who even contributed to the movement for the separate province of Orissa were not always free from the vices common to the contemporary Indian rulers. The ideals of democracy, self-governance and the right to self-determination which swayed the people of Orissa under British administration, did not remain away from the people of princely states. The factors contributing to the upsurge of a new consciousness in Orissa in late 19th century were equally applicable to the princely states. In fact, in the wake of the agitation for a separate movement, a strong base for popular movements in princely states was created. Particularly after the formation of a separate province of Orissa in 1936, it was natural that the people of princely states desired to come under that single administration. As a whole, it was felt that British administered territories were better off than the princely administered states even though there were few brilliant exceptions.

The Prajamandal movement began roughly in 1938. The Nilgiri agitation was the first most important one. The Congress and the Socialists patronised the Prajamandal movements everywhere. Mahatma Gandhi had sympathy for the people of princely states and after the Haripura session the Congress as a whole, supported the movement. The same Congress techniques were adopted everywhere. In Talcher the responsive measures were too harsh forcing nearly 60,000 people to migrate to British administered Orissa. In Dhenkanal people demanded grant of constitutional rights. In Ranpur the killing of Major Bazalgette was an important milestone in Prajamandal movement. In many other places like Khandpara, Nayagarh, Athgarh, Mayurbhanj and the Sambalpur group of states etc., people demanded constitutional rights, abolition of evil practices like 'Bethi', 'Begari', 'Magan' and 'Rasad' etc. The Prajamandal movement ultimately culminated in the merger of these territories with the province. The process of integration of the princely states with the Indian union began in every princely state of Orissa and within months of independence a fuller Orissa had emerged.

Review

A cross section of important historical works on the present area of focus is being reviewed with the fond hope that it will be useful addition to the forerun summary and shall serve to provide a perspective for analysis and conclusion. The coverage is only representative and not exhaustive. The works which have been excluded are not necessarily less important nor those which have been included are more important. The review is thematically arranged as follows; movement for a separate province, freedom struggle, Prajamandal movement and others. Presenting a review at the fag end of the thesis in contrast to the usual practice of placing it at the outset, may seem unusual. The reviews here are limited to the opinions and conclusions expressed by the scholars and these are placed here for an easy analysis of the present work's conclusion.

Sri S.C. Patra's *Formation of the province of Orissa, the success of the first Linguistic Movement in India* is one of the earliest monographs on the formation of Orissa as a separate province. The work basically traces facts from the archival records. In the conclusion he offers no views on the nature of the movement and leadership, save for holding the movement to be generally popular.

Nivedita Mohanty's *Oriya Nationalism, Quest for a United Orissa, 1866-1937* is a welcome departure from the general works in history of modern Orissa. She concedes that growth in education, vernacular literature etc. led to growth of political consciousness and a demand for a separate province.[1] She has attempted very briefly an analysis of the concept of nationalism. This is too skeletal and not followed up with an analysis in Orissan context either at the introduction or at the conclusion.[2] She generally accepts Pletkov's ideas ad defines it as a sense of oneness in culture and society.[3] She argues that language, religion, race, geography etc. either as a single factor or as a combination may create nationalism. In case of Orissa it was language for her.[4] The feeling of linguistic oneness is the foundation for her naming the movement for a separate province to be nationalist. She neglects other important aspects of nationalism in modern times like democracy, right to self-determination etc. She claims to be studying Oriya nationalism in the context of Indian nationalism and argues M.S. Das and Gopabandhu Das to be identified with two distinct strings of nationalism namely Oriya nationalism and Indian nationalism.[5]

She ignores the possibility of contradiction, overlapping, complementariness and such other complexities. She opines that while Bengal nationalism never ran counter to the Indian nationalism, she was not sure in case of Orissa.[6] As to the nature of the movement she held that it was basically a movement of the middle class intellectuals.[7]

Sri. K.M Patra's *Orissa State Legislature and Freedom Struggle,1912-1947* is one of the few well documented work on the freedom struggle in Orissa. As the book is devoted to state legislature, freedom struggle is only the second theme of the work. In spite of this justice has been done to both the themes. Sri Patra traces the growth of nationalism in Orissa to the rise of middle class and mass media amongst other factors.[8] He argues that the Chakradharpur session of the UUC changed the total perspective of the political scene in Orissa and drew its politicians into the mainstream of the national scene.[9] In other words, he argues that the linguistic movement and the movement for a separate province were basically regional and the Orissan middle class was isolated from the mainstream of freedom struggle. It was only in the 20's Orissa joined the freedom struggle without abandoning its aspiration for a separate province. This general conclusion seems to us to be valid.

As to the contradiction and inter-relation Sri Patra's most important argument is that the movement for a separate province and its leaders were never opposed to the freedom of India. Patra goes one step forward and argues that even if one concedes that the zamindars and proprietors had traditionally supported the autocratic rule of the British there is nothing to prove in Orissan context that they were opposed to the freedom. Similarly he holds that the leaders never sacrificed the interests of the country in spite of their strong regional identity.[10]

Sri P. Kar's *Indian National Congress and Orissa, 1885-1947* is the most important published monograph on Congress. Interestingly enough, it is only Sri Kar who argues that discovery of Orissa's past glory and culture through the writings of W.W. Hunter, John Beams, Pyari Mohan Acharya, Rajendra Lal Mitra etc. contributed to the growth of a new consciousness ; most other scholars have missed this aspect. The famine in his opinion loosened the caste feelings among the poorer section.[11] The growth of political association is also considered to be important by him.[12] Interestingly he argues that language agitation contributed to the development of Oriya literature.[13] To us the reverse seems to be more reasonable. If the language agitation contributed to the Oriya language, it was in the form of text books. Madhusudan Rao, Radhanath Ray, Fakir Mohan Senapati and Gangadhar Meher, the doyens of modern Oriya literature, all started writing atleast a decade before the language agitation. He further argues that political consciousness did not touch the common man in the second half of the 19th century. It was only confined to the elite.[14] In his opinion, all early Congress leaders of Orissa were moderates.[15] As to the contradiction between the freedom struggle and the movement for a separate province he holds that M.S. Das felt the necessity of a provincial organisation to espouse the cause of Oriyas and believed that the formation of Orissa as a distinct political unit would advance the cause of Indian nationalism.[16] Sri Kar holds that Gopabandhu Das transferred the constitutional programmes of UUC into an activist movement.[17] It is only Congress which was the first mass organisation.[18] For him UUC was basically an organisation of feudal elements and elites. He opines that the enlightened provincialism in Orissa and the Indian nationalism in Orissa were not contradictory, rather complimentary to each other.[19] As a whole, he feels that Orissa succeeded in establishing her own identity in the Indian body politic and also contributed to the broader freedom struggle of the country.[20]

Sri A.C. Pradhan's *Nationalist Movement in a Regional Setting, 1920-1934, The Rise of Congress to Power in Orissa* is comparatively a new addition to the existing literature on the subject. He holds UUC as basically loyalistic for it always paid rich tributes to the British Crown, it appealed to the British sense of justice and fairness. He further argues, it was predominantly an elite organisation consisting of rajas, zamindars and gentries. Yet in a way for Sri Pradhan it represented the people for the members shared common ties of language, religion and social custom. However, the author holds UUC far from being a mass organisation.[21] If one criticises UUC as being loyalist on the ground of paying tributes to the British Crown and believing their sense of justice and fairness, the early Indian National Congress can also be accused similarly. Further to hold the UUC as representative of the people on the ground that they shared a common aspiration for a separate province is also a bit far-fledged. The representative character of the rajas and maharajas had to face the bitter pill of the Prajamandal movement against them within three years of the formation of separate province. Thus, no representative character can be attributed to atleast the princes and zamindars. The elites like M.S. Das only represented the people. Sri Pradhan cites Gopabandhu Das' usage of the term 'Oriya nationalism and Oriya nationality'. For Pradhan humanism was the foundation of Gopabandhu's nationalism.[22] Hence Sri Pradhan indirectly suggests that humanism can solve the contradiction or act as a meeting ground for Indian nationalism and so-called Oriya nationalism. It must be held however that humanism may be an aspect of nationalism, but more important aspects are those of feeling of oneness, distinct identity, the aspiration to be self-governed to the exclusion of extra-territorial authority, ideas of democracy and liberty.

So the author also points out to the absence of industrial mercantile and working classes in Orissa and argues that trade was basically in the hands of marwaris and muslims. However, this impression seems to be based on a popular conception, atleast, a substantial class of small tradesman from the Vaisya caste existed both in Ganjam and Cuttack. The retained trade always remained with a predominantly Oriya class. Sri Pradhan concludes that in 19th century the emerging socio-political consciousness developed into regional and national identity. There was no inherent contradiction between the regional and national movements or loyalty. Sri Pradhan holds that there was a difference in the character of the leadership of the Congress and that of the UUC. He divides the Congress into two- one, naming as Satyavadi school dominated by the Brahmins and the other Bharati Mandir as dominated by the Karans.[23] This conclusion of Sri Pradhan seems unjustified when he himself concedes that there was no political grouping on the line of caste and four classes of intelligentsia, like lawyers, teachers, government servants and students formed the leadership. In fact, Dr. H.K. Mahtab, one of the most important leaders of Bharati Mandir was not a Karan. Further Sri

Pradhan argues that large number of zamindars were opposed to the Congress, yet it never started any anti-zamindary agitation. This Pradhan explains by pointing out to the presence of a rich propertied class within the Congress, unsympathetic to the peasants.

Sri Prabodh Kumar Mishra, in his book *The Political History of Orissa, 1900-1936*, holds that M.S.Das and the rajas and maharajas who led initially the UUC were basically moderates and followed different line from the Congress by placating the British. Sri Mishra feels that they followed such a policy as they felt more than the Congress agitation sincere pleading with the British would ensure the formation of a separate province. He feels this to be justified as events proved that the formation of a separate province of Orissa was more due to the work of M.S. Das, Maharaja of Parla etc. more than due to the Congress agitationists. Sri Mishra further justifies the early regional emphasis of the Orissa elite over the national cause for it was an immediate need and aspiration of the people and justified the higher premium. Sri Mishra adds that in the post 1936 era Orissa participated effectively in the freedom struggle. His opinion that the division of Orissa was due to the historical accident of the piecemeal conquest of the British does not seem to be sound for before 1803 Orissa had already been parcelled out to the Mughals, Marathas and the Nizams etc.[24]

Sri Chittaranjan Mishra, in his book *Freedom Movement in Sambalpur*, highlights the contribution of Sri Surendra Sai to a great extent. Basing on the contributions of Sri Sai he ventures to call the freedom movement in Sambalpur to be militant. The 1857 movement as a whole was an armed struggle, there is nothing special to term it as militant solely on the basis of Surendra Sai's contribution. Militant nationalism as accepted in general terminology is associated with the contributions of Lal-Bal-Pal, Aurobindo Ghosh, various secret societies, militant parties like Ghadar etc. and can not be applied to Sambalpur region. Unless one accepts a separate standard for Sambalpur, it is difficult to concede the existence of militant nationalism in Sambalpur. Interestingly enough, Sri Mishra admits the paucity of the non-governmental sources to place the history of Sambalpur region in proper perspective. Sri Mishra seems to have equated armament with militancy unlike others. He probably forgets that there were number of militant nationalists who never resorted to arms and all those who held arms can not be called militant nationalists. The best of the worst part of his conclusion is that "there is almost no records to highlight the Quit India movement in Sambalpur region. Except stray references here and there, there is no substantial source material to link the period with the rest. However, it is not entirely bleak and blank. This was probably a lull before the storm of complete Independence".[25] How far Sri Mishra is justified in drawing such an inference in the absence of records by his own admission is baffling.

Sri Bijay Chandra Rath in his work *Unrest in Princely States of Orissa, Dhenkanal and Talcher (1938-1947)* accepts the influence of Gandhian creed over the Orissan freedom struggle. He holds further that the people in princely states held the British responsible for the evils they suffered at the hands of the rajas and maharajas. This holding of British to be responsible makes the Prajamandal movement in his opinion, nationalist. However, this position seems to be incorrect. Long before 1938, i.e. the beginning of Prajamandal movement, the people held the kings to be responsible for the ills and generally held the British administered territories to be better off than the princely administered territories. Atleast, in Kanika, the people wanted the revenue to be fixed by the British government than by their ruler. The Prajamandal movement was nationalist not because people held the British to be responsible, but because they demanded democratic rights and representative government from their respective rulers. His generalisation on caste as a factor also calls for criticism. His view that all castes suffered equally under the British seems to be erroneous; all might have suffered, but not equally, the Brahmins and the higher castes were definitely better off. It must be remembered that the Brahmins continued to enjoy large tracts of tax-free lands. However, his view that caste and class distinction did not play any disintegrating role in Orissa seems to be valid.[26]

Sri P.K. Mishra's *Political unrest in Orissa in 19th Century (Anti-British, Anti-feudal and Agrarian Risings)* is basically concerned with the movements in the princely states. Sri Mishra characterises the political unrest to be anti-British, anti-feudal and agrarian. His observations for example regarding the movement led by Dharanidhar in Keonjhar leading to the control of the excesses of the Maharaja in Keonjhar; succinctly portrays however at times people preferred British administration to the feudal administration. This in our opinion goes to an extent to prove that every movement during the period was not necessarily absolutely anti-British.[27] The whole contention of Sri Mishra is that movements were basically anti-feudal and the British seemed to side with the feudal elements to suppress the people. Another important contention of Mishra is that several of these resistance movements and uprisings led to the growth of nationalistic consciousness in garjat and tribal areas in turn leading to the Prajamandal movement.[28]

Mrs. Satyabhama Pati's *Democratic Movements in India* is devoted to the Prajamandal movement in Orissa. Mrs. Pati holds these movements to be democratic though she never expounds the conception of democracy nor does she relate the nature of the movement with the same. However, one tends to agree with this nomenclature of Mrs. Pati for the leaders and the people demanded only democratic rights and abolition of feudal practices. Even though the demand for abolition of monarchy was not clear, yet representative government was the catchword everywhere. She has not made any subjective or otherwise observation regarding the nature of the leadership and the movement. She has also not expressed her views on the contradictory or complimentary nature of the three movements, namely, movement for a separate province of Orissa, freedom movement and the Prajamandal movement.

Having surveyed a few representative books on the three movements, few words may be added on some works of general nature. Sunit Ghose's *Orissa in Turmoil* attempts to trace the political scenario right upto the early 70's of the century and the three movements have been touched upon in the introductory portion. As his findings are an interesting departure, few observations on his work are appended here.

Ghose holds that Gopabandhu Das gave a different turn to the political movement of Orissa and placed on the broad canvas of the Indian Independence movement led by the Congress.[29] Similarly Ghose finds that the amalgamation of princely states as a consequence of the Prajamandal movement changed the socio-political character of the province. He holds that psychological make-up of the people of garjat areas is different, he recognises the problem of maladjustment not conducive to the development of the province. In a word political integration did not bring in emotional integration and a feeling of exploitation by the coastal people continued to exist in the non-Mughalbandi areas.[30] Further he points out that the famine brought into focus the neglect of Orissa. He wonders whether M.S. Das was more concerned to protect the interest of the educated people than others or whether the aristocrats fighting for the separate province of Orissa rub their shoulders with the commoners.[31] He feels that the famine in Puri in 1912 ultimately shook the faith of Gopabandhu Das and led to his conversion to the nationalist cause in a greater way.[32] Mr. Ghose accepts the general view that the Chakradharpur session of UUC marked the synthesis of the Congress and the UUC ideals. He concedes also a difference of class structure between the UUC and the Congress. Like Sri Bijay Rath, Sunit Ghose also points to the Brahmin-Karan fall out in Orissa politics and traces it to the period under our study.[33] Similarly pointing out to the lack of emotional integration Sri Ghose cites the conflict over the location of capital between Rangeilunda and Cuttack.[34] He holds Congress to be an urban based party. Sri Ghose relates the formation of Ganatantra Parishad in Orissa which subsequently merged with the Swatantra Party to the feudal character of the leadership in the movement for a separate province of Orissa. In other words, we may hold that not withstanding the differences in characteristics the leadership in Orissa in the first half of the 20th century held the interests of Orissa to be very dear to its heart. This leadership ultimately crystallized into three groups namely, the Congress, the Socialists and the rajas and maharajas aligned with a section of the educated elite who were not prepared to be under the shadow of the Congress party.

Sri J.K. Samal's *Orissa Under the British Crown, 1858-1905* is an attempt to analyse the nature of British administration. He holds that the famine exposed the lacuna in British administration and proved the danger of the policy of laissez-faire. Sri. Samal holds the famine to be turning point in the history of Orissa[35] which marked a change in British policy. This seems to be the generally agreed position of most of the scholars working on modern Orissan history. Even though the present scholar is not concerned with this question, yet it seems the change of the nature of British administration in India was more due to change of administration from the Company to the Crown, rather than due to the mere famine. Sri Samal finds the famine to be a blessing in disguise and on the whole holds the British land revenue policy to be helpful to the Orissa peasants. The growth in irrigation, navigation and communication etc. is held by him to be contributing factors in ending the geographical isolation of Orissa.[36] In spite of the fact that he opines that a wider context of general history the Crown's period did not provide scope for real economic growth of Orissa;[37] it seems Sri. Samal lacks the common perspective to identify the economic motives of the English behind little developmental work under them. While it is considered that some economic development took place, it is unwise to imagine that without the British such development would not have taken place. It is still irrational to argue that the Britishers were motivated by concern for colonial people rather than their own economic interests.

Sri P.K. Jena's *Orissa a new Province, History of Government and Politics in Orissa, 1936-1948* deals with the political history of Orissa from its formation to the independence of India. Sri Jena is critical of the politics of defection occurring in Orissa right from the beginning of the ministry making in 1937. He observes that the ministries both Congress and non-Congress between 1936 to 1948 had no clear-cut design for the growth of Orissa and except for the establishment of Utkal University and the Hirakud Dam Project they had no other concrete achievement. Sri Jena also points out to the growth of sub-regionalism within Orissa. The establishment of Hirakud was considered by the people of western Orissa to be in the interest of the people of Cuttack as a flood control measure. The predominance of Cuttack region in government offices of western Orissa was resented. Similarly the controversy over the establishment of the capital led to the conflict of interest between the north and south Orissa. Like Sunit Ghose, Jena finds that political unification of Orissa did not automatically promote emotional unification. It is felt by us that even after half a century of independence, sub-regional identities within Orissa are still quite strong. Sri Jena emphasises the illustrating contributions of Orissa to the freedom movement of India to be spectacular in the post 1936 era. He is particularly appreciative of the popular participation in Koraput district under the leadership of Lakshman Naik. He lauds the contributions of the socialists in Orissa during the freedom struggle.[38]

Discussion and Conclusion

In the last leg of the present work a humble attempt is being made in opinion formation and conclusion based on the foregone presentation. As to the genesis it is held almost unanimously that the 'Naanka' famine of 1866 was a turning point in the history of modern Orissa. It may even be equated with the birth-pangs of a more conscious Orissa fired with the vigour of greater self-identity. There are basically two issues concerned with the famine; one of the supposed change of British policy towards Orissa as a consequence of the tragic effects of the famine and the other of the famine acting as a catalyst for the new awakening. It is easy to concede the latter while the former contention needs to be debated. Even though it would be little out of place to debate on the nature of the British administration of Orissa, a few words may still be appended.

It has almost become customary on the part of the scholars of the history of modern Orissa to portray the change of British attitude in Orissa in the post famine era similar to that of Ashoka in the post Kalinga War era. Just in the wider context of modern Indian history it is impossible to concede that the British followed a policy of greater welfare in Orissa than the rest of India. If at all there was a change in the British policy it was partly due to the change from the Company to the Crown and mostly due to the changing economic interest of Great Britain in India. What is suggested here in terms of Orissan history is that the growth in transport and communication, irrigation and slight shift in the land revenue policy was not inspired by the sad effects of the famine in Orissa. It was in keeping with their general change prompted by desire to reach the interiors of India for a better collection of raw materials and marketing of their finished products; search for an outlet for their surplus capital through irrigation projects and the desire to create atleast a marginal surplus in the hands of the peasants to foster some purchasing power for the British goods at their end. Not withstanding the arguments for and against the change in the nature of British administration, it is fairly conceded that the famine gave the people of Orissa the first great opportunity in organised political activities. It made them conscious of the apathy and neglect of their interests at the hands of the government. It became a great theme of Oriya literature. It convinced them of the necessity of Orissa coming under a single administration and in term the formation of a distinct administrative unit. It fostered a greater feeling of unity cutting across the class and caste barriers. The famine can almost be considered to be a challenge to which the people of Orissa responded not through despondency but through a lively and vigorous movement filled with greater hope and aspiration. At the official level also the idea of a separate province dawned.

The genesis of the new awakening in Orissa can be traced to the factors beyond the famine. By the 20's of the 19th century a small but definite beginning had been made for the growth of western education in Orissa. Though the progress was slow by the middle of the century, quite a number of schools had come up. Calcutta also served as the home for emergence of an educated Oriya elite. Before the end of the 19th century, atleast one full-fledged college had come up in Orissa. The spread of education was the cradle for the genesis of modern Orissa.

The question of education in its natural corollary raised the issue of medium of instruction in Orissa leading to a lively debate. Just as the

Ilbert Bill electrified the educated Indian elite and greatly contributed to the formation of the Congress, similarly the question of medium of instruction slowly crystallized into an issue of Oriya identity generating the movement for a separate province on linguistic basis. It would not be wrong to hold that had Oriya been conceded as the medium of instruction and as the official language without resistance from the official side or the Bengali middle class which had a prime position in Orissa administration, the issue of Oriya identity would have been postponed to the post Independence era as in case of many other states and the educated elite in Orissa would have participated in the freedom struggle of India in full vigour in tune with the rest of India from the last three decades of the 19th century.

The spread of education in its wake brought a renaissance in Oriya literature. Coming in contact with the literary heritage of the West particularly English and the winds of change in other contemporary vernacular literature of India, Oriya litterateurs penned down free verse, new prose including drama and novels and touched almost every form of modern literature. To these and the growth of press, the contribution of domiciled Bengalis was spectacular. The presence of elite and educated class is questioned on account of the fact that there was only one college in Orissa in 19th century and one more was established before the 40's. It may be true that not many people graduated from Ravenshaw College and Parlakhemindi College. Yet it must be remembered that quite a large number of people went to Patna and Calcutta for higher education. The smallness of the elite class does not negate its impact on Orissa.

The famine, the spread of education, the growth of press and the language debate, all promoted growth of associations. By the 60's of 19th century it is interesting to note that a number of associations had come up, most of them were devoted to socio-cultural reforms and quite a large number of them were literary in nature. Unlike in Bengal or elsewhere, the early associations in Orissa were predominantly formed to protect the interest of the propertied class merely. However, there seems to have been no serious attempt in synchronizing the activities of various associations of Orissa. The UUC was not a supreme association of all these, but one which predominated the scenario in course of time. The elite in Orissa felt in the 80's that Orissa should have its own associations and not just be tagged with other all-India associations like the Congress. This feeling ultimately manifested in the formation of the UUC was prompted by the firm conviction that Orissa needed an association of its own to ventilate its aspiration for formation of a separate province. M.S. Das in particular was a firm democrat who believed in the constant expansion of the representative character of the existing administration. He was one of the ablest parliamentarians. He was not less nationalist, less democrat than any of the contemporary Congress leaders. In the 20th century a larger educated middle class was available in Orissa to take up the leadership. Gopabandhu Das was its best representative as M.S. Das was of the earlier lot. The discussion on genesis may be rounded off with the following observations :

Contact with the West, spread of education, rediscovery of past, development of press and communication, growth of political associations and the emergence of educated elite class are the general factors of the genesis of the new awakening in Orissa almost in tune with the Indian scene.

There were specific factors in the Orissan context like the predominance of language issue, greater economic backwardness and near total negligence and apathy on the part of British administration and a greater role played by the feudal elements in the language centred agitation.

The most important issue of course, is the nationalistic character of the movements of the present period of our study. As to the Congress-led freedom struggle in Orissa, there is no debate on its nationalistic character as it demanded abolition of foreign rule, establishment of democratic representative form of government and the right to self determination etc. The demand for formation of Orissa as a separate province and the consequent movement for the same raise the question of its nationalistic character or otherwise. It is felt by the scholar that nationalism in Orissa manifested first in the demand for a separate province and subsequently the demand for the Independence of India gained preponderant importance. There is no question of the separate province movement being non-nationalist or anti-nationalist; there is no question of the earlier movement merging with the freedom movement of India in 20's of the 20th century or there is no question of the earlier movement graduating or maturing into the freedom struggle. In tune with this opinion it is further held that the Prajamandal movements were yet another manifestation of the growth of nationalism in Orissa characterised by the demand for greater democratic rights and abolition of medieval feudal characteristics of a decadent administration, surviving as a protege of an imperial and colonial government. In other words, nationalism had multi-faceted manifestations in Orissa, divergent both in the time scale and thematic content. Presentation of our considered view before a full-fledged discussion may appear like placing the cart before a horse. This is done precisely with the hope of presenting a better perspective for appreciation of the following discussion.

Sri Aurobindo Ghosh, one of the most prolific theoreticians of Indian nationalism made the following observations and such other assertion of regional identity in 1907 :

"It is vitally important to Nationalism that these should awake. Behar, Orissa, the Central Provinces, Gujerat, Sindh must take their place in the advancing surge of Indian political life, must prepare themselves for a high rank in the future federated strength of India. We welcome any signs that the awakening has begun. It is for instance a cause of gratification that Orissa is beginning to feel its separate consciousness, and to attempt to grow into an organised life under a capable and high-spirited leader, although we consider his political attitude mistaken and believe that he is laying up for himself bitter disappointment and disillusionment come, then will the new political consciousness, the new organised life of Orissa become an immense addition of strength to the forces of Nationalism. Yet it remains true that the only way these provinces can make up for lost time and bring themselves of swiftly to the level of the more advanced races, is by throwing themselves whole-heartedly into the full tide of Nationalism, and we do not know that we ought not to thank Sir Pherozeshah for giving us a unique chance to light the fire in Gujerat."[39]

Sri Aurobindo was then an important leader of the nationalist or the so-called extremist faction of the Congress. From his observations it is apparent that Sri Aurobindo considered the rising in Orissa to be nationalist. He held that India would ultimately become a federal state and the regional identities were welcomed by him. He further took it as the first sign of nationalism in Orissa. He even appreciated M.S. Das' high spirit and his urge for building up a modern industrial Orissa. Yet he was critical of them of the Orissan movement and leaders like M.S. Das for he felt it to be fruitless to plead with an alien government. The other contention of Sri Aurobindo that implicitly Maharashtra and Bengal were more nationalist than Orissa or Gujarat is not tenable. His contention that Gujrat and Orissa should throw themselves in full swing to the nationalist movement at all-India level to qualify as an advanced race seems to exhibit a lack of understanding of Orissa's typical and special circumstances. It was neither necessary for Orissa nor was it possible for all areas to respond to the nationalist movement in a uniform manner. Gopabandhu Das also takes up the issue which Sri Aurobindo refers to and which is still being debated by the scholars of history. Gopabandhu exhibits the same urgency as Sri Aurobindo on the need for Orissa to participate vigorously in the nationalist movement.[40] Simultaneously, without considering the regional movement to be less nationalist or to be lower in character, Gopabandhu holds that the regional issue ought to be subordinated to the total interest of India just as national interest should be subordinated to the welfare of mankind as a whole. In other words, for Gopabandhu, humanism, nationalism and regionalism are all legitimate manifestations of human aggregation.[41]

Nivedita Mohanty's nomenclature of Oriya nationalism and other's use of the term linguistic nationalism in Orissa also call for critical analysis. In the considered opinion of the scholar it is wrong to use terms like Oriya, Bengali or Gujrati nationalism and to hold Indian nationalism to be competitive or contradictory with these or to be an aggregate of all these. The demand for a separate province of Orissa may have never meant seeking independence from the British, yet it never contained an iota of doubt to the existence of Orissa outside Indian union. Even the most ardent supporters of the British Raj within the UUC never questioned the ultimate goal for freedom of India. The awakening in Orissa was a part of the general awakening in India and as explained earlier here the manifestation of the awakening was not necessarily uniform in India. As the partition of Bengal led to the movement demanding withdrawal of the partition, the dismemberment of Orissa led to the movement for a separate province and the latter was as much a manifestation of nationalism as the former. Being anti-British can not be the sole criteria of nationalistic manifestation. The fundamental nature of nationalism is a feeling of unity of distinctness of the desire to be governed by themselves which the Oriya Movement adequately fulfilled. As noted earlier, the early Congress was not wholly anti-British, yet on that account it can never be considered less nationalist. Gokhale was as much a nationalist as Aurobindo Ghosh was. M.S. Das was as much a nationalist as Gopabandhu Das was. Difference in time and circumstance called for different stands. A narrow view of nationalism would only permit such scale of more or less, high and low, backward and advanced.

The similarity between the objectives of the Congress and UUC is striking. Both believed in constitutional means, promotion of unity among the people, formulating political activities etc. The UUC in addition looked forward to proper utilisation of natural resources of Orissa. The predominance of rajas and maharajas in addition to the educated elite was a typical characteristic of UUC. Further, though the inspiration may have come from the western educated Indians or the propertied class yet the issue was basically local and regional. The call for Swadeshi given by M.S. Das was not related with boycott of foreign goods but was based on the revival of traditional crafts and utilisation of the industrial potentialities of Orissa. With the advent of Gandhian era in Orissa, spinning wheels gained significance. Yet to us, M.S. Das' earlier stand on Swadeshi seems to be more robust and realistic in character.

M.S. Das' use of Bengali at home has made some to question his love for Oriya language. His use of Bengali was probably prompted by family consideration due to adoption of two Bengali girls. This matter should be placed at personal level and must not lead to criticism. However, in a larger perspective it must be remembered that the demand for a separate province of Orissa was not solely based on a language. Orissa had a long history of its own with a distinct cultural heritage. The leaders never demanded exclusion of Bengali and other linguistic minorities from Orissa. Similarly there were many amongst the Bengalis who were strong advocates of the formation of a separate province.

The nature of leadership and the popular content of various movements need to be examined. There was a distinct shift in leadership from the earlier UUC to the latter Congress. The UUC may have reflected the aspirations of common inhabitants of Orissa, yet the lower middle class and the common men on the lower rungs of the society neither participated in it nor were involved. This may partly be explained by the strategy adopted by the UUC. The UUC struck to constitutional methods of petitioning, ventilating grievances in the legislature, sponsoring deputation etc. and as it never launched any popular agitation, there was no question of mass participation. The rajas and maharajas and higher educated elite considered itself to be natural spokesman of the whole mass, if not the self-appointed leaders. They were not necessarily afraid of popular revolt but the very idea of popular revolt and resistance was absolutely foreign to their mind. The Congress in contrast came to be dominated by the educated elite, was not shy of involving the mass and launched several mass based programmes. The popular content in the Congress-led movements was higher. And the Congress increasingly became a popular organisation in later years. The feudal elements particularly the rulers were singularly absent from the Congress fold. As to the leadership of the Prajamandal movement, though it was led and engineered by the same class of leaders as that of Congress, it produced larger number of leaders from amongst the common folk and of humble origin.

Few other related issues may be touched upon. Sometime people are critical of the role of the rajas and maharajas. It is observed that the UUC dominated by them never called for merger of these states with the British administered territory. Thus, the sense of oneness and consequently the nationalistic character is questioned on this account. This is an invalid criticism for at that point of time it was inconceivable on the part of the princes to surrender their prerogative. Further, demand for abolition of the princely ruled territories was not yet vocal at all-India level. Cropping up of the Prajamandal movements shortly after the formation of Orissa in 1936 proves that at people's level there was a sense of unity. Further the kings wanted to come under the purview of British Orissa administration and the political agent at Cuttack in place of the Agent at Nagpur, Vizag or Calcutta.

Similarly the lack of emotional cohesion amongst various regions of Orissa is advanced as a negative factor of nationalism and feeling of oneness. It must be remembered that no state of independent India existed as such in pre-British or British era. There are various regions in every state with different make-up yet bound by strong strings of unity and harmony. Thus, presence of sub-regionalism does not disprove or negate nationalism. It must be remembered that India is still a nation in making in a way. Nationalism is a living process with natural complexities. This is equally applicable to Orissa.

The mass content was definitely higher in the Prajamandal movements even from the Congress-led movements. This was precisely because issues like abolition of 'Bethi' and 'Begari' etc. concerned directly the common men and their suffering at the hands of the princes was quite immediate to them. The leaders of Orissa partly encashed the impact of Gandhi on the people of Orissa. Gandhi was almost an incarnation of the divine, the chosen leader for attaining independence and messiah of the down-troddens. He definitely by highlighting the poverty and neglect of Orissa endeared himself. Gopabandhu and M.S. Das may have been projected as the best representatives of Orissan leadership, yet men like Lakshman Naik of Koraput or Dharanidhar of Keonjhar equally fired the imagination of the people and gave the movements the real popular character. The feudal elements who had played a very important role in formation of Orissa were interestingly enough relegated to a secondary position after the formation of a separate province. In 1937 it was the Congress which won the election; proving that though formation of Orissa was dearer to the voters, the question of independence was no less to them. Though the feudal elements formed the Ganatantra Parishad, they remained as opposition. The Maharaja of Parla who was instrumental in convincing the British authorities met his political death after independence. At times, many of the rajas were perceived by the people to be more oppressive than the British though men like Parla Maharaja were few brilliant exceptions.

The Prajamandal movements did not demand abolition of monarchy. Monarchy seemed to be firmly entrenched. The people carried the traditional respect for them. However, the people everywhere demanded democratic rights, formation of legislative assemblies and representative form of government. They demanded the abolition of medieval feudal administration.

To conclude, few generalisations may be made :

All the three movements namely the movement for a separate province, the freedom struggle and the Prajamandal movements were broadly nationalist in character.

The Prajamandal movements and the movement for a separate province of Orissa were also manifestations of the nationalist awakening in India reflecting the local aspirations, conditions and needs.

In the movements spread over nearly a quarter less than a century, leadership came from various classes, the feudal elements, the propertied class, the educated elite, the higher and the lower middle class, women, students and even the common men.

The popular contents of the movements gradually increased from the days of the UUC to the Prajamandal movements and the Quit India movement of 1942.

The movement for a separate province of Orissa was one of the earliest manifestations of regional identities in India and the ultimate acceptance of language as the basis for state formation in India has indicated the justification of the movement. It can not be considered narrow in nature.

It is firmly conceded that Orissa was created by the British move out of the convincing persuasion of the UUC and in particular by the visit of K.C. Gajapati to England than out of any fear of violent popular agitation. It is held that the British were ultimately convinced of the unnatural dismemberment of Orissa.

It is further held that Orissa was not created to balance the Hindu sentiment to counteract the creation of Sindh, a Muslim dominated state. Even today, far less in the yesteryears, the Hindu fundamentalists have no substantial influence in Orissa.

The Prajamandal movements brought into fore the obnoxious issue of continuance of the rajas and maharajas in India whose freedom fighters were undoubtedly committed to the ideal of liberty, equality, fraternity and democracy. The success of the movement and the merger of the princely states with Orissa paved the way for the general merger. It acted as the torch-bearer in this regard.

A new Orissa has emerged since independence. The years between 1866 to 1947 served as years of gestation. Though the pregnant hopes, ambitions and aspirations of the year of independence may not have been realised, yet the years between the last three decades of the 19th century and first half of the 20th century continued to be the most fruitful and creative epoch of modern Orissan history. It is through these movements and the awakening the modern Orissa has been born. Our analysis and understanding will not constitute the final words on this great epoch. The significance of the period would continue to attract the scholars of several disciplines in coming years.

References

1. Nivedita Mohanty, Oriya Nationalism : Introductory Note
2. Ibid : 14-15
3. Ibid.
4. Ibid : 23
5. Ibid : Introductory Note
6. Ibid.
7. Ibid : 76
8. K.M. Patra, Orissa Legislature : 2
9. Ibid : 35

10. Ibid : 290-293
11. P. Kar, Congress and Orissa : (These broad inferences are drawn from the introduction and conclusion chapters of the book)
12. Ibid : 22
13. Ibid : 27
14. Ibid : 32
15. Ibid : 46
16. Ibid : 74
17. Ibid : 78
18. Ibid : 101
19. Ibid : 228
20. Ibid : 235
21. A.C. Pradhan, Nationalist Movement : 18-19
22. Ibid : 27
23. Ibid : 231-244
24. Prabodh Kumar Mishra, Political History of Orissa: 212-21
25. Chittaranjan Mishra, Freedom Movement in Sambalpur : 302
26. Bijay Rath, Unrest in Princely States : 224
27. P.K. Mishra, Political Unrest : 162
28. Ibid : 189-193
29. Sunit Ghose, Orissa in Turmoil : 7-8
30. Ibid.
31. Ibid : 10-13
32. Ibid : 17
33. Ibid : 21
34. Ibid : 26
35. J.K. Samal, Orissa Under the British Crown : 27
36. Ibid : 356-357
37. Ibid : 360
38. P.K. Jena, Orissa a new Province : 251-260
39. Aurobindo Ghosh, Vande Mataram, 17.12.1907 : 645
40. Gopabandhu Das, Gopabandhu Rachanavali, Vol.IV : 1-5
41. Ibid, Vol. III (19.4.1919) : 8-49

BIBLIOGRAPHY

Primary Sources

A. *Manuscripts*

Home Political Proceedings, F.No.18 April 1922

__ F.No.18 June 1930

__ F.No.18 January 1931

__ F.No.5/62/1932

__ F.No.18/I January 1932

__ F.No.18/II February 1932

__ F.No.18/I January 1933

__ F.No.18/II February 1933

Home Public Proceedings, F. No. 38, 1868

__ Part A F.No.149-160 December 1903

__ Part B F.No.161-162 December 1903

__ F.No.135-136 January 1904

__ Part A F.No.155-167 February 1905

__ Part B F.No.75-78 January 1912

__ F.No.203-203A May 1920

Phillip-Duff Enquiry Committee Report,1924.

Proceedings of Indian National Congress (Micro),1903-1918, (Select reels).

Proceedings of the Legislative Council of Bihar and Orissa, 1921 - 1936.

B. *Parliamentary Debates, Proceedings, etc.*

British Parliamentary Papers, 1867.

British Parliamentary Papers (House of Commons), 1911-1912.

British Parliamentary Papers (House of Lords), 1911-1912.

British Parliamentary Debates (House of Commons), 1934-1935.

Debates, Bihar and Orissa Legislative Council, Vol. III, No. 4, 1921.

Debates, Indian Legislative Assembly, Vol. II, No. 7, 1921.

C. ***Selections from Government Records, Reports etc.***

Annual Administrative Report, Bihar and Orissa, 1919-1921.

Bengal Administrative Report,1905-06, Calcutta, 1907.

General Report on Public Instruction in the Lower Provinces of Bengal Presidency, 1858-59.

General Report on Public Instruction, 1869-70.

Government of India Act, 1935, Section 289(1-b).

Government of Orissa at Work (Work of the Congress Ministry from 18 July 1937 to 18 July 1938), Cuttack, 1938.

Indian Statutory Commission (Reports), 1930.

Indian Annual Register, 1937-1945.

Indian Round Table Conference, Proceedings of Sub-Committee, Calcutta, 1931.

M.K.Gandhi to C.F.Andrews, Jubbalpur, 1921.

Memorandum submitted to the States Reorganisation Committee, by the Government of Orissa, 1954.

Memoranda on Native States in India, 1910.

Montague Chelmsford Report, 1919.

Orissa District Gazetteer, Sambalpur.

Orissa Legislative Assembly Proceedings, 1942-48.

Orissa Records, Board's Proceedings, Acc.No.120, Commissioner of Cuttack to Government of Bengal, 22 December 1855.

Orissa Records, Dhenkanal Papers, Acc. No. 1026 S, Baishnab Charan Patnaik to Chief Minister of Dhenkanal, 21 June 1946.

__Raja of Dhenkanal to Political Agent, Orissa States, D.O.No.404-P/42, 29 August 1942.

__A.N. Mitchell to Resident, Eastern States, Calcutta, No. 466T, 31 August 1942.

__Raja of Dhenkanal to A.N. Mitchell, D.O. No. 460-P/42, 9 September 1942.

__Situation Report of the Dhenkanal State, No. 428-P/42, 4 September 1942.

__Raja of Dhenkanal to Commissioner of Police, No. 457-P/42, 9 September 1942.

__Raja of Dhenkanal to Superintendent of Police, 28 January 1943.

__Raja's speech in Oriya, 2 January 1943.

__Mandhata Gorachand Patnaik to Captain D.H. Biscoe, D.O. No. 99-CM/43, 9 February 1943.

Orissa Records, Kalahandi Papers, Acc. No. 5 Kal, Political Agent, Orissa States to Superintendent, Kalahandi, No. T/17 Con, 1 March 1916.

__No. 180 Con, 14 September 1915.

__Political Agent, Orissa States to Raja of Kalahandi, T/Con/141, 21 September 1919.

__D.O. No. TC/38, 23 February 1919.

__Raja of Kalahandi to Political Agent, Orissa States, No. 4 Con, 11 July 1919.

__Acc. No. 4 Kal, Resident , Chhatisgarh States Agency to Maharaja of Kalahandi, D.O. No. G-64-CR/37, 16 August 1938.

__Chhatisgarh States Agency to Maharaja of Kalahandi, Proceedings of the Orissa States People's Conference, 3-4 July 1938.

Orissa Records, Sambalpur Papers, Acc. No. 969 S, 'A Note on Ranpur'.

__Acc. No. 928 S, Notes on M. Worth, Political Agent, Orissa States, 15 February 1945.

Orissa Records, Acc. No. 1164 S, Talcher Speech by Resident, Eastern States Agency, Calcutta.

Orissa Records, W.W.C.C., Acc No. 10-60 (Select Nos).

Orissa Records, W.W.C.C., Files on Freedom Movement in Orissa, Orissa States Archives, Bhubaneswar.

Orissa States Enquiry Committee Report, Cuttack, 1939.

Proceedings of the Indian Legislative Council, 1919-20.

Proceedings of Joint Committee on Indian Constitutional

Reform, Vol.I, 1933-34.

Proceedings of Utkal Union Conference, 1903-1915.

Ravenshaw, T.E., Commissioner of Orissa to the Secretary to the Government of Bengal, Letter No. 90, 4 May 1868.

Report of the Joint Committee on Indian Constitutional Reform, Vol.I, London, 1934.

Report of the Motilal Nehru Committee, 1928.

Report of Reforms Enquiry Committee, 1924, Calcutta, 1929.

Report of Nilamani Pradhan, AICC-Files, Nehru Memorial Museum and Library, New Delhi.

Report of Pranakrushna Padhiary, AICC-Flies, Nehru Memorial Museum and Library.

Reforms Office, F.No. 47/1/34-R & K.W. National Archives of Indian (New Delhi), Secretary to Utkal Union Conference Committee to Reforms Commissioner, 24/2/1934.

__F.No. 46/36 G(B), National Archives of India

__Memorial to the Government of Madras, 23/2/1934.

__Telegram from Secretary of State to the Viceroy, No. 1687, 5 July 1934.

__Telegram from the Viceroy to the Secretary of State, No. 1555, 17 July 1934.

D. ***News Papers and Periodicals***

English

Amrit Bazar Patrika, 1904-1946.

Bombay Chronicle, 1922.

Harijan, 1933-34.

Star of Utkal, 1905-1937.

Vaitarani, 1926.

Young India, 1920-1930.

Oriya

Asha, 1915-1924.

Deshakatha, 1932-1940.

Prajatantra, 1925-1937.

Sahakara, 1931-1941.

Samaj, 1919-1943.

Sambad Vahika, 1885.

Sambalpur Hitaisini, 1875-1905.

Satya Samachar, 1930-1934.

Utkal Dipika, 1866-1931.

Utkal Prasanga, August 1972/1986/1988.

Utkal Sevak, 1920-1921.

Secondary Sources

Aitchison, C.U. (1931) ed. : *A Collection of Treaties, Engagements and Sunnuds relating to India and Neighbouring Countries*, Vol. II, Calcutta.

Andrews, C.F., Mukherjee, G.K. (1967): *The Rise and Growth of Congress in India*, Meerut.

Asirvatham, E. (1964) : *Political Theory*, Lucknow.

Bernard, Joseph, : *Nationality*, London.

Bhattacharjee, G.P. (1973) : *Renaissance and Freedom Movement in Bangladesh*, Calcutta.

Biswal, Bishnu Charan (1993) : *Some Aspects of Orissan Economy : A Study of Growth and Policy (1870-1931)*, Unpublished Ph.D Thesis of Utkal University, Bhubaneswar.

Buckland, C.E. (1901) : *Bengal Under the Lieutenant-Governor*, Calcutta.

Bury, J.P.T. (1960) ed.: *The Cambridge Modern History*, Vol.X, Cambridge.

Chandra, Bipan (1989) : *India's Struggle for Independence, 1857-1947*, New Delhi.

Choudhury, Gopabandhu (1969) : *Gandhi And Utkal*, Ahmedabad.

Choudhury, Ramadevi (1984) : *Jiban Pathe* (Oriya), Cuttack.

Choudhury, V.C.P. (1964) : *The Creation of Modern Bihar*, Patna.

Cobden Ramsay, L.E.B. (1910) : *Feudatory States of Orissa*, Calcutta.

Das, Durga (1969) : *India From Curzon to Nehru and After*, London.

____ (1972) ed. : *Sardar Patel's Correspondences*, Vol. II, No. 176,Ahmedabad.

Das, Gopabandhu (1977) : *Gopabandhu Rachanavali* (Oriya), Vol. III & IV, Cuttack.

Das, Nandkishore (1981) : *Mo Jibana O' Janjala Kahani* (Oriya), Cuttack.

Das, Nilakantha (1963) : *Nilakantha Granthavali* (Oriya), Cuttack.

Das, N.K. (1936) : *Madhubabunka Odia Gita O' Baktruta* (Oriya), Cuttack.

____ (1951) : *Utkal Gauraba Madhusudana* (Oriya), Cuttack.

____ (1958) : *Madhusudan's Immortal Works*, Cuttack.

Das, M.N. (1978) : *Indian National Congress versus the British*, New Delhi.

Das, Sailabala (1953) ed. : *Life of Madhusudan Das as seen by many eyes*, Cuttack.

Das, S.N. (1971) : *Desaprana Madhusudana* (Oriya), Cuttack.

Dash, S.C. (1964) : *Pandit Gopabandhu Das*, Cuttack.

De, S.C. (1964) ed. : *Diary of Political Events in Oriya*, Cuttack.

____ (1990) : *Story of Freedom Struggle in Orissa*, Bhubaneswar.

Desai, A.R. (1966) : *Social Background of Indian Nationalism*, Bombay.

Dhal, B.K. (1980) : *Bhulibu Nahin* (Oriya), Cuttack.

Dunning, W.A. (1974) : *A History of Political Theories*, Allahabad.

Dwivedy, S.N. (1972) : *August Biplab* (Oriya), Cuttack.

Ebenstein, W. (1960) : *Modern Political Thought*. The Great Issues, New York.

Fischer, Louis (1959) : *The Life of Mahatma Gandhi*, 2 parts, Bombay.

Ghosh, Aurobindo (1972) : *Vande Mataram*, 17-12-1907 (Sri Aurobindo Birth Centenary Library, Vol. I), Pondicherry.

Ghosh, S. (1979) : *Orissa in Turmoil,* Bhubaneswar.

Gopal, S. (1965) : *British Policy in India (1858-1905)*, London.

Grierson, G.A. (1968) : *Linguistic Survey of India*, Vol. V, New Delhi.

Grover, B.L. (1988) : *A New Look on Modern Indian History,* New Delhi.

Hallowell : *Main Currents in Modern Political Thought.*

Hunter, W.W. (1872) : *History of Orissa*, 2 Vols., London.

Jena, A.C. (1937) : *Dukhini Kanika*, (Oriya) Cuttack

Jena, P.K. (1988) : *Orissa a new Province, History of Government and Politics in Orissa, 1936-1948*, Calcutta.

Kamath, K.B. (1966) : *Linguistic Vivisection of India - Why not stop it still ?*, Bombay.

Kanungo, Binod (1979) : *Jatiya Kabi Birakishore* (Oriya), Cuttack.

Kar, P. (1987) : *Indian National Congress and Orissa, 1885-1947,* Cuttack.

Kohn, Hans (1955) : *The Idea of Nationalism*, Princeton.

Lipson Leslie (1970) : *The Great Issues of Politics*: An Introduction to

Political Science, Eaglewood Cliffs, Prentice-Hall.

MacIver, R. M. (1926): The Modern State, Oxford, Clarendon Press.

Mahtab, H.K. (1957) ed. : *History of the Freedom Movement inOrissa, 1857-1911*, Cuttack.

____ (1962) : *Odisha Itihasa* (Oriya), Cuttack.

____ (1972) : *Beginning of the End*, Cuttack.

____ (1972) : *Gandhiji O' Odisha* (Oriya), Cuttack.

____ (1972) : *Sadhanar Pathe* (Oriya), Cuttack.

____ (1977) : *Dasha Varshara Odisha* (Oriya), Cuttack.

Mansergh, N. (1970, 1971, 1972) : *Transfer of Power*, Vol. I, II, III.

Mansfield, P.T. (1932) : *Bihar and Orissa in 1930-31*, Patna.

Mansingh, M. (1962) : *History of Oriya Literature*, New Delhi.

____ (1973) : *The Saga of the Land of Jagannath*, Cuttack.

____ (1976) : *Fakir Mohan Senapati*, New Delhi.

Masselos, Jim (1987) ed. : *Struggling and Ruling : The Indian National Congress, 1885 - 1985*, New Delhi.

Mecus, Andrien de (1962) : *History of the Belgians*, (English Translation by G. Gordon) : New York.

Menon, V.P. (1961) : *The Story of the Integration of the Indian States*, Madras.

Mishra, Chittaranjan (1986) : *Freedom Movement in Sambalpur*, Delhi.

Mishra, Gobind Chandra (1967) : *Jatiya Jibanara Atmavikasa*(Oriya), Part- I, Cuttack.

____ (1970) : *Arddha Satabdira Odisha O' Tahnire Mo Sthana* (Oriya), Cuttack.

Mishra, P.K. (1983) : *Political Unrest in Orissa in 19th Century (Anti-British, Anti-feudal and Agrarian Risings)*, Cuttack.

Mishra, Prabodh Kumar (1979) : *The Political History of Orissa,1900-1936*, New Delhi.

Mishra, S. (1977) : *Side Lights on History and Culture of Orissa*, (ed) by M.N.Das, Cuttack.

Misra, Anant (1948) : *Talcher Andolan* (Oriya), Cuttack.

Misra, C.S. (1966) : *Satyavadire Satavarsha* (Oriya), Cuttack.

Mohanty, Gopinath (1967) : *Utkalamani* (Oriya), Cuttack.

Mohanty, Nivedita (1982) : *Oriya Nationalism - A Quest for a United Orissa*, New Delhi.

Mohanty, S. (1970) : *Satabdira Surya* (Oriya), Cuttack.

Mohapatra, Baikoli (1977) : *Odia Andolanara Itihasa* (Oriya), Cuttack.

Mohapatra, C. (1959) : *Odishara Patra Patrika* (Oriya), Bhubaneswar.

Mohapatra, J. (1972) : *Pandit Godavaris Jiban Charita* (Oriya), Cuttack.

Muir, Ramsay (1916) : *Nationalism and Internationalism*: The Culmiation of Modern History, London.

Mukherjee, P. (1957, April) : *Orissa Historical Research Journal*, Vol.VI.

____ (1964) : *History of Orissa in the 19th Century*, Cuttack.

Nandi, A. : *An Introduction to Political Science.*

Nayak, P.K. (1991) : *Biswanath Das and Indian National Movement*, Unpublished M.Phil. Dissertation, Utkal University, Bhubaneswar.

O' Malley, L.S.S. (1933) : *Bihar and Orissa District Gazetteers, Cuttack,* Patna.

Oxford University Press (1962) : *Oxford Illustrated Dictionary.*

Panda, Prahallad (1990) : *Biswanath Das : A bridge between Orissa Amalgamation Movement and NationalLiberation Struggle, Souvenir of Life and Works of Biswanath Das*, Berhampur.

Parida, Biswambar (1973) : *Mukti Sangram O' Odisha (1803-1948)* (Oriya), Cuttack.

Pati, Satyabhama (1987) : *Democratic Movements in India*, New Delhi.

Patnaik, Jagannath (1988) : *Feudatory States of Orissa, 1803-1857*, Allahabad.

Patnaik, Lalmohan (1941) : *Resurrected Orissa,* Cuttack.

Patnaik, N.R. (1992) : *Lakshman Naik, A Study in Tribal Patriotism*, Bhubaneswar.

Patnaik, S.N. (1972) : *Odisare Swadhinata Andolana* (Oriya), Cuttack.

Patra, K.M. (1971) : *Orissa Under the East India Company*, New Delhi.

____ (1979) : *Orissa State Legislature and Freedom Struggle*, New Delhi.

Patra, S.C. (1979) : *Formation of the Province of Orissa*, Calcutta.

Pradhan, A.C. : *Nationalist Movement in a Regional Setting, 1920-1934, The Rise of Congress to Power in Orissa*, Delhi.

Rao Narayan, K.V. (1973) : *The Emergence of Andhra Pradesh*, Bombay.

Rath, B.C. (1993) : *Unrest in Princely States of Orissa, Dhenkanal and Talcher (1938-1947)*, Cuttack.

Rath, M. (1971) : *Mrutyunjaya Granthavali - Karmayogi Gourisankar* (Oriya), Cuttack.

Rath, R.N. (1964) : *History of the Freedom Movement in Orissa States*, Cuttack.

____ (1964) : *Late Utkalamani Pandit Gopabandhu Das*, Cuttack.

Ray, B.C. (1948) : *Foundations of British Orissa*, Cuttack.

Rose, J.W. (1948) : *Poland, Old and New*, London.

Rout, S. (1982) ed. : *Nilgiri Praja Andolana Itihasa* (Oriya), Balasore.

Samal, J.K. (1977) : *Orissa Under the British Crown, 1858-1905*, New Delhi.

____ (1988) : *Princely States of Orissa, 1905-47*, Allahabad.

Samantray, N. (1964) : *History of Oriya Literature 1803-1920*, Cuttack.

Sarkar, Sumit (1983) : *Modern India*, New Delhi.

Satpathy, N. (1969) : *He Sathi He Sarathi* (Oriya), Cuttack.

Senapati, F.M. (1964) : *Fakir Mohan Granthavali* (Oriya), Cuttack.

Seten–Watson, Hugh (1964) : Nationalism and Communism: Essays, 1946-1963, London.

Sharp, Gene (1960) : *Gandhi Weilds the Weapon of Moral Power*, Ahmedabad.

Sharma, R.P. (1987) : *Modern Western Political Thought*, New Delhi.

Singh Deo, N.N. (1954) : *Singhbhum, Saraikella and Kharaswan Through the Ages*, Calcutta.

Singh, K. (1963) : *Prophet of Indian Nationalism* : A Study of the Political Thought of Sri Aurobindo Ghosh, 1893-1910, London.

Singh, K. Suresh (1972) ed. : *Tribal Situation in India*, Simla.

Singh, Purusottam (1986) : *Swadhinata Sangramare Banarsena* (Oriya), Cuttack.

Sitaramayya, P. (1944) : *History of Indian National Congress*, Vol. I, Bombay.

____ (1946), Vol. II, Bombay.

Stirling, Andrew (1904) : *An Account (Geographical, Statistical and Historical) of Orissa Proper or Cuttack*- Reprint, Calcutta.

Tagore, R.N. : *Gitanjali.*

Talcher Prajamandal Committee (1950) ed. : *History of Talcher Prajamandal,* Cuttack.

Two Bachelors of Arts (1919), (Patnaik, Niranjan and Pradhan, Chakrapani) : *The Oriya Movement,* Ganjam.

Zaidi, A.M. and S.G. (1981) ed. : *The Encyclopaedia of the Indian National Congress,* Vols. X, XI, XII, XIII, New Delhi.

INDEX